Praise for *Broke in America*

"A valuable resource in the fight against poverty."

—Publishers Weekly

"An exploration of why so many Americans are struggling financially . . . A down-to-earth overview of the causes and effects of poverty and possible remedies."

—*Kirkus Reviews*

"Clear, concise, and packed with facts, figures, and suggestions for action, *Broke in America* shows that poverty is not the result of individual laziness or 'bad choices' but of economic and social policies that produce inequality by design. The catastrophe of COVID-19, which is reducing countless people to desperation, makes this book especially urgent and necessary reading."

—Katha Pollitt, columnist for *The Nation*

"Kudos to Joanne Goldblum and Colleen Shaddox for a book filled with wisdom, compassion, and solutions. America is a country of paradox: the world's greatest wealth together with deeply entrenched poverty in its many forms, including homelessness, hunger, unsafe water, under-provisioned schools, and unaffordable energy, transport, health, and other basic needs. The authors open our eyes to these grim realities and how they can be overcome. This book provides a road map to a better America."

—Jeffrey D. Sachs, university professor at Columbia University

"*Broke in America* is a tour de force. The authors strip poverty to its bare truth. Millions of people in a nation of plenty cannot afford basic needs such as water, housing, food, energy, education, and mental health access. Thanks to Joanne Goldblum and Colleen Shaddox, there is no ignoring the immorality or the inhumanity of that—nor of the path forward. Their engrossing, well-researched, and compelling analysis delves into the role that discrimination, sexism, and racism play in trapping people in poverty, and outlines policies to help them ladder out of it. It is a timely call to action for anyone who dares to envision a world that does not resign children, seniors, or neighbors to poverty and suffering. In doing so, this important book should be a North Star for generations to come."

—Rosa DeLauro, US Representative, Connecticut

"Joanne Goldblum has been working for decades to bring diapers—a basic staple of childcare—to low-income families. Her new book, written with Colleen Shaddox, a writer and activist working to reduce the number of children the United States incarcerates, explains why America must fix the problem of poverty rather than blaming it on the people it afflicts. Goldblum and Shaddox also offer a road map to a better future."

—Emily Bazelon, national bestselling author of
Charged and *Sticks and Stones*

"In the richest country in the history of the world, an eye-opening and humanizing testament to the realization that no one should be poor. At a time of crisis when we are re-envisioning and reconstructing our relationship with government and with each other, this is the book we need."

—Mona Hanna-Attisha, author of *What the Eyes Don't See*
and pediatrician in Flint, Michigan

"At a tumultuous time in US history, many of us are asking ourselves what kind of country we want. I hope that we can work toward the vision laid out in *Broke in America*: a United States without poverty."

—Jodie Adams Kirshner, author of
Broke: Hardship and Resilience in a City of Broken Promises

Broke *in* America

Broke *in* America

Seeing, Understanding, *and* Ending US Poverty

JOANNE SAMUEL GOLDBLUM *and* COLLEEN SHADDOX

BenBella Books, Inc.
Dallas, Texas

BenBella Books, Inc.
10440 N. Central Expressway
Suite 800
Dallas, TX 75231
www.benbellabooks.com
Send feedback to feedback@benbellabooks.com

BenBella is a federally registered trademark.

Printed in the United States of America
10 9 8 7 6 5 4 3 2 1

Library of Congress Control Number: 2020035452
ISBN 9781637743454 (trade paper)
ISBN 9781950665464 (trade cloth)
ISBN 9781950665631 (ebook)

Editing by Claire Schulz
Copyediting by Miki Alexandra Caputo
Proofreading by Lisa Story and Greg Teague
Indexing by WordCo Indexing Services, Inc.
Text design by PerfecType, Nashville, TN
Cover design by Pete Garceau
Cover image © iStock / Soubrette
Author photos by Gale Zucker
Printed by Lake Book Manufacturing

For David, Jesse, Mollie, and Sherman

For Anthony, Charlie, and Russell

A note about names: We generally refer to people by their full names on first reference and last names on subsequent references. In some cases, we use first names repeatedly to distinguish between family members. In others, we use first names only in the interest of confidentiality. In a few cases we use pseudonyms to protect identities. Wherever we've done this, we have indicated it by using quotation marks around the name the first time it appears. We never used the real names of children. In some cases, we used pseudonyms because people divulged that they had broken the law, feared involvement with the child welfare system, talked about sensitive health information or their experiences with domestic violence or homelessness, or because they simply did not want to be identified as a person living in poverty.

"I just want people that read this book to understand that we're not losers. We're not lowlifes. We're human beings that want everything in life just like everybody else. It's just that we don't have the funds to back it up, as some people do. It doesn't make us losers, doesn't make us jerks. It makes us human beings who want better for ourselves. Just because of where we live doesn't mean we're losers or jerks. We're good people. If people just take the chance to learn that, understand that, and learn what we're going through, that's all I ask: to be treated decently."

—Shane Ward, a former truck driver who had to give up driving because of disability. He is now a full-time caregiver to his mother.

Contents

Foreword

The year 2020 exposed how thin the margins are for the average American. A seemingly robust economy that always did way more for those on top than everyone below cratered, burdened by a virus for which the nation was unprepared. Startling statistics that say an overwhelming majority of Americans had less than $1,000 in savings, and those numbers informed what we all should have known—financial insecurity has become a way of life in the United States, and its greatest test in recent memory is upon us.

I first met Joanne Goldblum in 2019, when few of us knew what was around the corner. I'll always remember how impressed I was by the simplicity of her message, the basic ideas of how things like diapers and feminine hygiene projects affected American lives, both in quality and mechanics. Children deserve to be clean. Parents shouldn't worry about such basic things. And the resources exist to make things better for all, should we simply commit to sharing them responsibly.

To improve the lives of all Americans, we must first care about them. For many, the first step toward caring is developing an awareness of the conditions under which many of our brothers and sisters live. Cowritten by Joanne and her colleague Colleen Shaddox, *Broke in America* is an important look into those lives, an exposure of what it takes for so many to simply hold on, let alone thrive. Privilege of many forms can insulate anyone from the daily struggles of others, allowing the fortunate to rest on reasonable—but fallacious—assumptions, like figuring everyone can provide essentials for themselves and their families, so long as they are responsible.

The truth is, poverty reflects no moral judgments. Failing to handle the basics is a failure of society before it speaks to any individual. Millions fight heroically to live but are shamed by those with no idea how hard it is for so many to get by. We stigmatize warriors to valorize those protected from the fight. We praise so-called "excellence" while downplaying the good luck it takes to achieve in America, but we turn our eyes away from the strength of those whom we barely notice.

Americans deserve better. *Broke in America* spells out how little so many receive. My hope is that seeing American life in these terms will inspire others, as I have been, to consider what we can do to make things better. And, in cases like mine, to reflect on why it took so long to realize both how necessary collective effort is, and the smaller things many of us could do to make a sizable impact.

Our country's future is uncertain. To protect ourselves and each other, we must examine our problems. *Broke in America* is a great place to start.

Bomani Jones

Introduction

In early 2020 poverty in the United States was exposed in a way it never had been before. When a global pandemic led local and national governments to close businesses and issue stay-at-home orders, unemployment swelled to levels not seen since the Great Depression. Businesses failed. For managerial and professional workers, who could work remotely, paychecks were more likely to keep coming in the pandemic. Meanwhile, in April 2020, the United States lost 7.65 million leisure and hospitality jobs, 2.1 million retail jobs, and 1.33 million manufacturing jobs.[1] Workers newly branded "essential" continued to labor in grocery stores and nursing homes where they risked their lives for wages below what they needed to pay their bills. COVID-19, of course, did not create US poverty; it merely brought it into the light. Like the virus itself, the economic toll of the pandemic was felt most acutely by people with underlying vulnerabilities.

Even before the novel coronavirus struck, most people in this country had less than $1,000 in savings.[2] In the middle of a strong economy, workers were existing paycheck to paycheck because income growth has lagged behind the cost of living for decades, while corporate profits and CEO pay soared.

Just as the United States should have done much more to prepare public health infrastructure to confront a pandemic, it should have done much more to ensure financial resiliency among its population. The current economic suffering is by no means inevitable, and neither is the suffering that has plagued lower-income US Americans for decades. Our contention is that poverty can be eradicated in this country. It persists, in part, because of horrible misconceptions about people in poverty.

A common saying—accepted as wisdom, available on posters and T-shirts meant to be inspirational—reveals a tragic misunderstanding about poverty and its causes: "Give a man a fish, and you feed him for a day; teach a man to fish, and you feed him for a lifetime." Antipoverty efforts should stop making assumptions about people's fishing abilities. Maybe the river is fished out. Maybe that man is too weak with hunger to pick up a pole. Maybe "he" is actually a "she," and the anglers' club that controls the river doesn't admit women. It is past time to stop judging and give that hungry person a fish.

Historically, the United States has approached poverty as a lack of knowledge, or perhaps of character and ambition, when in fact it stems from a lack of resources. We hope you'll adopt that definition as you travel with us across the country, from a dying farm town where the tap water is so dirty it looks like chocolate milk, to Los Angeles' Skid Row, where a quarter of the residents report eating out of garbage cans steps away from a new Whole Foods. Nearly all the research for this book was done before the pandemic. The stories you will read here are not the product of extraordinary times. Poverty is quite ordinary in the US.

When you focus on basic needs—water, food, housing, energy, trans-portation, hygiene, and health—and learn about the significant barriers that many US Americans face in obtaining them, you cannot help but realize that poverty is close to inevitable for low-wage workers and their children. Solutions fall short because they often try to "fix" people in poverty rather than eliminate poverty itself.

They don't need to change. The world does.

And it can. US policy has shaped a society where people can easily become trapped in poverty—not because this country lacks the resources to lift them out, but because it chooses not to. In the case of every basic need, there are clear barriers consciously erected that deny access for people in poverty.

When people don't have the necessities of life, poverty becomes quicksand. An educator who runs a program that trains women in poverty to qualify for high-paying manufacturing jobs told us that attendance suffers in the winter. Her students are sick during the cold weather because they cannot afford to heat their apartments. Too many absences, and they must leave the program. Parents who cannot afford diapers are turned away from daycare centers. Research shows that parents who cannot purchase enough diapers for their children miss an average of four work days a month. Poverty makes it harder to stay healthy, clean, punctual, well-fed . . . a litany of things that help you to earn a living.

The truth of poverty is generally hidden by economic and racial segregation where US Americans live, study, and work. We have spent our careers moving past those barriers: Joanne, as a social worker and later the founder of a nonprofit; Colleen, as a journalist. Even before we began writing this book, we were privileged to share people's journeys, to learn how the daily struggle for basic needs exhausted both tangible and intangible resources . . . and to marvel at how people keep going, day after day. We are deeply grateful to people who welcomed us into their homes, workplaces, and places of worship. We are grateful to people without homes, who sat with us on sidewalks and had brave and honest conversations. The strength and generosity of these people—the people for whom No Loitering signs were invented—leaves us awestruck.

This book combines heartbreak and hope, the twin streams always at the source of advocacy. The way things are is unfair and inhuman. That's the heartbreak. But poverty is not gravity. It's not a law of nature. It's not fate. That's the hope. In the following pages, you'll get a look inside the lives of people in poverty—for the most part, people in the deepest and most intractable deprivation.

Part I, "Basic Needs," examines concrete poverty, its causes, and its consequences. Each chapter also includes clear action steps that detail something you can do to drive change. Sometimes these will be highly personal. For example, in chapter 2 we'll talk about how many US Americans do not have access to clean water. Our action suggestions include refusing to drink bottled water because that industry is contributing to bad water stewardship in vulnerable communities. That's a personal action. We also provide a link to a blueprint for a fair water rate system that will ensure people do not lose access to water because they cannot pay for it. That's a public action that requires advocacy.

Part II, "Forms of Oppression," shows how the disadvantage of economic hardship is compounded for people oppressed by racism, sexism, and other forms of discrimination. We frequently acknowledge that in part I, but we focus on it intensively in part II, where we also spotlight the perverse role that government plays in the lives of low-income people and the complicated relationship between economics and mental illness. In order to truly understand US poverty, it is critical to understand how it reinforces and is reinforced by other forms of oppression.

Part III, "Solutions," includes a summary of policies currently being promoted within the US to expand economic justice. We offer evidence of how they have and have not worked elsewhere. The true solution to US poverty, however, is each of us, which is why we conclude with a primer on organizing and activism.

The final chapter of the book is a guide to advocacy, which is something everyone can and should do. Advocates are simply people who refuse to go away. Personal actions and advocacy are often seen in opposition to each other, but they can and should work together. For example, we suggest that you take action to end period poverty by starting a basic needs bank or working to supply your child's school with pads and tampons. That good action can be made even better by taking pictures of your supply drive and sharing them with your local news organization or legislator with information about how pervasive period poverty is in your community, how sales tax laws affect the problem, and why providing these products in public buildings will help people participate more fully in life.

As our nation and our world were thrust into the largest disaster of our lifetimes, wishes for a return to "normal" morphed into a recognition that many things would be permanently changed by the pandemic. It is a time to question everything we once accepted as simply "the way things are," from the handshake to the salad bar. As we rebuild our lives and our society, we must make no room for poverty. Nobody in the United States needs to be poor—not today, and not ever.

CHAPTER 1

Seeing US Poverty

Throwing Out the Caricature

If we want to address poverty—to understand and end it once and for all—we have to see it first. And that presents a challenge for many of us. Poverty has been largely invisible during the lifetimes of most US Americans who are not themselves poor.

That is changing. As poverty becomes more common, we will either confront it or become a nation resigned to overwhelming economic inequality. Even before the pandemic caused a prolonged shutdown of the US economy, a growing number of households were struggling to pay their bills. In short order, things are going to get much better or much worse.

Economic and racial segregation have always been common here. Slavery on these shores predates the founding of the United States; and some European arrivals came here as indentured servants. As we'll discuss in chapter 9, continued inequity is no accident. A century of government policy has carefully constructed homogeneous communities. People in poverty have had few housing options outside isolated neighborhoods. There is generally little reason for people who do not live in these neighborhoods to visit them. By definition, these areas do not have shopping or employment opportunities that would draw in outsiders. Upper-income US Americans are unlikely to have neighbors—or classmates, or coworkers, except perhaps subordinates—who are poor.

Literally unable to see their countrymen and women in different economic classes, US Americans with more money have bought into complex and damaging mythologies that blame people, not systems, by portraying low-income people as lazy, given to vice, or in some other way inherently flawed. Their conception of poverty and people in it is overly dependent upon representations in media. However, movies and television largely exclude them. A survey of the hundred highest-grossing US films found that only two directly addressed poverty: *My Fair Lady* and *Lady and the Tramp*.[1] When Hollywood does put lower-income characters in the picture, the results tend to reinforce negative stereotypes, as public policy expert Stephen Pimpare writes in a blog post entitled "The Poverty of American Film":

> When a character is poor or homeless, that is ordinarily the most important thing about them, and when movies try to explain why people are in such a state, the causes are rooted in individual failure or a dramatic, tragic event. There is almost never a sense of the political and economic forces that create poverty and make it a common occurrence. Blaming people for their poverty serves a function, obviating the need for policy change or a reallocation of resources. It relieves us, the viewer, of the obligation to press public institutions to operate more equitably. It reassures us that the world is as it is for a reason, and even if things are grim for some, it's ultimately their own fault or the hand of God. There is, either way, nothing to be done.[2]

2

Even journalism can be a poor source of information about poverty—for two reasons. One, there is not nearly enough reporting on the topic in the United States, with only a handful of news organizations making poverty an actual beat. And two, journalists come to their profession with the same biases that muddle the broader society, and that affects the work they produce. For example, a 2015 study of poverty coverage in *Newsweek*, *Time*, and *US News & World Report* found that African Americans were overrepresented in these stories, particularly when the stories focused on government assistance.[3] This suggests that things haven't changed all that much since 1976, when Ronald Reagan condemned a "welfare queen," an African American woman who fraudulently collected large sums in food stamps, veterans' benefits, and other government payments. The woman was real, but certainly not typical. Yet she became a symbol of people receiving welfare and a shorthand for racist condemnations of people in poverty, particularly women.

In fact, most Americans in poverty are white: more than 18 million individuals according to census data, while 11 million Hispanics and 8.6 million African Americans are in poverty as well. Yes, racial and ethnic minorities are poor at higher rates. But if you want to picture a typical American in poverty, picture a white person—more specifically, a white child. One in five US children live in poverty, as opposed to one in eight adults, according to census data. When it comes to the typical recipient of needs-based government assistance, again picture a white child. Whites are the largest group receiving aid from the Supplemental Nutrition Assistance Program,[4] which has 39.7 million recipients, and Medicaid,[5] which enrolls 70.6 million.[6] Temporary Aid to Needy Families (TANF) recipients tend to be minority, but this is a relatively small program with fewer than 2 million participants.[7] Racial and ethnic minorities are receiving this help at higher rates because they are in poverty at higher rates. But the color of poverty in the US is still most often white. Depictions of poverty, however, focus on people of color and play into stereotypes and prejudices.

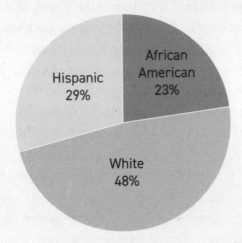

US Americans in Poverty by Race, 2020

Hispanic 29%

African American 23%

White 48%

Source: US Census data

HOW POOR IS POOR?

Now, all the data we just cited are based on government measures that do not capture the enormity of need in the United States. The federal poverty guidelines are set annually by the Department of Health and Human Services and used to determine eligibility for benefits. In 2020 a family of three was considered in poverty with an income below $21,720. The level is slightly adjusted for Alaska and Hawaii, but uniform across the contiguous United States and DC, despite widely varying living costs. It is also based on the cost of food, which has not risen as rapidly as the cost of other basic needs. The methodology for calculating the poverty line emerged from work published in 1963, when fewer women worked outside the home,[8] so the cost of childcare, additional commuting and clothing expenses, and other financial burdens are not captured.

All of this makes the poverty guidelines not a broad measure of poverty but a measure of how many US Americans have fallen into the deepest and most desperate circumstances. For example, a market report found that the median rent for a two-bedroom unit in the United States in early 2020 was $1,197,[9] which over the course of a year would consume *two-thirds* of the $21,720 that the poverty guidelines cite for a family of three. The US government considers housing "affordable" when it consumes no more than 30 percent of income (more on this in chapter 4). Because the poverty guidelines are so irrationally low, nonprofits and some government programs frequently set eligibility for their services at 150 or even 200 percent of the federal guidelines. But even this, particularly in higher-priced areas, is inadequate.

In contrast, this book follows a simpler definition: poverty is when a person cannot afford to meet basic needs. The Center for Women's Welfare has calculated the Self-Sufficiency Standard based on a more realistic basic needs budget and varying by community. This is a much more useful measure than the federal poverty guidelines. So far, the standard has been calculated for forty-one states. Where we live, in Connecticut, the project determined that the annual standard for a family of three, with one child in day care, would range from $63,896 in Windham to $81,937 in Bridgeport.[10] Even in the most affordable part of our state, a family would need close to triple the federal guidelines to meet their basic needs.

The US Census Bureau reported that 11.8 percent of residents, or 38.1 million people, were living in poverty in 2018, using the federal poverty threshold. If that were the full extent of the suffering caused by economic injustice in the world's richest country, it would demand major and immediate reform. Yet that is not nearly the whole story.

A full 38 percent of US Americans have difficulty consistently meeting their basic needs, according to a large Urban Institute study.[11] This would translate to more than 123 million individuals. The study defined basic needs as housing, food, utilities, and health care. It did not even address hygiene products, transportation, or many other clearly non-optional expenses.

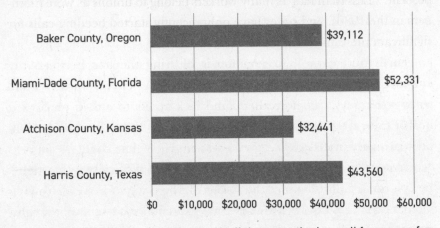

Self-Sufficiency Wages in Select US Counties

Baker County, Oregon — $39,112

Miami-Dade County, Florida — $52,331

Atchison County, Kansas — $32,441

Harris County, Texas — $43,560

Source: Center for Women's Welfare, selfsufficiencystandard.org; all figures are for one adult and a preschooler in 2020.

A 2019 industry survey found that nearly 70 percent of US Americans had less than $1,000 in savings.[12] This, of course, was during a period when the country was ostensibly approaching full employment. After COVID-19 created unemployment levels higher than the US had seen since the Great Depression, it is reasonable to surmise that many savings accounts have been decimated.

POVERTY IS GROWING AND SPREADING

US Americans are in this state because their earnings have not kept pace with the cost of living. This is not because there is not the money to pay them. The gross domestic product grew in seventeen of the last twenty years. Corporate profits have been consistently rising since the 1980s. CEO pay rose 940 percent between 1978 and 2018.[13]

Further down the organizational chart, it is a different story. US workers made only 12 percent more in 2018 than they did in 1978.[14] Meanwhile, rents for roughly the same period rose 45 percent, according to census data. Between 1984 and 2018 health-care costs increased 101 percent.[15] Less than half as many workers belong to unions as were members in the 1980s, and states have only recently started heeding calls for significant minimum wage hikes.

Furthermore, the gig economy is blurring the line between the employed and the unemployed. Too many US Americans make a good wage some days, but not others, and lack access to employer-assisted health coverage, sick pay, or retirement savings. In 2018 more than 20 percent of the national workforce was in a job that could be labeled "contingent" or "alternative," the Bureau of Labor Statistics reported.[16]

Work alone is often not a way out of poverty. Work, for a growing segment of the country, does not even pay enough to keep one's head above water. While education is strongly associated with higher wages, it is getting to be less and less of a guarantee of prosperity. The number of college graduates in poverty is growing. In 2017 the Census Bureau put the number of bachelor's degree holders in poverty at 3.3 million, or 4.3 percent. Remember, the census uses the official poverty threshold. So that's really 3.3 million college graduates in deep poverty, with considerably more experiencing poverty by our definition.

For most of US history, the country has avoided an honest discussion of economic injustice by segregating people in poverty and by heaping stigma upon them that serves to falsely blame them for their lack of resources. *Why don't they work harder? Why don't they go back to school?* That strategy will be less and less tenable as more Americans experience economic hardship. No longer will naysayers be able to point to "welfare queens," in part because government assistance is so pitifully low now that few families receive cash assistance.* More to the point, it is hard to

---

* In 2016 only twenty families received Temporary Aid to Families for Needy Children for every hundred that met the federal definition of poverty, according to the Center for Budget and Policy Priorities.

stigmatize people in poverty when they are your brother, your coworker, your neighbor.

We take no joy in reporting that more US Americans worry about putting food on the table. But this bad news is also an opportunity because it means economic hardship is becoming more visible across a broader cross-section of families and communities. You have a choice of how to respond.

The first option, despair, would be continuing to do what US Americans have always done—vote in large numbers against their own interests. For example, polls show that nearly half the country approves of eliminating the estate tax.[17] Yet less than 0.1 percent of estates are large enough to have the tax imposed on them.[18] Even people harmed by economic injustice support it. We believe this is because it is more desirable in many minds to identify with wealthy people than poor ones, who are so thoroughly stigmatized in our culture. Furthermore, since people of color are disproportionately low-income and overrepresented in media about poverty issues, racism encourages even whites in poverty not to identify with others in similar circumstances.

There is another choice: empathy and action. We can try something new. We can decide to work for economic justice—either because we realize that our interests align more with people poorer than us than with people richer than us or because it is simply the right thing to do. If people of all economic levels can come together and address the systemic injustices that rob US Americans of opportunity, happiness, health, and even years of life—we can build something better.

Today, there are babies with diets so low in iron that their brains don't get enough oxygen to develop properly. There are women who have made the calculation that it's worth being beaten up a few times a week rather than leaving partners who hit them and becoming homeless. There are houses aflame because someone who couldn't afford fuel for the furnace plugged in an ancient space heater. We have seen all these things. As you read the rest of this book, you will see them, too. Then we hope you'll understand that our collective duty to end poverty must not be ignored one moment more.

The next section of the book addresses basic needs: food, water, soap, transportation—things we generally take for granted in the US, though access to them is by no means universal here. That is why advice so often dispensed to people in poverty—stay in school, work hard, be thrifty—is both useless and insulting. How can you excel in school when you miss four days a month because you cannot afford tampons? How does working hard even help if your wages don't keep you fed? How can you be thrifty when the only grocery you have access to is a corner store where everything is twice the price it is in a supermarket?

Instead of worrying that helping people with basic needs will create dependency, policymakers must understand that material deprivation makes economic progress unlikely at best. Poverty is a self-perpetuating ill.

PART I
BASIC NEEDS

CHAPTER 2

Water

Running Dry

A mother of five, Valerie Jean Blakely likes to rise early and meditate before the demands of the day split her focus. So she was the first to see the Homrich truck turn down Woodland Street, just before 7 AM, in her Midtown Detroit neighborhood. The city had contracted with Homrich to shut off water connections to households with past-due bills. This was the summer of 2014, following a record cold winter. She and many of her neighbors had shifted their household resources to pay the heating bills while water bills mounted. Blakely's pipes had burst in the cold, leaving her with the added cost of repairs.

"I grabbed my phone and my camera and sat over the water access point," said Blakely. "I told them they could call the cops if they wanted to."

They did not want to. She remembers the technicians shrugging and proceeding to shut off nearly every other house in the neighborhood, while Blakely photographed them and posted the images on social media. She urged people to bring bottled water to her yard, which became a temporary relief post for families whose water had been shut off.

Years later, Blakely's activism has become more organized, and she is connecting with other advocates from coast to coast. They, too, live in low-income communities where skyrocketing water prices are causing many households to go dry. A variety of structural barriers keep low-income people—particularly when they are also people of color—from obtaining safe water for drinking, cooking, and hygiene, which we will discuss in more depth in its own chapter.

One in ten American households cannot afford their water bill, according to a 2017 University of Michigan study, whose authors predict that the rate will increase to one in three within the next five years unless action is taken.[1] The authors note that this estimate is conservative and factors could push the affordability gap much higher. While there are federal programs (albeit underfunded ones) to help people in poverty get food, housing, medical care, and heat, there is no national program to assist with water. The Environmental Protection Agency (EPA) found that seven out of ten water utilities offer no assistance to low-income customers.[2]

In some rural areas and a disproportionate number of Native American communities, there never has been plumbing. The Census Bureau has been asking about plumbing facilities since 1940, and the United States has never achieved 100 percent service. Currently, the Census Bureau estimates that 0.4 percent of housing units lack complete plumbing—a small percentage, but a total of more than half a million households.

Flint, Michigan, garnered national attention when high levels of lead were discovered in its drinking water. Around the nation there are many more communities where drinking water is polluted with toxins—and there is often little recourse for people who live in these places. A 2016 report by the Natural Resources Defense Council stated that 5,300 water systems, serving more than eighteen million people in the US, were in violation of the EPA's lead and copper rules.[3] While lead is the best-known contaminant found in drinking water, it is not the only dangerous substance that can flow through poorly maintained systems. More than ninety different contaminants are regulated by the federal Safe Drinking Water Act.

These deeply disturbing realities are made worse by climate change—bacteria love warm water—which experts predict will render more of the water supply undrinkable and potentially price poor and even middle-class families out of the market for this essential.

RISING PRICES, DRY TAPS

In Valerie Jean Blakely's home city of Detroit, water rates have increased 400 percent in twenty years. In 2017, after a restructuring of the

---

A Better Way: Lansing gets ahead of lead

LANSING, MICHIGAN, IS ABOUT fifty miles from Flint, roughly the same size, and also subject to the fortunes of the automotive industry. Lansing began replacing all of the piping in its water system in 2007, a ten-year project that cost $42 million. It was not required to do so by the EPA. This was a decision by city leaders, who knew that lines were old and contained lead. Because the project was spread over a decade and bonded, it was not traumatic for taxpayers. And because it was replacing so many miles of pipe, the city got good at it and the efficiency translated into cost savings.

Significantly, Lansing's water system is owned by the city, not a for-profit provider. Rates have risen in Lansing but are not unusual for the region. The cost of water in Lansing is less than half what it is in Flint. There is no detectable lead in water leaving the city's distribution system, according to the Lansing Board of Water & Light's *2017 Annual Water Quality Report*.

Water and Sewerage Department, it posted its lowest rate increase in decades—1.7 percent. But of course, that is on top of years of increases, and shutoffs continue—more than eighty thousand homes between 2014 and 2016. Detroit's infrastructure needs upgrades, but revenue shrank when the city's economic crisis caused it to lose wealth and population.

Utilities commonly try to meet their capital costs by raising rates, leading to an affordability gap, nonpayment, shutoffs, and finally an even smaller base of ratepayers to finance improvements to the system. Widespread shutoffs harm poor families without making the system itself any more sustainable. Shutoffs themselves cost money. In 2013 the city of Detroit and Homrich signed a two-year contract for $5.6 million. An investigation by the *Detroit News* in 2016 found that the contract had been extended multiple times, ballooning costs to $12.7 million without any public notice or city council approval.[4] "Think of how that money could have helped people," Blakely said.

Detroit's water crisis emerged because the city had underinvested in its water infrastructure for decades and is now playing an expensive game of catch-up. America's infrastructure, much of it constructed in the mid-twentieth century, is failing. States are not maintaining it, often at the same time that they are giving tax cuts. The American Waterworks Association, a trade association of water systems managers, estimates that the United States needs to spend $1 trillion over the next twenty-five years to upgrade its public water systems. There is little sign of this happening. For one thing, public investment tends to go to infrastructure that you can see: bridges, new schools, and so on. Furthermore, the United States does not fund infrastructure at even close to adequate levels. The American Society of Civil Engineers gave the country a D+ rating on its infrastructure in 2017 and estimated that an investment of $4.6 trillion is needed by 2025 to bring that grade up to a B.* Meanwhile,

---

* The report card comes out every four years, so an updated assessment should be available in 2021.

capital spending is falling in all but two states, the Dakotas, according to an analysis by the Center on Budget and Policy Priorities, a research and policy organization.[5]

The national failure to maintain infrastructure is a poverty issue, because public infrastructure equalizes opportunity and creates a minimum quality of life standard. A poor or nonexistent public transportation system is not a barrier to people who own cars. The more economically fortunate can send their children to private schools if public education is subpar. More to the point, people with more resources can compensate for bad water infrastructure. For example, lead in drinking water can sometimes be addressed with filters installed on a faucet head—if you can afford them.

While good infrastructure is more crucial for people in poverty, infrastructure is almost always worse in poor communities, where tax bases are weak. For example, school repair needs rise along with the percentage of students in the building qualifying for free or reduced-price student lunches (a common measure of poverty), according to the National Center for Education Statistics. A 2014 report by the center found that the majority of schools with 50 percent or more students qualifying were in need of significant repair.

In a two-month period in 2014, the Detroit Water and Sewerage Department shut off water to 7,500 households. This drew a condemnation from the United Nations, which considers water to be a human right and holds that people should not be shut off if they lack the means to pay.

The first UN special rapporteur on the human right to water and sanitation, Catarina de Albuquerque, said, "When I conducted an official country mission to the US in 2011, I encouraged the US Government to adopt a federal minimum standard on affordability for water and sanitation and a standard to provide protection against disconnections for vulnerable groups and people living in poverty. I also urged the Government to ensure due process guarantees in relation to water disconnection."[6] The release noted that the majority of households who had to go without water in Detroit were African American.*

Likewise, Baltimore, another black-majority city, is facing a crisis of water access. In 2016 Baltimore announced that it would need to spend $2 billion to improve its water infrastructure and tied that to a 33 percent hike in rates over three years. That comes after a 127 percent rate hike over the previous decade. That made "Fred Lee's" water bill a heavy lift—and an impossibility after he got a $6,000 water bill.

Lee's plumbing system almost certainly has a leak, but he cannot afford to fix it. "I live paycheck to paycheck," he explained. He suspects that his bill is also high because of a new meter that the city installed and that he believes is malfunctioning. He went to city hall to try to talk about the meter. He said that he met other residents with the same complaint but that he could not find anyone to talk to about it.

The city shut off his water, so he makes do. He spends about twenty dollars a week on bottled water to drink and flush the toilet. Now, Lee's Baltimore row house is in preforeclosure, in part because the city slapped a lien on it because of his unpaid water bill. Back when he had a manufacturing job, Lee had no problems paying his bills. But the company closed, and after two years of unemployment, he settled for a low-wage job in a bakery. "Being a bachelor, I can tough it out," said Lee. Several times he remarked how happy he is not to have a wife and children: "I wouldn't want them to suffer."

In Baltimore City, water is shut off when customers are $250 past due. A $750 balance earns property owners a lien and places them in jeopardy of losing their home to a tax sale. Lee said that he knows he can never pay his bill. He is just hoping that he is allowed to give up his

---

* The UN General Assembly recognized clean water and sanitation as human rights in 2010; however, the United States abstained from voting on the resolution. It's important to note that even some countries that do recognize the right are not providing universal access to their residents.

home without a hit to his credit—something that may make renting an apartment near impossible.

Owen Jarvis, managing attorney at St. Ambrose Housing Aid in Baltimore, helps people like Lee—or tries to. "The lack of a process handcuffs me. I can't do anything," Jarvis said with obvious frustration. The city used to offer informal conferences where consumers could bring in bills that they thought were inflated by error or leaks, according to Jarvis, but the process has been ended. If these issues are not resolved quickly, he explained, the user is likely to continue to get enormous bills that sink them deeper and deeper into debt.

"It's like tagging an animal for slaughter," he said.

UNPLUMBED AMERICA

Darlene Arviso drives the water truck that fills home tanks in her Navajo community, nestled into the Continental Divide in New Mexico.

Bizarre Policy: Residential users subsidize huge corporations

BOTTLED WATER IS THE most expensive way for a consumer to obtain water. Shutoffs actually boost the product's sales—think of Fred Lee's twenty-dollar-a-week purchase just to get water for essentials in his Baltimore home. But the companies that sell bottled water rarely pay much to obtain the resource.

Water bottlers, like manufacturers, and agribusiness, are "superusers" that utilities often grant much lower rates to than household users. The system rewards high use of a limited resource while also placing the cost of infrastructure maintenance and upgrades more heavily on the people who use the least water.

"People are happy to see me," she said. The community began partnering with the nonprofit Dig Deep in 2013 to install a tank-based system that provides running taps in houses but delivers the water via truck rather than waterlines running down streets, which is cost prohibitive in this rural area. The system gets put in house by house as money is raised for the project.

According to the Johns Hopkins Center for American Indian Health, 30 to 35 percent of households on Navajo reservations do not have plumbing.[7] In 2017 the US Census Bureau placed the total number of housing units without complete plumbing at close to 3 million. That's only about 2 percent of the homes in the country—but still a huge number of people doing without running water or a toilet.[8]

Arviso was raised without plumbing. Growing up in New Mexico, she and her brothers took turns using the same tub of water once a week for bathing. When all the children were finished, the same water was used for clothes washing. There was no school in the community, so they took long bus rides to study alongside children who had very different lives and teased the Navajo kids about their hygiene. "Maybe that's why I didn't go very often," Arviso said with a laugh. She never did finish high school.

In Kivalina, Alaska, another rural native community, a few families also have a tank-based system installed as part of a pilot project. Seven homes in town have been outfitted with experimental systems that combine rainwater collection, storage, and gravity to produce running water in a washbasin. A toilet directs liquid waste into an underground collection area outside the home. Solid waste is held in bags, dried, and brought to the landfill.

Public facilities were opened for people to wash their clothes and themselves. Most households still rely upon the public "washateria" where residents of the native village can do their laundry. But Kivalina resident Colleen Swan reports the showers there have not worked in years. People clean themselves in basins of water that get used by the whole family, whether they have been repairing an ATV or butchering an animal (subsistence hunting is a critical part of the local economy). They cart their solid waste to the town dump in "honey buckets," plastic bags that often break and leave a smelly trail. Some people do not let their children play outside during the spring thaw, when accumulated waste melts and flows down the streets. Waves of disease frequently run through the village school.

One Kivalina resident who uses the new system said on her evaluation, "I'd like to see the whole town get the system because, especially during the springtime—it's a real bad time of year—we have a bad problem with human waste when you're walking on the road. I don't even like my kids to be playing out because it's so bad, you know. So when I'm walking down the road I just cover my mouth and walk, because I don't want to smell that."

Another said, "It's a real hassle to try to haul that to the dump with the pee and anak [feces] together. You have to make sure the bag doesn't tear, and we make a whole trail out to the dump with pee and anak, and it just takes a lot of space and a lot of time and a lot of work."[9]

Because of the small sample size, no evaluation was done to determine whether providing access to running water and better waste disposal improved health for the Kivalina residents who got the first systems. Anecdotally, participants reported that it did. "It's way better than using honey buckets and washing with the same dirty water. We don't get as sick as before, because before that we just, you know, just use the same water over and over to wash, and now it's real good," one homeowner said. A second homeowner with six children reported, "I can say we haven't been going to the clinic as much as we used to."[10]

In Darlene Arviso's southwestern community, tank-based systems are also well received. As in Kivalina, it is common in this New Mexico community for people to cobble together a living between the land and part-time income-generating enterprises. One woman on Arviso's route got herself a food service license and makes tamales, tortillas, and rolls to sell in town—a business that could not have existed without access to potable water.

Each community, though, is dependent on grants or private gifts to bring service to more houses. Federal grant programs are anemic, as the EPA budget is at a forty-year low in constant dollars. According to the federal Indian Health Service (IHS), it would cost $2.8 billion to provide adequate water and waste service to every American Indian and Native Alaskan home in the country. Given IHS's budget and population growth, its current efforts are not making a dent in the number of unserved households.

WATER UNFIT TO DRINK

"The crops get better water than the people do here," said Janie Jones, nodding toward the lush green fields in the distance. Here in Tensas Parish, Louisiana, an African American majority area, the per capita income is about $10,000. Jones has been organizing in the county seat, St. Joseph, where what came out of the tap for years was brown and opaque. Periodically, residents would be warned to boil their water.

That, unfortunately, would have concentrated the lead levels. After years of drinking and washing in muck, the town got a new state-funded water system, largely because Jones, of the Council on Policy & Social Impact, collaborated with a Louisiana State University professor to prove that the water contained lead. However, after the system was installed, the now-crystal-clear water continued to have contaminants. Water rates doubled, leading to an increase in shutoffs.[11]

Just as having no water causes health problems, so does having bacteria or lead, a neurotoxin, in the water. The EPA calls for action when lead in drinking water reaches fifteen parts per billion. Though lead can be acquired from a variety of sources, including paint or even the dishes we eat off, scientists agree that there is no safe level of lead.

But the material was legal to use in constructing water systems until 1986. The Environmental Defense Fund estimates that six to ten million US American homes have drinking water supplied through lead pipes. Adrienne Katner, the scientist who discovered the lead in St. Joseph's water, estimates that there are "hundreds of St. Josephs" throughout Louisiana. But the cost of replacing lead pipes is considerable, leaving some utilities and government entities hesitant to look for lead, she said, and even prone to use testing methods that are less likely to detect it. State inspectors had pronounced St. Joseph lead-free many times before Katner found otherwise.

While lead is dangerous to people of all ages, prenatal and childhood exposure is linked to lower IQ, stunted growth, behavioral health problems, and special education needs. Iron immune deficiency, common in children from low-income households because of poor diet, increases risk of lead poisoning by making the digestive tract absorb more heavy metals. In 2010, the Pew Charitable Trust calculated that the United States would save seventeen dollars for every dollar it invested in lead abatement through reduced costs in health care, special education, and the criminal justice system, coupled with increased earning potential for young people with higher IQs. The economic benefit would be $192–$270 billion for a single birth cohort, according to Pew.[12]

The US failure to invest in infrastructure is singular among developed nations, according to Virginia Tech civil engineering professor Marc Edwards. Edwards helped bring to light lead drinking water crises in Flint, Michigan, and Washington, DC. Countries like Canada and Germany find "a way to maintain a basic level of civilization," Edwards said. "Civilization ended a long time ago for people in Flint."

Edwards can hold forth on the millions of miles of lead pipe still in service in the United States, on practices that actually speed their corrosion, on EPA testing procedures that he says miss lead, on water utilities that turn a blind eye to developing problems, and on new bacteria that pose a risk to water quality. But he keeps coming back to that word *civilization*. "If you don't have a system to bring clean water into cities and sewage out, civilization as we know it will cease to exist," he said.

Edwards also finds encouragement that, while water system upgrades are expensive, proactive maintenance is a relative bargain. It is three to four times more expensive to replace a pipe after it has failed, according to Edwards: "If we were more proactive about addressing these issues, we'd actually have more money at the end of the day." (See the A Better Way box on page 15 for more information on how one community proactively replaced lead pipes.)

POOR ACCESS, POOR QUALITY, POOR HEALTH

Each year, 1.7 million people die because they do not have access to safe drinking water and sanitation, according to the World Health Organization.[13] But the problem is much more recognized in resource-poor nations than in the United States. Anecdotally, people talk about health crises in US American communities brought on by not having access to water. It is difficult to document. There are people like Fred Lee who also lack access to health care and therefore go undiagnosed and uncounted. Valerie Jean Blakely works to get food-safe hoses for her Detroit neighbors so that a hose can be run from a house with service to one without. Those hoses get replaced regularly before they can become contaminated. But she also works hard to get people on payment plans with the city and restore service quickly. "After eleven days, people get sick," she said.

There was one study showing the effects of water shutoffs in Detroit, but the full results have not been shared publicly. A preliminary study by the Henry Ford Health System's Global Health Initiative found a connection between water shutoffs in Detroit and people contracting waterborne diseases, with people on blocks that had experienced shutoffs one and a half times more likely to suffer. The study relied on reports of hospital visits to track illness. Patients who dealt with illness at home or through a primary care provider were not captured. Henry Ford Health System's announcement of the findings contains tips that might appear in a brochure distributed in the developing world: "You can use rubbing alcohol to clean hands and wounds as much as possible. Consider asking neighbors or friends to come use their shower to bathe yourself and your family." Henry Ford did not release the full study, a move that activists say is the result of pressure from the city. One of the authors declined to be interviewed by us, and the organization's press office did not respond to queries.

When the study was due to be released, advocates were ready to have a press conference, explained Peter Hammer, director of the Damon J. Keith Center for Civil Rights at Wayne State University Law School. Hammer believes that the city threatened to withhold approval for Henry Ford building projects if researchers shared their full results. "I don't have a smoking gun, but it doesn't take a lot to imagine the mayor or the mayor's people calling up Henry Ford and saying: 'You cut this crap, or we're going to make it very hard for you to get anything through the city,'" Hammer said.

Detroit Mayor Mike Duggan's office did not respond to a request to reply to this and other accusations leveled by activists.

Instead of scientists from Henry Ford, the press conference featured Dr. Wendy Johnson, director of La Familia Medical Center in New Mexico.

"I wish I didn't have to be here because I wish there were local public health officials and board medical professionals that could say what I am going to say," Dr. Johnson said in the news conference, according to the *Detroit Free Press*.[14] "The folks that are suffering from these water shutoffs aren't just staying in their houses," she said. "They're going out shopping in grocery stores, taking care of kids, delivering food to you at lunch time, cleaning the office buildings, they're cleaning the hotels, they're cleaning homes, they are in the community living their lives. And that puts the entire community at risk. So the water shutoffs are a public health crisis of enormous dimensions."

WHO OWNS THE WATER?

Though many taps are dry in Midtown Detroit, the region does not lack for water. In fact, Nestlé has large water bottling operations in the Great Lakes, drawing on the same natural water systems that feed Detroit. Nestlé paid a $5,000 one-time application fee to begin operations as well as an annual $200 permit fee for the groundwater well it operates in Michigan, but there is no meter running. The company draws water for free now—and sells it to consumers by the bottle.

"Why does Nestlé get it for free . . . and make millions while the people in Detroit have been shut off because they can't afford it?" asked Jim Olson, an environmental lawyer who founded For Love of Water (FLOW), an advocacy group dedicated to protecting the Great Lakes. "Everybody else on the system who is not selling it is subsidizing their profit."

It is common for large bottlers to pay less for water than residential customers. Niagara Bottling entered into a contract with the Metropolitan District Commission (MDC), which supplies Hartford, Connecticut, and its suburbs, to begin a bottling operation on the Barkhamsted and Nepaug Reservoirs. Niagara would pay the same as residential customers for its first 500,000 gallons—but then a substantially discounted rate would kick in. It is also getting a discount on sewage fees. This is by no means the sweetest deal in the industry. On federal lands, bottlers typically draw water for free.

MDC held that water use rates had been falling for decades, largely because of conservation. So like Detroit and Baltimore, it was faced with raising rates to finance system costs. Selling to a large user, MDC reasoned, would bring in a large chunk of revenue—even with a discounted rate—and stop rate hikes for homeowners.[15] MDC set up a discounted rate for Niagara in 2015, which it rescinded during a drought a year later. The water authority proposed reinstating a 20 percent discount for Niagara in 2018 but withdrew the plan after public outcry. Even with several years of MDC being paid full rates for Niagara's use, the authority raised consumer rates 11 percent in 2019 and 13.43 percent in 2020. At least in this case, having a superuser did not spare regular ratepayers a hefty increase.

Groups like Save Our Water CT decry "corporate takeovers" of water. This is what has advocates like Jim Olson both angry and worried. For most of US history, water was seen as a "public trust," he said. Anyone could access it to drink, tend their livestock, or water their crops. European settlers and their earliest descendants would make their homes near rivers or lakes where they could get water directly or easily sink wells to access it. As the population grew and this became impractical, water systems emerged to transport the water from reservoir to tap, Olson said, but the water itself remained (and he argues remains still) a public resource.

Who should manage those systems is an open question. The trend in communities is toward public ownership of water systems, according to Mary Grant, who manages Food and Water Watch's Public Water for All campaign. Private ownership used to be much more common. The firm we know as JPMorgan Chase got its start as the Manhattan Company, a private water supplier founded by Aaron Burr and associates, whose poor service was linked to 3,500 cholera deaths in New York City. The story of water in the US shows increasing preference for public water systems over time, Grant explained, and that preference continues today, even in conservative regions. "It's seen as a tax cut," she says, when a community switches to public ownership and invariably lowers rates.

But Grant fears that a political preference for market solutions could reverse what she sees as an entirely positive trend toward public water utilities. Food and Water Watch collaborated with the NAACP to pass an ordinance mandating public control of water in Atlantic City because the groups feared then-governor Chris Christie would invite private investment in the water system. Atlantic City's tax base is less than half what it was in 2010 after the departure of five casinos.[16]

Just as water bottlers have an advantage in accessing water, so does agribusiness. This is particularly evident in California, where 40 percent of available water goes to crops, compared with just 10 percent going to the state's cities. Farmers can access ground sources of water, often through publicly financed projects, as well as pump it from below ground. That pumping is associated with wells going dry in communities where farmworkers live, and groundwater contamination in those areas linked to pesticide and fertilizer use is common.[17]

STEALING WATER TO STEAL LAND

On the face of it, no one benefits from denying US Americans access to potable water. When Detroit shut off ratepayers, its water revenue dropped and its ability to finance system upkeep weakened. When children in Flint, St. Joseph, and communities all over the country drink water with lead in it, costs in health care and other services far exceed the cost of repairing the water system, as the Pew study demonstrates. And finally, in communities with no access whatsoever, health, education, and economic development all suffer, as the experiences of native peoples in Alaska and New Mexico attest.

Across the country, community advocates charge that water access or quality crises are worsened by a desire to encourage residents to vacate land that is coveted by developers; a disenfranchisement so severe that there is no pressure to relieve the suffering of the community; historical injustices that forced marginalized groups onto land with poor water access; and racism. Often several of these factors work in tandem.

Valerie Jean Blakely refers to her central Detroit neighborhood as a "sacrifice zone," where low-income, predominantly African American residents are considered impediments to development and gentrification. Again, Mayor Michael Duggan's office did not reply to a request for comment. Blakely pointed to closures of neighborhood schools and libraries as further evidence that the city wants to empty out her neighborhood to make way for the much-touted "New Detroit."

As the battered city attracts investment, the African American population is dropping and the white population is increasing.[18] As Blakely and her longtime neighbors were finding it hard to stay in the neighborhood, employers like Wayne State University and local medical centers were offering their employees incentives to move in.[19] Employees who already resided in the neighborhood could get a $1,000 rent credit. But those moving in qualified for $2,500.

"You have to construct what I call dystopian scenarios (to get residents to move)," said Hammer, of the Damon J. Keith Center for Civil Rights. Detroit went from one hundred neighborhood schools in 2004 to just nine in 2016, he noted.

"If you deprive people enough, they are willing to trade their rights for lights that turn on, potholes that get filled," he said, explaining that residents lost agency within the city when it declared bankruptcy and an emergency manager assumed control. Voters had chosen this course of action, which makes perfect sense to Hammer. "It's very hard for people to look from their own life experience and see that voting has ever made a difference in their lives," he said. Though the city always had an elected mayor, the power to control budgets remained under the control of an unelected financial review commission for three years.

In Tensas Parish, Louisiana, there has never been a bankruptcy declaration, but there is a historical disenfranchisement. The large agricultural holdings that dominate the area are still called "the plantations." But today there is less need for manual labor on these spreads and little else in the way of employment opportunities in town. The descendants of persons formerly enslaved who make up the majority of the parish tend to seek jobs with the local detention center or with the parish school system.

Though St. Joseph is an African American majority town, Mayor Elvadus Fields Jr. is only its second black mayor. Fields grew up in

Farmville, Louisiana, which he describes as "outside the plantation system." Fields was educated as an agricultural agent and moved to St. Joseph in 1961 to perform services like vaccinating and castrating livestock. When he interviewed for his first job in the community, he was informed that "N——s don't vote here." (A records check showed there were no African American voters on the rolls in Tensas Parish until 1964.)

"If I wanted to vote," Fields replied, "I would have stayed in Farmville."

Fields can provide a history of every house. That one is where the beloved home economics teacher Miss Efflie Layton lived for many years. It's still in good shape. But many of the houses were inherited by children, nieces, or nephews who never showed up to claim them. These are houses without potable water in a town where there are no jobs. They weren't worth the back taxes.

Many of the houses are vacant—windows missing, crumbling steps, blue tarps covering the holes in the roof. Others that look much the same are occupied. It's hard to tell without knocking on the door.

Josephine Washington, the mayor of neighboring Clayton, which faces many of the same problems as St. Joseph, believes that generations of poverty have created a fatalism here in Tensas Parish. She described the prevailing attitude as "I ain't got nothing. I ain't gonna have nothing no how."

RATES THAT PEOPLE CAN PAY

In low-income Philadelphia neighborhoods, residents were plagued by water shutoffs that resulted in tax liens. Some thought they could never get out from under the liens and abandoned their homes. In 2017 the city instituted the Tiered Assistance Program (TAP), which links water rates to income for the neediest residents. Bills can be as low as fourteen dollars per month. So long as a customer on TAP is paying monthly bills, past-due balances will be frozen and the city will not take action on liens related to water bills.

"You'd rather keep people in their homes," said Joanne Dahme, then a spokesperson for the Philadelphia Water Department. "You don't want vacant property on blocks; that brings down property values."

There were assistance programs in Philadelphia for low-income customers before TAP, but to qualify, residents had to already be delinquent on their water bills. The new system aims to avoid debt and make water affordable for all residents. It is financed by higher rates for residents who do not receive assistance.

There were already conservation programs available to low-income customers that did things like fix leaks and install low-flow showerheads. Participation is mandatory for TAP customers with exceptionally high use.

The program is brand new, but there is speculation that it could pay for itself by ensuring that the city collects at least some water revenue from every household, discouraging blight, saving the cost of shutoffs, and improving the public health. Dahme underlined, however, that it remains to be seen how the numbers shake out. The city is committed to TAP nevertheless. "We do recognize that having water access is the number one essential for people to stay in their home, but also to have a healthy home," she said.

Significantly, the Philadelphia plan was developed by the same consultant who drafted a rate plan for Detroit in 2005 that would both guarantee access to low-income users and promote conservation. Detroit obviously did not adopt the plan.

A number of policy and academic groups advocate that utilities charge users who consume the most water the highest rates—the exact opposite of communities where water bottlers, industry, and agribusiness consume millions of gallons at deep discounts. The scheme would encourage conservation and favor people over industries. The city of

Davis, California, recently voted down such a system, and few others have adopted it.

KILLING COMMUNITIES

The UN considers water a human right. Up in Kivalina that fact is not lost on Colleen Swan. "We're living in third-world conditions here in rural Alaska," she said. "This is the United States."

The nearly four hundred people who live in Kivalina, Alaska, are there because of government decree. Their ancestors were nomadic hunters. In 1905 the US government built a school in what is now Kivalina and gave the nomadic hunters living there a choice: send your children to a government school, or go to prison and have them taken from you. From the start, Swan said, elders told the government that Kivalina was a bad place to plant a community.

Swan said that village elders quickly realized that the barrier reef they were on was eroding, but that the government paid no heed. With climate change, the ice barrier that protected the spit of land is melted for more of the year, and erosion is accelerating. The village will disappear within the next decade. "You wonder how people can sleep at night when they have made people's lives miserable," she said and wondered aloud how her culture would be preserved, as there are no definite plans yet for relocating the village.

But even now, she says, young people are leaving. Being extremely isolated, employment opportunities are scarce, and some people have to go to the mainland to work as miners for months at a time. People don't stay in a community without water, whether it's in Detroit, on the Mississippi Delta, or in rural Alaska, because denying people water is denying them life.

What Can I Do?

1. **Ask about water access and safety in your own community.** Don't accept officials telling you that funding for system maintenance or improvement does not exist. Remember the lesson of Lansing. Smart, proactive maintenance of a water system benefits everyone. Campaign for responsible upgrades to your system.

2. **Advocate for the right to water—regardless of ability to pay.** Every community should have a system where poor people are not priced out of the water market. There is a wonderful blueprint for a fair payment system online. You can find it at Peopleswaterboard.org. Look for "water affordability program." Detroit failed to adopt it in 2005, but Philadelphia's system uses many of the principles.

3. **Reject privatization.** For-profit utilities on average charge higher rates than public ones.

4. **If you can avoid it, don't drink bottled water.** In most cases, bottled water is no more safe or pure than tap water; often, it comes from the same place. (The exceptions, of course, are areas like St. Joseph and Flint, where lead in the water supply is a threat, or in areas that are experiencing boil advisories.) But the industry seeks to privatize water resources, often paying lower rates than consumers. It wastes water—much of which evaporates during the bottling process—and 80 percent of water bottles are not recycled.

5. **Take the #4Liters challenge.** Most US Americans use more than 100 gallons of water a day. Dig Deep, the nonprofit that brought water to Darlene Arviso's community, asks people to

live on four liters a day to raise awareness about what people like Fred Lee live with every day. Visit www.4liters.org.

6. **Demand that schools and other public facilities be tested for lead in drinking water.** Your local school board is a good place to start. The least we can do is provide clean, safe drinking water in all our public buildings.

CHAPTER 3

Food

Hungry in America

In hospitals throughout the United States doctors treat young children for failure to thrive, often abbreviated FTT. These are children who are not gaining weight and growing normally. Dr. Deborah Frank, who specializes in treating FTT, noted, "For the longest time, it was a mother-blaming diagnosis." The common assumption was that mothers were not adequately feeding and caring for their children. "What we call failure to thrive, the rest of the world calls malnutrition," she said.

Dr. Frank is a pediatrician, director of the Grow Clinic for Children at Boston Medical Center, and founder of a food bank at that institution. The food bank was an extension of her practice. "I really hate telling mothers how many times their kids need to eat and having them burst into tears," she said.

Dr. Frank can trace the politics of hunger by looking at patient charts, she said, as she sees FTT increase when safety net programs are under attack. Think about the term "safety net." It implies something essential, something that no responsible society would ever compromise.

Hunger is a public health issue. But the federal government's response to it has never reflected that. The United Nations recognized the right to food in 1948 under the Universal Declaration of Human Rights. But once again, the United States lags behind the international community in affirming that a basic need is a human right. During World War II, Congress turned its attention to hunger but framed it narrowly as a problem of war readiness. The National School Lunch Act passed in 1946 reads in part (emphasis ours):

> It is hereby declared to be the policy of Congress, as **a measure of national security** to safeguard the health and well-being of the Nation's children and to encourage the domestic consumption of nutritious agricultural commodities and other food, by assisting the States, through grants-in-aid and other means, in providing an adequate supply of food and other facilities for the establishment, maintenance, operation, and expansion of nonprofit school lunch programs.[1]

During World War II, the military found itself rejecting too many draftees because they had physical problems traced back to their malnutrition as children. A full 40 percent of the men found unfit to serve had problems rooted in their early diets. Generals testified to get the bill passed.[2] The original inspiration to feed children properly in this country was that we might need them to fight in future wars.

In successive administrations of both parties, government nutritional programs such as food stamps, or the Supplemental Nutrition Assistance Program (SNAP), and the Special Supplemental Nutrition program for Women, Infants, and Children (WIC) grew. By the time Ronald Reagan was elected, childhood hunger in the United States was at an all-time low. But Reagan quickly reversed that gain. His first year in office, he cut the school lunch program by $1.46 billion, nearly 40 percent. That same year, his cuts threw one million people off food stamps. These savings funded corporate and personal income tax breaks.[3]

Nearly half the food banks and most of the soup kitchens operating today under the Feeding America umbrella—the largest antihunger organization in the country—came into existence in the 1980s in response to the need created by such cuts.[4] Hungry US Americans now had to rely on the kindness and resources of their neighbors rather than the government. The need grew even greater after President Bill Clinton kept his promise to "end welfare as we know it," restricting access to cash aid. The same legislation placed new restrictions on who can receive food stamps.

Programs like SNAP and WIC are essential and do improve the health of millions of people in the US, but they have never been properly scaled and are perpetually the targets of shortsighted cost-cutting. The private nonprofits that attempt to fill the gap are often small and poorly resourced, which leads them to limit service. One of us, Colleen, used to run a food pantry. Her supervisor objected that the same women were coming in month after month. "It's an emergency food pantry," he would say. "You can't have an emergency every month!"

Actually, you can. SNAP benefits do not last an entire thirty days. People get hungry at the end of the month, seek help from a nonprofit, and do exactly the same thing month after month—because there is no alternative. But the charitable hunger relief network is inadequate to supply all the nutrition that every family in need requires. That's why there are babies, right here in the United States, with dangerously low weights. The World Bank estimates that 0.5 percent of the US under-five population is underweight, more than 100,000 children, an emergency that has never been acknowledged as such.[5]

Dr. Frank came to work at what was then Boston City Hospital as a fellow to the renowned pediatrician T. Berry Brazelton in 1981, just as the Reagan cuts were beginning to take effect. Young mothers could no longer qualify for WIC if they lived with their own mothers. She had parents tell her, "We used to drink milk when we had WIC, but we can't afford it."

Dr. Frank knew that the children in her care could not grow and gain weight if they did not have quality food, but you can't prescribe a full grocery cart. She decided to get politically active. "I don't like people hurting my patients," she explained. Dr. Frank began talking with the press and doing research to show the effects of government funding on hunger. She demonstrated that 10 percent of the children receiving WIC or attending Head Start programs in Boston had symptoms of malnutrition. National data sets are always two years out of date, she said, so she organized physicians like herself who serve the poorest children in a number of US communities. They produce data six months out, and they clearly show matches between cuts to nutrition programs and surges in FTT and other health problems affecting children.

Eventually, Dr. Frank started a food bank at her hospital, so now she actually can prescribe food to a family. But she is quick to point out that it is only a stopgap—three days of food every two weeks to a family that knows poverty all month long. Though food is clearly a medical necessity for an underweight child, there is no way to bill it through insurance. Boston Medical Center raises $1 million annually to support the food pantry. Again, it is the kindness of strangers, not a recognition of human rights, that is feeding malnourished US American children.

Dr. Frank gets angry just talking about it. She referred to the late nutritionist Jean Mayer, who said, "Of all the dumb ways of saving money, not feeding children is the dumbest."

STARVING YOUNG BRAINS

Most people in the US, even those with plenty of income, have diets that are lacking in some vitamins or minerals. For people in poverty, those deficiencies can be severe because of the cost and other barriers to getting high-nutrient foods. Iron deficiency is the most common nutrient deficiency in the United States and the world and is particularly prevalent among women of childbearing age and children. This is a recipe for disaster.

One in four US American one-year-olds are not getting enough iron.[6] The odds of suffering from iron deficiency anemia (IDA)—a dangerous condition that impedes brain development—increase significantly when a family lives with food insecurity.[7] When blood is low in iron, it cannot transport oxygen efficiently to the brain. It is tantamount to holding poor children underwater. IDA also makes children more susceptible to lead poisoning, a danger kids from low-income families already face at much higher rates than their more affluent peers, by making the gastrointestinal tract absorb more heavy metal. (See chapter 2.)

The harm of IDA is lifelong. A baby with IDA does not get sufficient oxygen to the brain. Nobody recovers from that. A study compared twenty-five-year-olds who had suffered from iron deficiency as infants with peers who had not.[8] The young adults who had been iron deficient were less likely to have completed high school or to be married. They reported poorer emotional health and more feelings of dissociation or detachment.

How is this happening? In some cases, a child may suffer from a medical condition that prevents the absorption of iron. It is more likely that the child is not getting an iron-rich diet or is being nursed by a mother who is herself suffering from anemia. Iron-rich foods, such as green vegetables and meats, are expensive.

HUNGER IS A TRAUMA

Not surprisingly, living with food insecurity is traumatic. Multiple Canadian studies have shown a link between experiencing hunger and depression and suicidal ideation.[9]

Antihunger advocate Rachie Weisberg uses pop culture to demonstrate the stress of going without food:

Earlier this year, Snickers ran a commercial where a bunch of young men are playing football with an irritated older woman. The scene is confusing at first, but, as soon as the woman bites into the Snickers, she "morphs" back into her original self—a young man. The Snickers tagline then runs across the screen stating, "You're not yourself when you're hungry." While this is a silly example the overwhelming stress associated with hunger is no laughing matter. Unfortunately, food insecure parents are often forced to make the decision between feeding their children and going hungry themselves.[10]

We spoke with many parents who talked about cutting back on their own food to shield their children. Despite these sacrifices, research shows that children are aware of and harmed by living with food insecurity. In one study, researchers interviewed children who spoke of voluntarily limiting their own eating and trying to make money to buy more food, even if they were too young for legal employment.[11]

A high school boy ate no more than one meal at home each day. He was often hungry and described that he felt "angry, mad, go to sleep basically, that's the only thing you can probably do and after you wake up, you feel like you've got a bunch of cramps in your stomach and you'll be light-headed."[12]

HOW SCARCITY PROMOTES OBESITY

The narrative of children going without meals may seem at odds with the high rates of obesity among people in poverty. Actually, they are two features in the same story: food insecurity is associated with binge-eating disorder and obesity.[13] Furthermore, high-calorie, low-nutrition food is typically much cheaper than healthier options.

The Federal Crop Insurance Program cost US taxpayers an average of $9 billion annually between 2012 and 2017, according to a report by the nonpartisan Congressional Budget Office.[14] That is a terrible investment going to support low-quality food, overwhelmingly corn that will fatten animals and sweeten beverages. Among a great many other uses, corn is the raw material of fast food.[15]

But crop subsidies are not to blame for most of the price differential between foods, despite popular opinion. Farm production accounts for only eight cents of every dollar US consumers spend on food, according to 2018 data from the US Department of Agriculture (USDA).[16]

"It's a really vexing problem. If there were easy answers, people would have already pursued them," said Jayson Lusk, an economist and head of the Department of Agricultural Economics at Purdue University.

There are many reasons why farmers would rather grow corn than kale or berries. The growth of grains, or row crops, has been mechanized. A single worker can seed and harvest acre upon acre. Fruits and vegetables usually require human workers to plant, tend, and harvest them by hand.[17] Though many of these workers are paid outrageously low wages, the cumulative effect is still expensive. So is the refrigerated shipping that fruits and vegetables require. While a single buyer may purchase mass quantities of grain, fruits and vegetables generally get transported to supermarkets to come home with individual shoppers. Some will rot on the trip, and still more will go bad in the store. According to the USDA, a staggering 31 percent of the US food supply goes to waste at the retail and consumer level.[18]

Federal agricultural research dollars have been weighted heavily toward grains, said Lusk. Placing emphasis on developing fruit and vegetable varieties that were more advantageous to farmers—easier to grow in more places, maturing faster, and so on—might help a bit, he told us, though he thinks change to consumer eating habits would be easier to achieve on the retail side. He noted that higher-income people consistently eat better diets. "Make people richer," he quipped.

Lusk wrote *The Food Police: A Well-Fed Manifesto About the Politics of Your Plate*, in which he takes on the likes of writer Michael Pollan, celebrity chef Alice Waters, and other proponents of fresh, local, and organic foods. The movement "adds cost without adding nutrition," he said.

In other words, if you can get children in a food-insecure family eating broccoli, that is a victory. If the broccoli came from the freezer, it's still a victory. If it came from a local organic farm, chances are that their parents could not have afforded it. Programs that give people in poverty access to farmers' markets are laudable steps toward inclusion. But advancing a movement toward local, organic foods is not addressing the nutritional needs of food-insecure people. The public needs to stop pretending that it is—and instead take a close look at why people eat the way they do.

SCHOOL NUTRITION, AN ESSENTIAL AND IMPERFECT SOLUTION

The National School Lunch Program serves thirty million students a day with free or reduced-price lunches. School breakfasts and increasingly available suppers are also mostly feeding children who qualify for free meals.

Feeding thirty million children who may not otherwise have access to a healthy meal is an unquestionably good thing to do. Kids who eat a school breakfast have higher math scores and improved memory compared to kids who do not.[19]

But school nutrition programs are short on funding. This can produce substandard meals, meals that kids refuse to eat, or both. All school meals must include one-percent or fat-free milk, the only product singled out for such treatment, in defiance of high rates of lactose intolerance among students of color.*

---

* The legislation that created the new standards was the target of lobbying by many food industry groups, according to data gathered by the Center for Responsive Politics, including the International Dairy Food Association and the sugar industry, who successfully collaborated to keep chocolate milk in cafeterias.

Dan Giusti is formerly head chef at Noma, a Copenhagen eatery regarded by some critics as the world's best. The biggest challenge of his career has been producing a $3.43 lunch (the federal reimbursement) that includes a carton of milk as well as the staffing to cook and serve the meal. Giusti founded Brigaid, a company that puts chefs into school kitchens. He started in New London, Connecticut, and expanded operation to the Bronx. "We're very far away from great," Giusti said.

He is still puzzling out how to get good meals to kids under the constraints of a school program—and get kids to eat them. He firmly believes that charging chefs with bringing their skills to the challenge is "the only way to figure it out." Chefs are constantly responding to feedback from students. Dishes that the pros consider successes will be struck from the menus if the students do not like them.

He is frequently asked about serving local, seasonal ingredients. "My whole career has been rooted in working seasonally and locally, but if that's your priority, then your priorities are out of whack," he said. He added that some schools have the capability to use local and fresh ingredients, but not all do.

WHAT HAPPENED TO DINNER?

The idea of happy, broccoli-eating children comes with a host of assumptions: An adult who has the time and energy to cook dinner. A store nearby that sells broccoli, or transportation to get to such a store. A refrigerator, a stove (or at least a microwave), running water, a knife, cutting board, and other kitchen supplies. And finally, the adult responsible for grocery shopping must either be certain that the kids will eat broccoli or flush enough to be willing to take a chance that the vegetable will go to waste. Those are a lot of assumptions.

"Tonya," a fourteen-year-old from New Britain, Connecticut, eats fast food nearly every day. We met Tonya in a summer program that encourages physical activity and healthy eating for girls. She usually gets

A Better Way: School kitchens become community kitchens

DAN GIUSTI'S CHEFS PREPARE a weekly dinner open to the whole community, in part because he cannot stand to let a perfectly good kitchen sit idle after 1 PM. It is five dollars for a "legit meal"—and many diners pay ten dollars so that someone without cash can eat as well. These Wednesday-night dinners have become popular and have got him wondering about how many underused kitchens can be put to work preparing affordable meals for overworked, low-income families.

there well before the program's 7:30 AM start time because of her family's schedule. Both her parents are certified nursing assistants who work double shifts. The family's only car is in the shop, so they are borrowing the children's grandmother's. To make the arrangement function, Tonya's parents must get up early and drive to the next town to take the grandmother to her job, before dropping Tonya and her younger brother at different camps and beginning their own sixteen-hour workdays. Somewhere in there, the grandmother must also be picked up and taken home. It is no wonder that the kids' dinner comes from a drive-through.

As Tonya described her routine, the girls around her nodded. One is being raised by an aunt working three jobs. Fast food was a frequent option for all of them. Incidentally, they did not complain about this. They enjoyed the food—which may well become a lifelong preference. They did express sadness that they could not spend more time with their parents.

A nightly home-cooked meal is becoming increasingly rare in US families across the economic spectrum. Researcher Eddie Yoon tracks how US Americans feel about cooking and finds the love of the activity is in decline. By 2017, 50 percent of respondents to his survey said that they hated to cook. He likened it to sewing, a onetime standard household chore that has become a niche hobby.[20]

Despite typical work schedules and cooking habits, SNAP assumes that recipients should spend more time on meal preparation than the average US American. A report by the Food Research and Action Center (FRAC) points out a number of reasons why SNAP benefits must be far more generous to work in the real world.[21] The report focuses on the Thrifty Food Plan (TFP), a monthly diet developed by the USDA that purports to allow for healthy eating on an extremely limited budget. SNAP benefits are based on the TFP. "Healthy," of course, is relative. The plan does not account for medical conditions such as diabetes or high blood pressure that require special diets. The family allowance does not change with a child's age. Recipients get the same assistance to feed a five-year-old as a sixteen-year-old. Monthly SNAP benefits simply do not pay for a month's worth of groceries, though they do significantly reduce hunger, the experience of families across the country shows. Cash value is not the only weak point in the TFP.

Time, as the authors show, is a limiting factor. For example, celebrity chef Mario Batali took the SNAP challenge—living for a month on what a program participant could purchase—and had to go to four stores to find the necessary ingredients to abide by the TFP. Batali lives in New York City, where stores are located closely together, and he presumably has transportation. Many SNAP recipients lack these advantages. Studies have shown that food preparation time is considerably higher under the TFP than what most US American households do. Virginia Tech researchers calculated that it would take 13.1 hours a week to prepare meals under the TFP, compared to 4.41 hours spent on this chore in the average household.[22]

The TFP clearly is an abstract developed by academics and bureaucrats, not by people trying to actually feed themselves or their families. The TFP allows for 5 percent food waste in its budget. As noted earlier, food waste is much higher on average in the United States. This leaves families without enough food to meet their needs. It also may preclude trying new foods in favor of safe bets that parents know children will eat.

"Sheree" is an unemployed mother of four. She lives in Section 8 housing, receives SNAP, and gets cash assistance to pay her utility bills. Aside from some occasional help from her children's father, from whom she is separated, the utility assistance is the only cash she has.[*]

She has one picky eater in the family, a seven-year-old son. "Some of the stuff will go to waste," she said, shaking her head. Sheree spoke about sitting down with her children before shopping trips and trying to agree on a list. But her son will often refuse food that she thought he would eat. Waste is a huge concern for Sheree as her resources do not last through the month. "We have had times when we have had to eat real light," she said. Without help from a local food bank, where she volunteers to give back, those light meals would be skipped meals.

"If you're not sure your kid's going to eat it, you're not going to put some expensive vegetable in front of your kid," said Marlene Schwartz, director of the Rudd Center for Food Policy and Obesity at the University of Connecticut. "For a low-income parent, that's a huge deal."

Schwartz is a proponent of including more fruits and vegetables in school lunches so that children can be introduced to them. Opponents say that this will lead to waste. She counters that 30 percent of all food served in school cafeterias is thrown away already. "For me, the cost/benefit of waste compared with the increase in kids' willingness to eat that for the rest of their lives—it's worth it," she said. Schwartz is referring to a large body of evidence that food preferences are formed in childhood. "People like food that's familiar. That's a very human phenomenon," she said.

---

[*] Living with no income at all has become increasingly common since the Clinton-era overhaul to the welfare system. An excellent picture of what this looks like can be found in *$2 a Day: Living on Almost Nothing in America* by Kathryn Edin and H. Luke Shaefer.

> ## Bizarre Policy: Meal plan built on microscopic portions
>
> **THE THRIFTY FOOD PLAN,** which serves as a basis for SNAP bene-fits, was developed by researchers, who apparently never stepped inside the kitchen: researchers noted that "the weekly market bas-ket for a reference family of four allots approximately 0.64 ounces of 'frozen or refrigerated entrees' and approximately 2.1 ounces of 'all cheese'—which, respectively, translates to about two-thirds of a fish stick and two slices of cheese for a family of four for a week."[23]

So if kids grow up on pasta because it is cheap, easy, and palatable, it is likely to be a favorite throughout their lives. If they are not served leafy greens in childhood, they are less likely to eat them as adults.

"These moms are doing the best they can," Schwartz underlined, but they are faced with an environment where a healthy diet is hard to achieve.

LOTS OF FOOD, MOST OF IT BAD

The teens we spoke to in New Britain described a neighborhood with fast-food restaurants and gas stations that offered packaged snacks and drinks. Sheree, the mother of four, has no car and must rely on high-priced, low-selection bodegas unless she is lucky enough to get a ride to a supermarket. Ron, who lives on Los Angeles' Skid Row, finds that unhealthy foods from a corner store are the main option if he misses a free meal at a nonprofit, which sometimes happens when he has an appointment outside the neighborhood.[24] All these people are living in food deserts, areas where healthy, affordable food is difficult to obtain.

In Ron's neighborhood, the closest grocery store is a Whole Foods, evidence that the fringes of Skid Row are becoming gentrified. A study by the Los Angeles Community Action Network (LA CAN) found that most Skid Row residents prefer to leave the neighborhood to shop at Food4Less and 99 Cents Only Stores, where their money goes further.[25] The average monthly income of people participating in the study was $448. The most accessible sources of food were vending machines, ubiquitous in single-room occupancy hotels.

Housed residents were obviously more likely to cook at home, but they also faced barriers like lack of access to a kitchen, the insufficiency of their SNAP benefit, and the difficulty of getting real groceries (as opposed to packaged snack foods) in a neighborhood dotted with corner stores and lacking supermarkets.

Skid Row is full of charities offering free foods. Yet 80 percent of respondents said that they skipped meals because of lack of resources, and 27 percent said they did so often. In addition, 25 percent said that they had resorted to eating out of trash cans or dumpsters. Why are so many people going hungry in a landscape with so much free food?

There is time, one of the factors that so often stands between people and nutritious food. Take Ron, who sometimes misses meals at nonprofits because of appointments. Mealtimes are limited at all the nonprofit providers, meaning that residents with appointments, work, or school can miss out. Additionally, some of these institutions require people to attend church services or other programming in order to eat. There is also an informal system of food giveaways—well-intentioned people handing out food from the back of their cars or pickup trucks. These tend to be high-fat, low-vitamin meals, such as pizza or hot dogs. The more ambitious meals can be dangerous, according to the report, as they do not do well without refrigeration. Many residents report getting sick after eating food given away on the streets. One store owner told the LA CAN researchers that he sells out of Pepto Bismol on Mondays and Tuesdays, after the weekends when street food giveaways are heaviest.

THE HIGH COST OF HUNGER

As we'll discuss more thoroughly when we talk about health, nutrition is a bargain. The United States spends about $1 trillion on Medicare, Medicaid, the Children's Health Insurance Programs, and Affordable Care Act marketplace subsidies. In contrast, it spends about $68 billion on food assistance programs. Increasing access to healthy food is a smart way to chip away at that $1 trillion. Food assistance alone won't do it, though it's an excellent start. As we've seen, free time and access to healthy choices through convenient and affordable transportation make it more likely that people will eat healthily. There is no end of public education programs urging US Americans toward a lower-fat, more plant-based diet. But eating habits won't change unless that ideal diet— or something close to it—fits into the already extremely stressed lives of people in poverty.

What Can I Do?

1. **Advocate for nutrition.** SNAP, WIC, and the School Nutrition Program are perpetually on the chopping block. You can let your public officials know that these programs need *more* funding and that you support them.

2. **Raise wages.** That really is the solution. When stimulus money went to extra food stamp allotments in the wake of the Great Recession, food security increased. Similarly, when people make more money, they buy more and healthier food. Increases in minimum wage and other pro-worker policies will make for better-fed US Americans. More money can also translate to more time, so often the barrier between a family and a good meal. Imagine if the parents of those girls in New Britain did not have to work double shifts.

3. **Support community eligibility for school meals.** If a high enough percentage of students qualify for free school meals, a district can opt to provide, and get federal support for, free meals for all. That means no stigma and no child left out because of red tape. Contact your board of education or superintendent to find out if your school district could qualify.

4. **Support universal school meals.** A bill was put forward in 2019 to amend the Child Nutrition Act of 1966 and the Richard B. Russell National School Lunch Act to make breakfasts and lunches free for all children. Ask your members of Congress to support this bill.

5. **Eat lunch at your child's school.** Even in more fortunate communities, meals served in school may be some children's primary access to nutrition. Kids do not have power. You do. Have lunch in the cafeteria. Are children eating the food? Would you eat the food? If not, get involved. Find out if there is a way that parents can support the staff to do better.

6. **Buy lunch for someone else's child.** In school districts around the country, there are children who, for various reasons, are not receiving free lunches but cannot afford to pay. Stories have emerged nationally of children being turned away or shamed. Contact your school administration to see if there are children who owe the lunch program money. Offer to do some fundraising to make sure that every child is fed and respected. Meanwhile, investigate community eligibility.

7. **Support summer food programs** by donating or volunteering.

8. **Advocate for the Low-Cost Food Plan.** The Thrifty Food Plan is unrealistic and keeps SNAP benefits low. The USDA should switch to the Low-Cost plan, which would provide more realistic benefits.

CHAPTER 4

Housing

No Place to Be Poor

T he man with the tousled hair held a toothbrush. Michael, forty-four, looked like any guy about to head into the shower, but he was standing in line on the sidewalk. He was waiting for a hot shower provided by a nonprofit out of a converted city bus. It is a weekly treat for Michael, who volunteered matter-of-factly that he expects to be homeless for the rest of this life. "You get the choice of eating or paying rent," he explained. "So I decided to eat."

The Department of Housing and Urban Development (HUD) has long held that housing (including utilities) should not consume more than 30 percent of household income to be considered affordable. HUD arrived at the number by weighing the cost of other necessities such as food, transportation, and health care. So long as housing costs stay at or below 30 percent of income, no one should have to make the terrible sorts of choices that shape Michael's life. But today, many US Americans, more than forty million of us, pay in excess of 30 percent of our income for housing; and nineteen million pay more than 50 percent. So around the country people who are far more prosperous than Michael are choosing to skimp on necessities to keep a roof over their heads.

Choosing housing over other necessities is often a sound decision. If you live on oatmeal during a bad stretch, the grocery store will still be willing to sell you vegetables when times get better. It is not so with housing. Once a person loses housing or even gets into a conflict with a landlord, it can be difficult to secure a lease again. Being right in a dispute with a landlord will likely not change the situation. Just ask "Liza Cooke," who is still paying rent and has not even considered suing the building owner for the furniture and clothes that she lost in an infestation of bedbugs, because she does not want to be labeled a "troublemaker" and thus discourage a new landlord from renting to her. We met her in a shelter, where she is living because conditions at her apartment became too unhealthy.

US Americans are struggling to stay housed because wages have not been growing significantly for decades while housing costs have soared. Workers made only 10 percent more in 2017 than they did in 1973, after adjusting for inflation.[1] And it should be noted that even that lackluster growth was not distributed fairly among people of color, women, and low-wage workers.

Meanwhile, the median US home sold for $65,300 in 1970 and $119,600 in 2000 (in 2000 dollars), according to the US Census—an 83 percent increase. The census tracked the rise in rent for the same period from $415 to $600, a 45 percent increase. Obviously, both rent and sale prices are higher in sought-after areas where there is more access to jobs, good schools, and other quality-of-life plusses.

The situation is even worse for US Americans of color. The history of racism in housing is long, ugly, and far from over. We discuss this in depth in chapter 9. A 2018 study found that African American and Hispanic homeowners were much more likely to hold high-cost mortgages from exploitive lenders with high foreclosure rates.[2] HUD sent undercover staff on a search for sale and rental property in 2012 and found that African American, Hispanic, and Asian staffers were consistently shown fewer units by brokers, giving them less choice in price and quality.[3]

More than half a million US Americans are homeless, according to HUD, though of course counting people who are homeless accurately is close to impossible. Any day, you can find someone speaking or writing about the intractability of homelessness or proposing a byzantine network of services necessary to ameliorate it. But in most cases homelessness is less a complex social problem and more a math problem. Wages are not nearly sufficient to support the cost of housing. Simple. It is inevitable that this imbalance will cause homelessness, as well as people settling for poverty-quality homes, going without food and other essentials, and living in situations where they are victimized.

This is, of course, not to say that mental health and substance abuse disorder never play a role in rendering people homeless. Services to address these problems are too few and too hard to access. But the fact remains that even for people who obtain excellent and effective services, finding an affordable place to live may still be an insurmountable barrier to good health.

As a nation, the United States is doing virtually nothing to change the situation. While wealthier US Americans have their housing subsidized through the mortgage interest deduction, the government spends far less on programs to make housing available to lower-income people. Policy and what one advocate calls "the commodification of housing" encourage surging prices that literally leave too many people out in the cold.

THE HOMELESSNESS BLAME GAME

If you do not have a permanent place to call home, a place where you don't need to exchange sex for shelter, a place where no one can decide to kick you out on a whim, then you are homeless. Most homeless people do not live on the streets, which is why their numbers are probably vastly underestimated. There are homeless eighteen-year-olds who have aged out of foster care and stay on friends' couches—until the host or the host's parents tire of the arrangement. There are families put up in motels on an emergency basis. There are people who get short-term rentals during the winter and camp out in the summer. You probably pass people on the street without identifying them as homeless. They work in the restaurant where you grab a coffee or lunch. They wash your car. They make up the crew that emerges from your contractor's truck.

As we have said, poverty is typically seen as a failure of character—that's the big lie that got us angry enough to write this book. The character assassination against people who are homeless is far worse than what is typically aimed at other people in poverty. *They drink, do drugs, are violent, are crazy. They'd rather sleep on a grate than do a day's hard work.*

Of course, some of these people do have mental health or substance abuse problems, just as some housed people do. But most do not. The most frequently cited figure is that one-third of people who are homeless are also mentally ill.[4] We notice the man talking to himself in an agitated voice on the subway (who, by the way, may be sleep deprived or simply frustrated with a bureaucracy that isn't helping him) and make him the archetype of all people without housing. The federal Substance and Abuse and Mental Health Services Administration estimates that among people who are homeless in the short term, most do not have a mental illness or substance abuse disorder. When homelessness is chronic, the rates increase: 30 percent have a chronic mental illness, and 50 percent have a substance abuse disorder.[5] The connection between higher mental health need and chronic homelessness raises the possibility that at least some of the time the stress of homelessness is causing illness—rather than the other way around.

Most homeless people are homeless because they cannot afford housing. As we've illustrated, many US Americans cannot afford the housing they currently occupy. The average housed US American and the average homeless one have quite a bit in common.

Paul Boden, executive director of the Western Regional Advocacy Project (WRAP), neatly summarized the cause: the government has dramatically cut its support for affordable housing. WRAP's report "Without Housing" documents $50 billion in cuts to affordable housing between 1979 and 1983.* "Racism, poverty, and addiction all existed before 1982," said Boden. "What did not exist was a homeless shelter." He added that the homeless shelters that cropped up in the 1980s were funded by the Federal Emergency Management Administration (FEMA), the nation's disaster relief agency, implying that the crisis of homelessness was temporary.

According to "Without Housing," "From 2001 to 2008, the George W. Bush administration continued this trend while claiming to be pushing for the end of homelessness. He modestly increased HUD homeless assistance targeted at 'chronically' homeless single adults, but substantially cut funding for public housing, Section 8 and other HUD affordable housing programs."[6]

The single biggest government program to support housing is the mortgage interest deduction (MID), which primarily benefits upper-income people—as well as the builders, finance companies, and other businesses that profit from home sales. In 2013, 73 percent of the program benefited the wealthiest 20 percent of Americans.[7] The deduction is available for interest accrued from first mortgages up to $1 million. For homes purchased after December 15, 2017, it was amended to cover the first $750,000 of a mortgage. It's no wonder that the wealthy, who are more likely to own homes and expensive ones at that, benefited more than low-income families who are less likely to fill out the itemized return necessary to access the benefit. Recent changes in standard deductions

---

* Read "Without Housing" online at wraphome.org/what/without-housing/. It is periodically updated with new proposals to fight further cuts to federal housing assistance.

make middle-class households less likely than they were to itemize. The MID costs the federal government more than $70 billion in collectible taxes in a typical year. In contrast, HUD spends $22 billion helping low-income people pay their rent through Section 8 and other programs. The MID also drives up the price of owner-occupied homes because potential buyers calculate tax savings into their budgets when making purchasing decisions.[8] Thus, they can afford to pay a higher asking price. So the biggest housing assistance program our government runs actually makes housing more expensive.

Filers must itemize their tax returns to claim the MID, something that is much more advantageous for upper-income taxpayers. At lower income levels—and without the help of a savvy accountant—the standard deduction is often bigger than what an itemized return will yield. An analysis by Matthew Desmond found that households with $100,000 or more in income claimed four-fifths of the total value of the MID and property tax deductions.[9]

So the issue is not that the government does not have the money to help low-income people obtain housing. It does. It just chooses to reduce the tax obligation of well-off people. Public housing and housing vouchers like Section 8 get people into housing. We know this. But according to the National Coalition to End Homelessness, only one out of four people who qualify for this type of assistance receives it, owing to lack of funding.

THE HIGH COST OF HOUSING

The MID, as noted, drives up the cost of housing. So do a number of other government policies. The National Association of Home Builders holds that 25 percent of the cost of new housing comes from regulation, most of it at the site level (in other words, local planning and zoning). The Obama administration also weighed in on regulatory burden. Its 2016 report "Housing Development Toolkit" warned that overregulation threatened to stifle gross domestic product growth by driving labor away from places where job growth is robust. The report says:

> Locally-constructed barriers to new housing development include beneficial environmental protections, but also laws plainly designed to exclude multifamily or affordable housing. Local policies acting as barriers to housing supply include land use restrictions that make developable land much more costly than it is inherently, zoning restrictions, off-street parking requirements, arbitrary or antiquated preservation regulations, residential conversion restrictions, and unnecessarily slow permitting processes. The accumulation of these barriers has reduced the ability of many housing markets to respond to growing demand.[10]

The report notes that overregulation limits economic and racial diversity. But, of course, that's the intention. Communities will often choose senior housing as their only affordable housing option because it keeps communities whiter.

In addition to regulation, housing prices are affected by what Boden calls "the commodification of housing." For some of us, a house or an apartment is a place to hang our hat. For others, it's a way to make money—often lots of it.

While we were doing our research in Los Angeles, we stayed in a one-bedroom apartment in a downtown complex where units rent for more than $2,000 monthly. The building also did business with travelers. We paid $193 a night, which would come to nearly $6,000 if the place stayed continually occupied over the course of a month. It was a ten-minute walk to Skid Row, where advocates estimate that five thousand homeless Angelenos occupy a 0.4-square-mile area. With rental subsidies, that building could fill overnight with permanent residents, but profits would take a nosedive.

Short-term rental services like Airbnb and VRBO are taking permanent housing off the market. Around the country, cities are figuring out how or if to regulate them. Los Angeles began doing so in 2018. This is, of course, just one example of how real estate is for many an investment—not a home. The subprime mortgage market that brought on the housing crisis is another. Borrowers were not sufficiently, and were sometimes fraudulently, vetted, creating a large cohort of buyers who could not afford their loans. The problem was hidden so long as prices kept rapidly inflating, something that predictably could not go on forever. The original lenders had often bundled these subprime mortgages as securities and sold them off, so they were out before the defaults started in large numbers. It was not their mess to clean up—it was yours. The federal government devoted $700 billion to financial bailouts in the 2008 crisis, with additional bailouts of Fannie Mae and Freddie Mac. In fairness, some of that money was returned, with interest.* However, note that the United States spends about $22 billion on Section 8 in a typical year. Government places far more importance on the business of real estate than it does on housing.

ALL THE JUSTICE YOU CAN AFFORD

General Dogon no longer goes by his "government name." When he was incarcerated, younger men started calling him "General" in tribute to his skills as a jailhouse lawyer. He is a good tour guide in Los Angeles's Skid Row, where he has lived, unhoused and now housed, for much of his life. His mother lived in less densely populated South-Central L.A., but he always preferred to stay with his father on Skid Row. "Downtown was like Las Vegas to me, the part of the city that never sleeps," he recalled. Skid Row may sound like a landscape of despair to an outsider, but there is an active art scene, culture, and sense of community

---

* ProPublica is keeping an updated tally of where the money went and how it was repaid. Go to Propublica.org and search "bailout tracker."

Bizarre Policy: Funding segregation

COMMUNITIES MAY MANIPULATE THEIR participation in affordable housing programs to exclude people of color. For example, a Connecticut report found that a number of communities in the state were using HUD Community Development Block Grants (CDBG) to construct affordable housing. In a single year, every CDBG grant in Connecticut went to support senior housing. "Given that seniors in majority-White municipalities are overwhelmingly White, such grants do not appear to affirmatively further fair housing," the report concludes.[11] When communities are forced, often through lawsuits, to construct affordable housing, they often fulfill the obligation through adding senior units that accommodate elderly residents of the town rather than new families who could benefit from schools, job opportunities, and other amenities.

amid overwhelming poverty here. It's something Dogon fears the city will wipe out as downtown land becomes scarcer.

The sidewalks of this warehouse district are lined with tents augmented with plastic tarps, cardboard, and bits of carpet. An American flag woven into the design is a sign that a veteran is in residence. There is no space between tents, and it can be difficult to know where one ends and another begins. It looks more like a refugee camp in some conflict-torn nation, the footage of an urgent appeal from a humanitarian organization: *Please open your heart! Please help!*

Everyone knows the General, who is an organizer with LA CAN. He points to some metal projections at the roofline of a brick building where sprinklers are mounted. He called it the "XL 5000" with a laugh. The owners installed the sprinklers to turn on whenever a homeless person dared to make camp at the side of the building. These are not gentle sprays. The building's paint has been stripped off where the jets hit. Dogon recalled the sprinklers being "like Niagara Falls." The owner has stopped using the sprinkler, however, Dogon explained. It actually attracted people, who brought soap if they had it and used the opportunity to wash up. Dogon cracked up at the memory of what passes for a victory around here.

Dogon is a natural advocate. While incarcerated, he successfully sued the state to start providing basic recreational equipment so that men could exercise. The victory cut down on fights by giving men an outlet for energy and frustration. When he returned to Skid Row, he soon ran into trouble with private security guards, hired to patrol the "Business Improvement Zone," an enterprise meant to transform Skid Row into a desirable commercial locale, as so much of downtown L.A. already is.

When Dogon would go outside to have a cigarette, guards would approach him and tell him, "We just want people to smoke and walk." In other words, a man—who happens to be African American—smoking in front of his own home was a problem.

He first showed up at LA CAN after confronting security guards who were twisting a woman's arm. They said she had drug paraphernalia. "You gonna break her arm because she got a pipe in her hand?" Dogon asked them. It turned out to be eyeliner. LA CAN gave him a camera and a clipboard and sent him out to document harassment of Skid Row residents by security guards and police.

Arrests of homeless people in Los Angeles jumped 31 percent between 2011 and 2018—a period when overall arrests across the country and in L.A. were falling. Most of the alleged offenses were minor, and nearly inevitable consequences of being on the street.

LA CAN has partnered with WRAP to promote a Homeless Bill of Rights that would stop arrests for "infractions" like sleeping, eating, or urinating in public—things people living on the street cannot help but do. It also would require states to provide affordable housing and access to sanitation. WRAP is pushing similar bills in Colorado and Oregon. "WRAP has become experts on what it means for a bill to be dead," Boden said, noting how hard it was to even find sponsors.

There is some good news, too, regarding the rights of people on the streets. In December 2019 the US Supreme Court refused to hear and potentially overturn *Martin v. Boise*, despite urging from cities.[12] *Martin v. Boise* upholds the right of people to sleep in public when no alternatives are available. While cities have been aggressively expanding municipal laws to criminalize the noncriminal act of rest in public places,[13] the courts have moved to protect the rights of people who are homeless from policing and criminalization.

In practice, however, people without homes still face criminalization. Dogon described incident after incident of Skid Row residents arrested for simply being homeless. One woman has been arrested 109 times for sitting or sleeping on the sidewalk, he said.* These charges come with $140 tickets with escalating penalties for nonpayment and sometimes jail time. Homeless people can build up six-figure debts, which of course will never be repaid but will make it nearly impossible for them to rent an apartment.

HOMELESSNESS IS A MATH PROBLEM

The concentration of homelessness on Skid Row is overwhelming, but it does not begin to encompass all the people who are homeless in L.A. There are mini tent cities on freeway exit ramps all over the city and throughout the county. Beautiful Santa Monica has one of the largest shelters in the state and many more homeless people sleep by the famous pier that stretches into the Pacific Ocean. Almost 58,000 people are homeless every

---

* We attempted to find the woman and interview her, but people on Skid Row said she had not been seen for a month.

night in Los Angeles County, according to government estimates, a number that jumped 23 percent between 2016 and 2017. "We've been seeing the tsunami coming for a long time," said John Maceri, executive director of The People's Concern, a housing nonprofit. He cited high rents, low vacancy rates, stagnant wages, and the death of state-financed affordable housing in California as contributing to the crisis in L.A. County.

Both at the city and county level, residents have voted to increase their own taxes to create funds dedicated to addressing homelessness. Various ballot measures are funding services for homeless people (policing is considered a service) and new affordable units. The goal is for public investment to create ten thousand new units in L.A. County over the next decade. There are close to sixty thousand people homeless there right now, according to government counts, with more joining them every day. Again, there is a math problem here.

New construction is emphasizing permanent supportive housing, units where tenants will have access to a range of services to help them with substance abuse disorder, mental illness, and other challenges. The average cost of these units is $400,000.

Some advocates would rather see a higher volume of less-expensive units. "Homelessness is a visible manifestation of extreme poverty," said Boden. "Housing, health care, education, and a living wage. Almost everybody I can think of—if they had three of those four things, everything would take care of itself."

SICK SITUATIONS IN UNHEALTHY HOMES

The unaffordability of housing puts some people on the streets. It puts others into situations that compromise them in many ways. All too often, it makes them sick. Angelov Diaz came into the emergency room at Boston Medical Center (BMC) seven times in his first eight months of life.[14] He and his mom were sleeping in her mother's living room. Allergic to the dogs that roamed the home and to many of the foods that were on the family table, the baby boy with the curly black hair was underweight and had trouble lifting his head. The apartment was home to an extended family and had so little floor space that Angelov did not learn to crawl. Besides, the boy would become ill when he got near the carpet, a repository for dog dander.

Dr. Megan Sandel did the only thing that could really help—and something that almost no other doctor in the United States has the power to do. She wrote the Diaz family a prescription for housing.

BMC is making a $6.5 million investment in affordable housing in greater Boston. Under Massachusetts law, BMC had to dedicate a percentage of a huge expansion project to a "community benefit." Dr. Sandel pushed hard for a housing initiative. Dr. Sandel explained that 5 percent of patients account for 50 percent of health care costs. Within those 5 percent, 40 percent are on the street or, like Angelov and his mother, in unstable or inadequate housing. "One of the things that's interesting about hardships is that they're amazingly expensive to the health-care system as well as to society," Dr. Sandel said. That creates leverage. Why not invest in removing hardships, rather than in expensive health care that will not work?

"Housing is a foundational social determinate that is going to make all your other interventions work better," she explained.

BMC is not becoming a landlord but is partnering with the Boston Housing Authority, providing free case management for disabled residents, paying for health-related improvements—like pest control for renters with asthma, or accessibility upgrades—and creating an equity fund to support new units.

"You'll see more hospitals following suit," Dr. Sandel predicted, particularly as payers concentrate more on health-care outcomes, which she argues will improve relatively rapidly and cheaply when patients' basic needs are met. But for now, BMC is far ahead of most hospitals.

Medical-legal partnerships where doctors and lawyers collaborate to advocate for patients are another way that hospitals can help patients get into healthy housing. For example, in New Haven, Connecticut, the mold in his apartment's carpeting made "Javier's" asthma worse. His doctors kept prescribing higher doses of steroids. The boy predictably gained weight and came to hate school because of the teasing he now endured over his size. He also developed diabetes. The only thing that the steroids did not do was control his asthma. His mother missed so much work taking him to the ER that she was fired. She begged the landlord to fix the mold problem and searched for an apartment that would not make her son sick. But a nice place was hard for the newly unemployed woman to swing. Finally, the Hartford-based Center for Children's Advocacy (CCA) provided her with a lawyer, who pressured the landlord to remediate the mold. Today Javier is breathing easier, feeling better about school, and losing weight. The only reason that carpet was replaced was because he was a patient at Yale New Haven Hospital, where there is a medical-legal partnership with CCA. There are currently fewer than four hundred medical-legal partnerships in a country with more than five thousand hospitals.

LOW-OPPORTUNITY NEIGHBORHOODS PERPETUATE POVERTY

Dr. Sandel describes low-income families who make "toxic trade-offs" to keep a roof over their heads. This can be literally true, as lower-cost housing is more likely to carry environmental risks, including lead poisoning in children. But families who live in lower-cost communities also suffer higher crime and worse schools and enjoy fewer job opportunities and less access to all the things that make life healthy and pleasant, such as well-maintained parks, convenient grocery stores, and libraries with the wherewithal to sponsor free or low-cost family programming. A wealth of research shows that children raised in poor neighborhoods have lower academic achievement.[15]

University of Delaware researcher Yasser Arafat Payne has done extensive studies of Wilmington neighborhoods plagued by crime and poverty. In a 2013 project, he found that most residents of the focus neighborhoods were unemployed and that even among those with jobs, most were doing low-wage work that did not allow them to meet their basic needs. Payne's work includes an interview with a nineteen-year-old who was job hunting:

> Richard alerted me to fact that a number of residents in South-bridge do not have basic resources or the capacity to effectively seek employment. He exclaimed that basic resources like a "computer," the "internet," a "car," or access to transportation, are not conveniently available to most residents in Southbridge. Also, given that this neighborhood is located in the margins of the southern end of Wilmington, a lack of access to transportation prevents many residents from traveling into larger Wilmington. As Richard points out, the "good payin' jobs," are actually located in the, "middle of the city."[16]

We'll delve more into the education and transportation problems inherent in poverty housing in chapters 6 and 13. But one solution seems so obvious that we will deal with it right here: Why not simply put more low-income housing in neighborhoods with better schools, access to jobs, and other life-enhancing features?

Local papers often write of an affordable housing "problem" or "crisis." In fact, the shortage of affordable housing in advantaged communities is not a "problem"—it is what communities are deliberately trying to achieve. The most cost-effective way to create affordable housing is in multifamily units. However, the most well-resourced communities often do not allow multifamily projects—or allow them only in a few areas of town.

PUTTING UP WITH ABUSE

Poor access to housing makes people stay in places that are not healthy. It also makes them stay with people who are abusive.

This is the first month that Sam and her husband, Bob, have been late paying the mortgage on their Cape Cod–style house in rural Connecticut. The couple asked that we identify them by their first names only. The place was a bargain that they found in foreclosure. They had to haul out carpets soaked with urine from the wild animals who had claimed the small house in the woods, but the mortgage payment was cheaper than their rent. Their home has been cold because a series of administrative errors have held up their fuel assistance. Bob has been putting $30 worth of diesel a day into the oil tank to keep the furnace on, at least a bit.* "It's always a heart attack because we've had so many issues," he said. He lost his job after a knee injury and has found nothing after three years of searching. He is taking online courses to work toward an associate's degree that he hopes will qualify him for better opportunities. Sam runs a dog-grooming business, but her revenue is a poor match for her expenses. She's looking at a storefront with lower rent today.

There are plenty of reasons to be scared when you can't pay your mortgage. But it's particularly traumatic for Sam, who has often put up with abuse in exchange for housing.

When she moved in with her mother, Sam's own daughter was an infant. Sam described her mother telling her, "You're crazy. You're going to kill that baby. The child is going to turn into Satan and have a forked tongue." The mother had once been admitted to a psychiatric hospital, but Sam's father arranged an immediate release. Sam is sure that her mother has a serious mental illness, though she has no diagnosis to go on. Because the mother took charge of Sam's paycheck, escaping to a place of her own was difficult.

---

* Many standard furnaces will operate on diesel. Cash-strapped households often resort to this workaround when they don't have the means to buy large quantities of heating oil.

She finally moved in with a boyfriend whose emotional abuse turned physical in time. He cleaned out their joint checking account, took the car, and left. Sam drifted between friends, but having an infant and large dog did not make her an attractive houseguest for everyone.

Along came "Greg," a coworker who welcomed Sam and her charges. At first, Greg made himself out to be a platonic friend, but that changed. "He wanted a relationship with me," Sam said, and very quickly he got one. "I'm rushing into these situations where I can't be on my own," she said. Eventually, she married Greg and had a child with him. He spent money like water, which worried Sam. He cheated. He threw her across a room and tried to pin her to a stove burner. But she felt she couldn't get out because of the debt that Greg had accumulated in both their names. She couldn't afford an apartment, let alone pass the necessary credit check to sign a lease. Finally, they got a $9,000 tax refund, which she immediately applied to the credit cards. She took the kids and left.

Many women, like Sam, find themselves forced or pressured into unwanted sex or other abusive situations because they need housing. For example, a survey of homeless women in the District of Columbia found that 29 percent had practiced survival sex (trading sex in exchange for a basic need) and another 28 percent said that they were forced or pressured into performing sex acts.[17] A survey of women who were homeless in Los Angeles found that 19 percent had practiced survival sex, though the authors of the study noted that nearly a third of the women declined to answer the question and hypothesized that many were ashamed to report they had used sex to obtain basic needs.[18]

Sam's story also highlights the extreme risk of homelessness posed by domestic violence. According to HUD, 57 percent of women experiencing homelessness cite domestic violence as the immediate cause, while the dynamics of control and abuse create financial instability and trauma that can make rehousing difficult.[19] Like Sam, "Jayla" has also experienced violence from a partner, but her search for housing is still ongoing.

STRESSED FAMILIES IN TIGHT SPACES

Jayla wore a black t-shirt with metallic gold lettering that coordinated with her jewelry. It said FLAWLESS. Her hair was pulled tight into a ponytail on the top of her head and cascaded down in curls. This is a woman who takes pride in her appearance and in keeping a spotless house. Right now, however, she is living with a cousin, a woman so messy that Jayla feared the house would become infested with rodents.

"Living with people is not what I want," she said.

The cousin did not have room for Jayla's children, who are with other relatives. Her fourteen-year-old son is "acting out like crazy," she said, and was expelled for having drug paraphernalia. Jayla believes that she is losing his respect because she cannot provide a home for him. Plus, it's difficult to parent from another household. Her mom, whom the boy lives with now, goes to work early in the morning and never checked to make sure that he was going to school.

Jayla was one of many people we talked with who described bad family situations that they tolerated to keep a roof over their heads. She'd once lived with someone who sold drugs out of their apartment. "I didn't want my kids around that, but I had nowhere to go," she said.

Though most of Jayla's kids are living with her mother, the last thing in the world she wants is to hand off parenting responsibilities, as there is a long history of trauma in her family.

"I'm trying to break the cycle with my kids," she said. "I'm not going to give up."

THE STRUGGLE TO REENTER
THE HOUSING MARKET

When Jayla talked about her will to persist, her social worker, Lorna Rodriguez, held her thumb and index finger an eighth of an inch apart and said, "We're this close." Jayla has one overarching goal—to reunite with her children. In order to do that, she must first find a job and an apartment. Both are big reaches for her.

Jayla described an abusive relationship with a man she lived with. As he tried to choke her, she fought back and was arrested for assault.* She spent 120 days in jail before the father of her children finally bailed her out. A private attorney told her that he could easily get the case dismissed—for $3,000, which she does not have. Her public defender has urged her to take probation if it's offered. But that would leave her with a felony conviction and forever ban her from public housing.

Though she has not been convicted of a crime, the assault charge still shows up on a record search when potential employers do background checks. She's completed a number of vocational training programs to try to qualify herself for a job, but she is not getting interviews. She'd like the chance to explain what happened that morning, but she believes that potential employers are seeing the charge and passing over her application.

There are other barriers to housing. Before her incarceration, Jayla was once evicted for nonpayment of rent. Her son was getting into trouble in school—and she left work one time too many to respond.† She lost her job and then her apartment. A past-due electric bill has also earned her a black mark.

Competition for affordable housing is stiff. There are only thirty-six available affordable units for every one hundred extremely low-income renter households, according to the National Low Income Housing Coalition.[20] Landlords can be extremely selective.

---

* In May 2018 Connecticut law changed in recognition that far too many abuse victims were being arrested for fighting back. Under the new "primary aggressor" law, police might not have arrested Jayla.

† Time and again, we interviewed parents who had lost their jobs because they were attending to their children.

THE WEATHER'S WORSE WHEN YOU'RE POOR

Severe weather, occurring more frequently on this warming planet, threatens those few affordable units. "It's really unfortunate in our country that the real estate market is most affordable in the places that are most at risk," said Liz McCartney, cofounder of the St. Bernard Project (SBP), an organization that began in an effort to get people displaced by Hurricane Katrina back into their houses. In New Orleans, Uptown and the French Quarter claim the high ground with stately mansions, universities, and the restaurants and bars that continue to make the city a tourist destination. People in poverty have always lived in low-lying areas, in New Orleans and pretty much around the world. Poor homes get flooded when natural disaster strikes. In New Orleans, only the very wealthy were spared. Middle-class, and predominantly black, neighborhoods on the eastern side of the city also ended up underwater. African American homeowners were more than three times as likely to be flooded out than white ones.

When Katrina struck the city, "Alice Stark" and her husband lived in New Orleans East, in the brick house where they had raised their children. Before Hurricane Katrina, New Orleans East was a middle-class African American neighborhood. The couple loved their close-knit community and were determined to rebuild and return after Hurricane Katrina devastated the neighborhood in 2005. Stark finally made it back in 2011 with the help of SBP; her husband had a fatal heart attack while they were living in a FEMA trailer.

Stark is poor now, but she was not before Katrina hit. She had a good clerical job with the New Orleans Board of Education, where her husband worked as an accountant. After the storm, the school system laid off its workers. Employees like Stark and her husband generally relied on significant late-career boosts in pension to create comfortable retirements, but they did not have a late career.[21] We said that poor housing usually takes the brunt of storms, but in this case the middle class got flooded out as well. In New Orleans, only the sliver by the river—the high ground that made up the richest (and whitest) parts of the city—escaped unscathed. Racism and economic oppression are each other's evil twins. Sometimes it is difficult to say for certain which you are encountering; they love to work as a seamless pair. That is abundantly apparent in the way that New Orleans was rebuilt. Black neighborhoods like New Orleans East were neglected in the rebuilding efforts, so much so that there was talk of the neighborhood and the adjoining Ninth Ward seceding from the City of New Orleans.

In her excellent book *The Shock Doctrine*, Naomi Klein argues that Katrina created an opportunity for "Disaster Apartheid," a chance to displace black residents and make room for whites relocating to soak up the unique culture (largely created by African Americans) of the City That Care Forgot.[22] After the storm, the city's black population dropped by nearly seventy-five thousand, while the white population quickly returned to nearly its pre-Katrina level. New white residents were college educated and affluent. Katrina gentrified New Orleans. In 2010 the city elected its first white mayor since 1978. New Orleans remains majority black, but that majority and its power are dwindling.

Was the exodus of black New Orleanians, as Klein argues, the intended result of policy that made it harder for them to rebuild? Consider the analysis of Road Home, the federal program to help Katrina-displaced homeowners, offered by Alden J. McDonald, president of Liberty Bank and Trust, a local institution that built its business on making loans to black customers:

> Compensation would be based not on the actual cost of rebuilding, but on the appraised value of a property. The cost of restoring a 2,000-square-foot house in mostly white Lakeview, just west of City Park, or Gentilly, a black middle-class neighborhood to its east, would be the same—but the Road Home payment would differ. In Lakeview, that home was valued at a little over $300,000. A

Lakeview couple who received a $150,000 flood insurance payment would receive the full $150,000 from Road Home. But in Gentilly, a similar home was valued at closer to $160,000. If a Gentilly couple received a flood insurance check of $150,000, they would receive only $10,000 from Road Home. It wasn't just the poor, McDonald understood early on, who would have trouble rebuilding, but also middle-class people who didn't have the savings or family wealth to make up the shortfall and fix their homes.

"If we use pre-Katrina assessments for compensating people, nobody in the black community is coming out anywhere near whole," McDonald said at the time. By the time a federal judge reached the same conclusion, nearly five years later, it would be largely too late. All but $148 million of the original $10 billion had already been spent. (The federal government agreed to set aside another $500 million specifically to help homeowners shortchanged by Road Home.)[23]

While black New Orleanians waited for help, something else happened. House prices and rents increased. Their drowned city was the place to be, and they could no longer afford it.

Property taxes doubled and projections are that water rates will double by 2020. That is likely to fuel the black exodus further.

Stark is an enormously positive person. "I'm thankful I get up every day. It could be worse," she said. She is back in her gleaming home full of family pictures, and the Saint Bernard Project did some renovation to accommodate her scooter. Stark fell while living in a trailer and emergency crews had difficulty extracting her from the narrow hallway. The initial prognosis was permanent paralysis, but she was determined to get movement back and has had some success.

She does get down when she discusses house taxes. The city continued to levy taxes on her home, even in the years that she could not possibly live there. As of 2017, she owed more than $10,000 in back taxes, which she has been trying to pay down whenever she's a bit ahead. But that is not often. Her daughter encouraged her to sit down and draft a budget. Stark shook her head. With disability and a small pension, she is living on less than $20,000 a year. She got no life insurance when her husband died because the school system canceled the policy after the layoff.

"I'm always working in the negative," she said.

The city has been trying to recoup taxes by putting delinquent properties up for sale. Currently, the city is accepting bids on nine hundred properties where the owners are behind on taxes. So far, Stark's house is not one of them.

HOME SWEET INVESTMENT

Housing is an area where the rich definitely get richer. If you can afford a home and a conventional mortgage, chances are that you will get not only a place to live but a growing asset that could help fund your retirement or be used as collateral to finance your or your children's education. The government will give you a generous tax break to help make this possible.

If you can afford to rent or own in a desirable neighborhood, you'll have access to better schools, better jobs, safer streets, and other benefits that will add to your family's prosperity. If you cannot, then you are out of luck. The chances of finding a home you can afford comfortably are slim. Government policy—from housing finance to local zoning—makes it so. If you do find an affordable place there will be trade-offs, in access to education and employment, in the health of your environment, and even perhaps trade-offs that make you accept toxic relationships.

Housing inequity is a result of poverty—and it creates poverty. It is also a result of conscious government policy. When it comes to housing, our tax system is helping the wrong people.

What Can I Do?

1. **Zone for affordable housing in every town.** Local zoning restrictions play a role in preventing construction of affordable housing. It is easy to get into this game. In many communities, seats on planning and zoning commissions are not even contested. The federal "Housing Development Toolkit," available online, offers an easy guide to establishing housing-friendly regulations.

2. **Support a living wage.** What's affordable entirely depends on what you make. As we discussed—housing prices have risen, but wages have been basically flat since the 1970s. You can support laws that make it easier for workers to unionize or that increase the minimum wage.

3. **Fight for subsidized housing.** HUD has increasingly been getting out of the business of affordable housing. Tell your members of Congress that the federal government has a responsibility to revisit housing policy to stop supplementing the wealthiest at the expense of the poorest.

4. **Support tenant unions.** As we showed, renters are often at a disadvantage when dealing with landlords who provide substandard housing. Find out how to form your own tenant union. The Minnesota group Home Line has an excellent online guide to help you. Go to Homelinemn.org and search for "Form a Tenant Association."

A Better Way: Housing people, not cars

ZONING REGULATIONS TELL YOU what a town values, whether it's open space, affordable housing, or commercial development. In most communities, zoning regulations limit affordable housing—sometimes unintentionally. For example, it is common to require off-street parking in multiunit complexes. The logic is that occupants will need vehicles, which is often a safe bet in a country that invests so woefully in public transportation, as we discuss in chapter 6. But in larger cities with good transit infrastructures, this might not be the case. Space for cars reduces the space available for humans. Developments have fewer units and therefore higher prices.

A number of cities are easing or eliminating minimum parking requirements as a no-cost way to increase their affordable housing stock. In 2017 Buffalo, New York, became the first to completely abandon parking requirements. The change has not been in play long enough to track its impact, if any, on the housing stock.

New York City mayor Bill de Blasio has relaxed some, but not nearly all, parking requirements. Most New Yorkers already use public transit, and in much of the city street parking is free, though not always easy to find. When constructing a new forty-three-unit residence designed for low-income tenants, Dunn Development surveyed incoming renters and found that only 30 percent owned or had access to a car. Nevertheless, city zoning in 2011 required the developer to provide parking, according to a report by the Furman Center. To recoup some of the cost, the developer rented the spaces to tenants at forty dollars per month. Only nine of the required eighteen spaces were taken.[24]

CHAPTER 5

Power

Shut Off

W hen National Grid came to shut off the power, Shane
Ward asked for time to switch his mother from her electric-
powered oxygen enrichment machine to tanks that didn't
require electricity. But the power was cut immediately, Ward said, and
his mom went into a seizure. Months of caring for his very ill mother in
their Pawtucket, Rhode Island, home without hot water, refrigeration,
or heat followed.

Theirs became one of the 2.2 million US households to experience
shutoffs every year, with another 14 million dealing with utility payments
in arrears.[1]

"I don't trust the National Grid. They're a joke," said Ward. "They put
profits before human rights, before human dignity. Their main concern is
how much they're going to be in the black, every quarter. When you put
financial before human beings, there's something wrong with that."

National Grid declined to comment.

Ward is decrying exactly the way that power utilities are arranged in this country. Electric and natural gas are by and large for-profit industries here. That's an arrangement that is most common in high-income countries, though worldwide, public ownership is the norm.[2] In addition to rates paid for power, residents support utilities indirectly through tax subsidies to the fossil fuel industry, which are estimated at $20 billion annually.[3]

Utilities tend to be monopolies, so consumers cannot shop around for more affordable electric rates or for features like budget plans that could get them through lean times. National Grid, a British-based company, is the only provider of electricity and natural gas in most areas of Rhode Island.

There is some public regulation of utilities, generally by appointed commissions on the state level. The Federal Energy Regulatory Commission has jurisdiction over interstate matters. Nevertheless, keeping the lights on can be a challenge for people living in poverty. The government says that energy is affordable at 6 percent of income. A report by the American Council for an Energy-Efficient Economy calculated that low-income households pay 7.2 percent for energy, about twice the percentage of median-income households and three times that of wealthy ones.[4] Some low-income households carry even heavier burdens. For example, a 2015 analysis found that Mississippi households with less than $50,000 in pretax income—the majority of households in the state—were paying 18 percent of their income for electricity.[5]

There is also racial inequity in shutoffs. Among all households at or below 150 percent of the federal poverty guidelines, 11.3 percent of African American–headed households experienced shutoffs, compared with 6 percent of Caucasian-headed households. A report by the NAACP concluded, "These disparities may be the result of institutional racism; uneven levels of consumer education; differences in savings, available income, or outside assistance; and geographic density of customers based on race."[6]

Ward talks about "borrowing from Peter to pay Paul," as he juggles medical bills, the mortgage, and his power bill. That's common among people struggling with utility costs. If they are paying the electric bill, they are probably behind on the phone bill. Housing instability is also strongly linked to utility struggles, as customers with delinquent power bills can have difficulty securing a lease. We saw that in chapter 4, where a years-old unpaid electric bill was one of the barriers keeping Jayla from finding housing and reuniting with her children. Finally, utility poverty can play havoc with a resident's health, as Judith Jorge knows all too well.

SICK AND COLD

At seventy-three Jorge is no longer working as a certified nursing assistant but does not consider herself retired. She'd like to be working. In fact, she had a part-time job lined up when she fell down a flight of stairs and was seriously injured. Months later, she is still using a walker.

Her body is rejecting some of the pins that were used to fix her broken ankle, and more surgery may be necessary to fix the problem. She also lives with a painful hernia, arthritis, chronic obstructive pulmonary disease, and cataracts. Some of her illnesses are aggravated by poor air quality or extreme temperatures. While air conditioning and heat can help manage both those environmental factors, Jorge hesitates to turn either on because she cannot afford the bills.

She keeps the heat low, often turning off the central heat and relying on a single space heater in her bedroom. Two winters ago, she had pneumonia, an illness she blames on her cold apartment. "The house is very cold, and it hasn't been insulated," Jorge said. She applied for a free energy assessment to look for ways to improve her apartment's efficiency, but her landlord objected and put a stop to the technicians' work. "I was trying to help the owner. I almost got evicted," she said.

In the summer she eases her breathing with the help of a window air conditioner that a friend lent her. That's in the kitchen, since Jorge's bedroom has no windows. She runs the unit more than she would like. "I have to think of my health," she explained.

She is surviving on Supplemental Security Income, distinct from Social Security in that it is designated for elderly or disabled people with little or no income—all boxes that Jorge ticks. In 2019 the monthly benefit was $771. Her car expenses eat up one month, and with medications and rent, the check does not go far enough.

Though she's always worked, none of her jobs ever offered pensions. Jorge thinks back fondly to when her children were young and she'd scrimp to give them a treat, dinner at Ponderosa. "Those were the best times," her son recently told her, and she agrees. She wishes she could help her adult children more and resume sending money to a cousin in Puerto Rico. Jorge believes the only way she can do that is to move to an affordable place that includes utilities. We met Jorge at the George Wiley Center in Pawtucket at a meeting of people concerned about their electric and gas access. Many people expressed a wish to find a low-income unit that includes utilities.

"The thought that I have to move again," Jorge wearily lamented, "it's unbelievable."

Energy insecurity is most harmful to elders, chronically ill people, and children, who have less capacity to regulate their body temperature than adults, according to Diana Hernández, an assistant professor of sociomedical sciences at Columbia University's Mailman School of Public Health. Two factors are intensifying that harm, Hernández said: climate change, with its associated weather extremes, and the increased management of seriously ill people in their homes. "What if you are living on an oxygen tank?" she asks. "What if you have to refrigerate your insulin?"

She noted that uncomfortable temperatures can make it difficult to sleep, a hardship that can contribute to cognitive problems, particularly in elderly people.

Hernández became interested in utilities when she was working on her dissertation, which focused on the connection between health and housing. "I was doing these home visits, and there was something about these energy stories that was very much present in people's lives and very much absent from the academic literature."

She has now published studies that document people with shut-offs experiencing worsening asthma, anxiety, and depression; unsafe, improvised heaters; and monitoring from child protective services. But Hernández noted that despite the harms associated with energy insecurity, it receives relatively little attention:

> Similar to food insecurity, where affordability and access to quality food matters, energy insecurity is determined by access to decent, efficient and affordable housing. Both are embedded within larger contexts of material deprivation and neighborhood disadvantage. Still, food is generally considered indispensable whereas energy is often perceived as an amenity. As most people would cringe at the thought of hunger-prone families, few shudder at the notion of poor households living in the cold and in the dark, accruing debt to fulfill a basic need.[7]

BAD DEBT AND BAD HOUSING

"Donna Green" owes National Grid just over $5,000. With the help of the George Wiley Center, the mother of two advocated to stop a shut-off and get herself onto a payment plan. Instead of putting down the 35 percent on the debt that the utility had demanded, Green will have sixty days to make a 15 percent down payment of $760, which is much better—but may still be beyond her reach.

Green has been laid off from her job, which is why she fell behind in the first place. She is getting $289 in unemployment benefits weekly and $330 in SNAP benefits monthly. She is paying $1,100 rent.

Though it's summer, she does not run the air conditioning. "All I do is yell at my kids about the lights."

Green had a job interview in two days. If she needs to continue her job search, losing power will be a huge barrier. Think of the things you might use to find and land a job: a computer, phone, washer and dryer to launder your best outfit, a blow dryer to style your hair for an interview—all require electricity.

We interviewed a number of people dealing with energy debts in the thousands of dollars. It's Shane Ward's "borrow Peter to pay Paul" logic. Utility shutoffs usually come with some kind of process that takes time. So if a family must choose between groceries and paying the gas bill, they are likely to pay for the groceries first. Utility bills pile up month after month. Sometimes a windfall, such as an income tax refund, will allow a household to pay off the bill. Other customers, like Jayla, have the bill hanging over them for years—preventing getting new service, housing, or credit.

People in poverty also have high utility debt because they have high utility bills, as a result of living in poorly constructed and insulated housing with low-efficiency heating and cooling systems and appliances.

Green once lived in an apartment where her monthly electric bill was $500, though she was scrupulous about turning off lights and turning down thermostats. Her electrician brother looked at the electrical box for her. "It was the oldest wiring in Rhode Island," she recalled. She called National Grid and the company advised her to talk to her landlord. "She refused to do anything," Green said.

People who own their own homes have an incentive to make upgrades that will save energy. These repairs will likely pay for themselves over time and will make the home more comfortable. Landlords who rent to people with many housing options also have an incentive to provide energy-efficient units; sky-high bills might inspire their tenants to find new digs. But as we discussed in chapter 4, people in poverty have fewer options. If they are in a place where they can pay the rent, that's a big thing to give up, as affordable units are in short supply in most communities. Moving is expensive, typically requiring a security deposit and first and last month's rent.

So, of course, Jorge's and Green's landlords resisted energy upgrades. Their only incentives to do them were ethical in nature.

RATEPAYER ACTIVISM: PEOPLE POWER

"Don't put me in a nursing home," Shane Ward's mother begged. He didn't understand. His mother made that plea on the day that he took her to fill out her retirement papers. He wondered why a college graduate would need help with basic forms. Not long after, his mother walked out of the house at night to stand barefoot in the snow and sing Christmas carols. Ward and his sister slept by the doors so that their mother couldn't wander out of their shared Cape Cod at night. The Alzheimer's disease was compounded by a parade of illnesses: cancer, epilepsy, chronic obstructive pulmonary disease (COPD), and now, the doctors suspect, Parkinson's disease. Ward has COPD as well. And emphysema—his lungs are so bad that he has passed out during coughing spells, a development that marked the end of his career as a long-haul trucker and an intensification of his family's financial struggles. His mother's medical bills mounted.

"What threw me in the downfall is I had a sewer pipe that burst," Ward recalled. He was concerned that breathing in unhealthy air would make him and his mother sick, given the lung issues they have in common. "So I have to get that fixed. When I borrow the money to get that fixed, it's over eight hundred and seventy-five bucks right there. It threw me in a tizzy." There was no way he could pay for the repair and keep the utility bills current. "I said, 'No, screw it! I got to take care of my mom. Take care of other things, keep her going, pay for her medication.' Whatever she needed. That's what I did."

In 2014 the family's power was shut off. Ward and his sister established a "bucket brigade" to warm up water on an outdoor grill for his mother's sponge baths. Her dirty linens had to be hand-washed in cold water in the bathtub. A refrigerator full of food spoiled.

The shutoff came despite a certification from her doctor that losing power would put her health and life at risk. Ward contacted the George Wiley Center, which had already been organizing for decades around utility access. He began speaking up at public meetings and protests, often accusing National Grid of playing "Russian roulette" with lives when it shut off customers. The family joined a class action suit with other customers who said that, given their medical conditions, their shut-offs were illegal. As a result of that action, the house's power is back on. But the story does not end there.

Ward's mother has had a series of recent hospitalizations for pneumonia and blood clots, with every hospital stay ending with new pre-scriptions to fill. "The bills just keep adding up, and adding up, and adding up," said Ward. He estimates that he's six months behind in his utility bills. While he lives with his mother, there's unlikely to be a shut-off. But his debt will keep climbing.

He's in favor of a percentage income payment plan (PIPP) proposal that would provide power to people living at or below 150 percent of the federal poverty guidelines at a rate that is a fixed percentage of their income. The George Wiley Center has been promoting PIPP, as has the Providence chapter of the Democratic Socialists of America (DSA). But a PIPP bill has been unable to get traction in the legislature for two years running. There are PIPP plans in Ohio, Colorado, New Jersey, Nevada, and Illinois.

The Providence DSA is also advocating that the power company move to public ownership. California DSA members are making the same proposal regarding the troubled Pacific Gas and Electric. "Utilities are a human right," said Providence DSA member Anna Castner. "People deserve to have heat, and they deserve to have light." In addition, the DSA "Nationalize Grid" campaign seeks to achieve zero use of fossil fuels under public ownership.

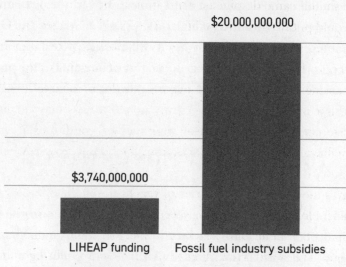

US Government Spending on . . .

$20,000,000,000

$3,740,000,000

LIHEAP funding   Fossil fuel industry subsidies

Sources: Department of Health and Human Services and
Environmental and Energy Study Institute

Castner notes that some Rhode Island towns have bought their street-lights back from National Grid, a small example that private resources can become public ones. But she knows that moving a shareholder-owned company to state ownership will not happen overnight. "I think it's important to keep that as a goal for us," she said. "Right now, we are fighting about shutoffs and rate hikes."

Together with the George Wiley Center, DSA members have been packing Public Utilities Commission meetings, which according to Castner takes some organizing since meetings tend to be held during the day in a building not accessible by public transportation.

National Grid does have a discount plan now for low-income customers, but that plan is criticized for enrolling only half of eligible accounts. Jorge has inquired about energy assistance repeatedly but said that she's been told that to get help she needs to already have unpaid bills.

A review of various assistance plans around the country finds that most people who are eligible for help do not receive it. The majority of funding for energy assistance in the US comes from the Low Income Home Energy Assistance Program (LIHEAP). LIHEAP is a federal program that gives block grants to states to offer energy assistance to low-income consumers, but the funding has never been equal to the need. In fiscal year 2014 LIHEAP served just 16 percent of eligible households during the winter heating season.[8]

FORCING POLLUTION ON PEOPLE WITH LESS POWER

Monica Huertes believes that National Grid was allowed to site a new natural gas plant liquefaction facility in her Providence neighborhood, near the port, because the area already had so many polluting industries. "Things are already there, and so they're like, 'Why not just dump it there?'" she said. Huertes, a social worker, became coordinator of No LNG in PVD (No Liquefied Natural Gas in Providence). She believes that the facility poses a high risk for explosion. The state Department of Health was prepared to ask for a health impact assessment as part of the facility's approval process. In an unsent letter to the Federal Energy Regulatory Commission,* director of the Rhode Island Department of Health Nicole Alexander-Scott wrote, "The traditional process does not look at the broader picture, including the history and future of this region. The Port of Providence has a long history of environmental problems that concentrate many of Rhode Island's most concerning environmental and safety issues in neighborhoods that are racially and economically disadvantaged."[9]

---

* Alexander-Scott, according to an email obtained by independent journalist Itai Vardi, told her staff, "At this time, every state agency in the Governor's administration has been asked not to submit a letter."

The facility ended up being approved, in part because it was so difficult to generate neighborhood opposition, according to Huertes. "It's hard to mobilize people who work 9 to 5," she said. "When people are dealing with food insecurity, they're not going to mobilize over something that's a 'maybe.'"

That's right. And that's one reason why polluting power plants are so often sited in low-income communities. The result is a great chain of injustice. Low-income people are more likely to have power plants built in their neighborhoods. Those power plants can contribute to a number of chronic diseases that people in poverty suffer from at higher rates, including cancer and heart disease. Some of those diseases require electrical equipment, like ventilators, or are exacerbated by extremes of temperature. And these people are the ones most likely to lose power because of nonpayment and thus lose access to potentially lifesaving technology.

The location of power plants in low-income neighborhoods is also tied to the practice of redlining, when government policy encouraged developing high-pollution projects in African American neighborhoods. (More about that in chapter 9.)

The discriminatory siting of these facilities hasn't ended. A 2018 study by Food and Water Watch looked at plant siting in Pennsylvania and found a historical pattern of locating them in areas with high numbers of people who were low-income, minority, or had not graduated from college. It found that planned fossil fuel facilities in 2018 were concentrated in rural, economically distressed areas. Many of the newer ones used fracking, which poses new risks to communities. "The gas power plant building boom will lock in fossil fuel dependence and environmental injustice for decades to come," the study predicted.[10]

POWER DENIED

While his mother dozes in and out in the next room with Judge Judy on television for company, Shane Ward worries about how he is going to balance the bills. "Utilities is killing us. It's utilities. Electric and gas, it's outrageous. But you need it. You got to have it for the stove, you got to have it for the hot water, for your showers. Entertainment. Life support. You need it. It's basic needs that should not be denied to anybody. You know? What can you do? Either sink or swim. And as far as I'm concerned, I'm swimming. I'm not going to sink."

It took a federal lawsuit to get Ward's power back on, to keep him from sinking. That's not realistic for all the fourteen million US households behind on their energy bills. The UN Sustainable Development Goals include universal access to affordable, reliable, and modern energy by 2030. The UN goals primarily address low-income countries. But without major policy change, the US will not come close to meeting that benchmark.

What Can I Do?

1. **Work in your state or community to get every building energy rated.** Energy ratings, already standard throughout Europe, let buyers and renters know what they are signing up for. We repeatedly interviewed low-income people who were shocked by the energy bills they received when they moved into homes where little had been done to promote efficiency.

2. **Support sliding-scale rates that make energy affordable for everyone.** In most states, a public agency reviews rate increase requests and offers opportunities for public comment. You can take that opportunity to ask for rates linked to income, or a percentage of income payment plan, so that energy is affordable for everyone.

3. **Ask your state legislator to look into how your state's public utility regulator operates.** Are meetings in the

evening? Are they widely advertised? Are they in venues accessible by public transportation? Are there effective conflict of interest regulations to ensure that commissioners are not too closely linked to industry? All these things can be legislated.

4. **Ask for increases to the Low Income Home Energy Assistance Program.** LIHEAP is a federal program that gives block grants to states, territories, and tribes to offer energy assistance to low-income consumers. The program is perpetually underfunded, however. When funds run out for the year, people in need are out of luck. You can contact your members of Congress and tell them LIHEAP matters to you.

5. **Make LIHEAP qualification automatic.** LIHEAP grantees have the option of automatically enrolling households that qualify for Temporary Assistance for Needy Families, SNAP, Supplemental Security Income, or certain types of veterans' benefits. Automatic enrollment ensures that more people who need and qualify for energy assistance get it. Find out what the policy is where you live.

6. **Advocate for assistance that starts before people become delinquent.** Energy assistance programs typically kick in after a person has missed payments, meaning that a household has already acquired debt and taken a hit to their credit score. Poor credit scores put people at risk for predatory loans, sending people even deeper into poverty.

7. **Oppose new fossil fuel plants.** These plants, linked to a host of illnesses, are usually sited in communities that have been robbed of political power by poverty and racism. Stand up against them whether they are in your neighborhood or not.

A Better Way: Solar for everyone

LOW-INCOME HOUSEHOLDS COULD SAVE on their energy bills and develop some independence from power companies if they had solar capability. But solar requires an up-front investment that is out of reach for families who struggle to pay a utility bill in the first place.

Some communities are using workforce development programs to provide the installation of solar systems for low-income homeowners or on affordable rental units. This saves owners the cost of labor and develops more workers for a green industry. It generally draws on existing pots of money. Green City Force in New York City uses AmeriCorps members to perform the work.

As you will read in chapter 10, however, it is important that these workforce development opportunities are made available to women and minorities who frequently face barriers to entering tech and construction industries.

CHAPTER 6

Transportation

Access Denied

Baltimore resident "Fred Lee" lives about a half hour by car from his job at a bakery outside the city. He relies on the bus—and route changes are making his commute more than an hour long. He's up at 4:30 AM every day to get to work by 6 AM. After a long day and long commute home again, he's exhausted: "I think, 'When's the point where I'm going to have fun in my life?'"

Location, location, location. That is what gives real estate value. A run-down ranch house with easy access to a commuter rail, shopping, and recreation is worth more than a large, pristine Victorian cut off from jobs, health care, and groceries. So the places that people in poverty can afford to live are typically geographically farther from amenities. They are also "transportation deserts," with poor access to the trains or buses that could help them overcome geographic barriers. What public transportation does exist is often not affordable or does not run on schedules that accommodate the shifts common in low-wage work. Because public transportation is not a viable option, more low-income people are purchasing cars—and entering into predatory lending arrangements to finance them.

Several factors create transportation deserts:

- **Changing patterns of wealth.** The "inner city" used to be a synonym for an impoverished area, complete with racial subtext. Not so anymore. Urban centers are increasingly gentrified, while lower-wage workers are forced to move out to cities' edges or suburbs where housing is cheaper. But transportation systems tend to be most robust in the urban core.

- **Underinvestment in infrastructure.** As we discussed with water, the US has underinvested in its infrastructure for decades. That means that rail lines are in poor condition, as are buses. It also means that many routes have not been updated to serve current travel patterns. The largest public infrastructure investments go to highways rather than mass transit.[1]

- **Racism.** Communities of color often have particularly bad access to transportation.[2] This reinforces segregation by literally stranding some people in underserved neighborhoods.

There is something beyond the practical at work when it comes to transportation. When we interviewed people with poor access, they frequently used the word "freedom" to describe what they wanted. The ability to move at will from one place to another is a pretty good definition of freedom. People who lack free movement feel that they are not living like adults or like full members of society.

When Stephanie LeBeau was laid off, she could not afford to maintain a car. She worked hard to get back on her feet by enrolling in community college and getting a part-time job, but she had to depend on her mother for essentials like getting to work and school. Living in rural Vermont, she did not have access to public transportation. That's more than an inconvenience. "Being able to just go do it and not have to ask permission is a great feeling—independence," she said. "Nobody really realizes until they don't have it." She often couldn't borrow her mother's car for additional things, such as enrolling her daughter in dance classes or getting together with friends. "I was left out, a lot." Research has often shown that low-income mothers experience social isolation, which cuts them off from potential sources of practical and emotional support.[3]

DECADES OF DEFERRED MAINTENANCE

We begin by looking at public transportation, because it is accessible without an up-front investment and because public transit is widely promoted to reduce carbon emissions. But in much of the United States, public transit is seen as the way poor folks get around—and so investments in it fall far short of what's needed to provide reliable, convenient service.

Unlike many parts of the country, New York City is designed around mass transit. Yet New Yorkers have some of the longest commutes in the country—nearly an hour, on average.

"The lowest-wage service jobs which are driving the job growth overall—that's who's getting killed by this," said Danny Pearlstein of the Riders Alliance, an advocacy group pushing for more convenient and affordable mass transit in the city.

Low-wage workers tend to live in areas far from the central business district that are less served by public transportation; many do not have nine-to-five schedules, and so are coming to and from their jobs at times when trains and buses run less frequently. Finally, they are hourly wage employees. A salaried professional who arrives late will not lose pay as a result. Someone who must log comings and goings on a timecard will.

New York City's subway system is designed to get people up and down the narrow island of Manhattan. You can go way down to Brooklyn or way up to the Bronx and Queens, though service is more frequent within the richest borough, Manhattan, which is no longer the city's center of growth in either population or jobs.

Today, the NYC subway has the worst on-time performance of any major transit system in the world. A decades-long failure to invest in public infrastructure has led to breakdowns and general inefficiency. For example, the signals that should show a train's position on the tracks are so outdated that transit workers must guess where trains are.[4] To avoid collision, they space trains farther apart, which slows the system. Unscheduled breakdowns are a fact of life. The Riders Alliance takes life-sized cardboard cutouts of New York governor Andrew Cuomo's image on much-photographed subway rides—a poignant way to drive home that the governor has little firsthand experience with transit delays. (He lives in Albany and has a state car.) The group has encouraged people to use the hashtag #CuomosMTA whenever posting on social media about the frustrations of their daily commute.

"Our elected officials all drink the same water we drink. They do not take the subway," said Pearlstein. "The political class is exempt from that." The Metropolitan Transit Authority (MTA), which operates public transport in New York City, is a state agency—meaning its budget is determined by the governor and legislators, who for the most part represent constituents outside the city. Pearlstein and other activists charge that this arrangement has robbed the city of a viable system. "For generations, the state budget officials have been stripping money out of the MTA," he said.

In 2017 Cuomo declared a state of emergency around the subway system, and the state committed $8.4 billion to fix it. The MTA has issued a plan calling for a major overhaul that is generally getting high marks from the system's current critics, though there is skepticism. The plan will take more than a decade to complete, noted Pearlstein. "There will be economic downturns and upturns," he said. To fund the upgrades, state money needs to keep flowing to the city in lean years.

Upgrading the bus system is even more important for low-income workers, though improvements to bus systems tend to be much less popular with the general public than investments in rail, as we will discuss later. A study by the Center for an Urban Future found that health-care workers had even longer commutes than the average New Yorker, with home health aides, who make an average of $25,000 a year, suffering the most:

> Most home health aides live in parts of the city that lack ready access to public transit or make for extremely long and complex commutes. For example, a Center for an Urban Future analysis of census data shows that the largest concentrations of health aides live in poorly served neighborhoods such as East Flatbush and Canarsie in Brooklyn; East Tremont/Crotona Park in the Bronx; and Jamaica, Hollis, and St. Albans in Queens. Nearly 20 percent of the city's entire population of health aides lives in one of these three census-defined neighborhoods.[5]

The report found that poor transit service in their neighborhoods was putting some workers at risk of losing pay or even their jobs:

> In fact, they can get docked pay for being late, says Maria Castaneda, secretary-treasurer of 1199 SEIU and a longtime organizer of nurses and other healthcare workers. "Once you are late, even for 10 minutes, you are docked 10 minutes on your paycheck," she says. "And if you have excessive lateness, it can lead to discipline—even termination."[6]

Castaneda's local did a survey of home health aide members in 2017 about stress. The number two cause of stress that respondents reported was transit, second only to having a death in the family.

New York City presents a serious, and well-documented, case of underinvestment in mass transit. But it is far from unique. The US Department of Transportation estimated that at current levels the spending backlog to maintain the public transit infrastructure we have now will grow from $98.8 billion to $116.2 billion by 2034.[7] That does not include new routes, though, as we discussed, poverty is moving out of high-concentration city centers. The problem of public systems not meeting the needs of residents in poverty is common, from the Big Apple to the Big Easy.

HARD COMMUTES IN THE BIG EASY

If you go to New Orleans, you'll probably take a streetcar at some point, a breezy ride on a beautiful antique vehicle that winds its way from the French Quarter, through the Garden District, and finally Uptown. These are the touristy spots to eat, shop, drink, and admire antebellum mansions. The streetcars do not offer practical transportation between working-class neighborhoods and jobs.

By 2018 New Orleans' streetcar system had been fully restored and indeed surpassed the level of pre-Katrina service. Yet thirteen years after the devastating hurricane, only 41 percent of bus service was back online.

When the storm hit, buses were not evacuated, leading to two-thirds of the fleet being lost. The first people to return to the city were the relatively well off. They had cars and sometimes also lived in the upscale neighborhoods along the streetcar line. People who depended on buses returned more slowly, if at all. Income from fares was cut in half.

"The storm took people who were already teetering on the edge and pushed them over," said Alex Posorske, executive director of the advocacy group Ride New Orleans.

While bus service struggled, more than $75 million in city and federal funding was invested in expanding streetcars, which were seen as essential to the city's tourism industry. Of course, the people who work in that industry tend to live in the city's outer reaches, which are not served by streetcars. The most common public transit in these neighborhoods are buses, which Posorske complains too often run between unmarked stops where riders wait in the tropical climate without roofed bus shelters to shade them.

New Orleanians who rely on public transit can only reach 12 percent of the region's jobs in thirty minutes or less, according to a Ride New Orleans study. In contrast, 89 percent of the region's jobs are reachable in that time frame for workers with cars. Extend the commute to an hour, and 99 percent of jobs are reachable by car—but only 42 percent by public transit. The transit system stops at the parish line (the Louisiana equivalent of a county boundary) and makes a public transit commute even more problematic for many residents. In 2018, however, some bus routes began offering service between parishes. Nevertheless, for people in outlying parishes, access by transit is dismal. In the adjacent parishes of Jefferson and St. Bernard, only 4.6 and 0.6 percent of the region's jobs, respectively, are accessible in a half-hour commute by public transit.

Charming as streetcars may be, they are undependable for daily commutes. Posorske noted that they frequently get stuck, requiring traffic to go around them—if possible. Passengers must climb three steps to put cash into a fare machine. For those who cannot climb the steps, the process for the driver to deploy a midcar lift will take four minutes. Ride New Orleans successfully organized against a city proposal to extend a streetcar line running along the riverfront and serving a convention center. The line would have represented a departure from the city's own transit plan, which calls for investment to be directed to buses.

Among transportation policy wonks, buses are beloved vehicles. But politicians show a marked preference for rail. Posorske blamed "some classist and definitely some racist attitudes" for the preference. He believes the thinking is "Buses are for poor people. Buses aren't for people like me. But I would ride a streetcar!"

BUSES ARE FOR OTHER PEOPLE

Along with an economic divide in ridership, passengers of different races use different modes. Caucasians who use public transit are more likely to use rail, while black or Hispanic riders are more likely to use the bus.[8] Data show that people who earn less than $50,000 annually are more likely to use the bus. Above $50,000, the preference flips to rail.[9]

Journalist Amanda Hess detailed how racism limits public investment in bus systems:

> As minority bus ridership rises, the racial stigma against the transportation form compounds. When Atlanta launched its Metropolitan Atlanta Rapid Transit Authority (MARTA) system in the 1970s, some hissed that the acronym stood for "Moving Africans Rapidly Through Atlanta." Today, though 78 percent of MARTA riders are black, many black residents still struggle to access the city bus lines, which fail to stretch deep enough into the sprawling black suburbs. (One critic has characterized the lingering problem as "transportation apartheid".) And the racial stigma against buses lingers even in lines that have not yet been built and boarded. When a new bus route was charted through a white Tempe, Arizona, neighborhood a few years ago, neighbors complained that the line would attract serial killers and child rapists. Also: "bums," "drunks," and "Mexicans," who the commentators feared would soon be "drinking out of our water hoses."[10]

Jarrett Walker, a transportation consultant and proponent of buses, believes that the crux of the problem is bad transit systems—that when systems are pleasant and efficient, use transcends race and class, and stigma is not a factor. When they are not, more privileged people will opt out of public transit. "There are places where everybody rides buses, and those tend to be places where buses are really, really useful," he said in an email. "Where buses are largely useless, only poor people ride them, so of course they get that reputation."

Buses are cheaper than trains and can easily be rerouted—no track to lay. Increasingly, though, Walker is not defending buses as a better alternative to rail—but to "microtransit," such as vans that users can summon on demand. He points out that 70 percent of the cost of a bus is labor. A driver in a full-sized bus on a fixed route is more efficient, to Walker's thinking, than a driver responding to demand wherever it arises. The trick is to get the routes in the best places and have them run frequently.

A Better Way: Employers step up

WHEN EMPLOYERS HELP WORKERS get to the job, they can reduce traffic around their locations, save money by requiring less land to build parking garages, and improve loyalty and productivity.

A few examples:

- Barnes-Jewish and St. Louis Children's Hospitals provide transit passes for employees and guarantee them a ride should they need to return home for an emergency. The hospitals avoided adding more employee parking and saw gains in recruitment and retention.

- Bluegrass Industrial Park is located in downtown Louisville, but many people who work there come from the western and southern sides of the city. Employers in the park collaborated with the state to design bus routes that would increase access to jobs at the park and got grant support from the federal government. The route now operates eighteen hours a day.

- Cincinnati Children's Hospital Medical Center provides shuttle service from a downtown transportation hub to its campus. The administrative cost of the program is roughly equal to that of adding one new parking space.

- CVS has hired tens of thousands of workers who had been on public assistance. The company places workers at the store closest to their residence.[11]

CRIMINALIZING RIDERS

While investment in transit systems may lag, government is often willing to pay millions to police these systems. Since people with lower incomes disproportionately use public transportation systems, they often become the targets of overpolicing. As 2019 came to a close, New York's Metropolitan Transit Authority announced it would be hiring five hundred additional police officers over four years at a cost of $249 million.[12]

These new officers will be charged with, among other things, catching riders who do not pay their fares. "Arresting hardworking people who cannot afford a $2.75 fare is, in effect, the criminalization of poverty," US Representative Alexandria Ocasio-Cortez and other legislators said in a letter to Governor Cuomo. "Further, it will be these same communities that will be most affected if the subway system is bankrupt or if there are additional route cuts."[13]

Criminalizing fare evasion is particularly disturbing considering that many students take public transportation to school. Public school students who live a mile or more from school in New York can ride public transit for free. But that does not include the cost of an adult to accompany a young child.

Until 2017 California was arresting students who failed to pay fares. "They don't have the cash to pay for a ride to school or maybe to a job, they get a ticket and next thing they know, the ticket can be hundreds of dollars, and they don't know how to pay that," Andrew Lamar told the daily news site Streetsblog USA. Lamar is a spokesperson for California State Senator Robert Hertzberg, who sponsored the decriminalization bill. "Kids would end up either being convicted of some misdemeanor or spending time in juvenile hall. The whole cause of this was getting a fare evasion ticket. That punishment is far too harsh for the crime."[14]

Reports analyzing arrests by transit police find that enforcement targets minority riders. A study of the Minneapolis Metro Transit system found that police gave citations to black adults at five times the rate of white adults and arrested blacks at seven times the rate of whites. Native Americans were cited at five times the rate and arrested at eight times the rate of white riders.[15] Minneapolis is not unique. Data show racial inequality in transit policing from New York to Seattle and many points in between.[16]

GOING SOLO WHEN PUBLIC TRANSPORT ISN'T AN OPTION

When we talk about transportation, by and large we mean "public transportation." Obviously, automobile ownership offers more flexibility, though that too is frequently lessened by poor infrastructure that does not move cars efficiently through congested areas. In 2019 Kelley Blue Book reported that the average price for a new compact car was $20,000. Given that car ownership also comes with taxes, insurance, maintenance, and fuel, it can be an enormous burden for people in poverty.

Nevertheless, most workers living in poverty still use an automobile to get to their jobs. According to the US Census, in every metropolitan area other than New York, cars are by far the most common means to commute even for the poorest residents. This is because public transportation is typically less accessible and dependable than it should be. In low-income neighborhoods, getting to work on public transit can be an odyssey, robbing riders of their time and their wages.

The nonprofit Good News Garage has given out more than five thousand used vehicles to New England families living at below 250 percent of the poverty line. The organization takes donated used cars, reconditions them, and offers families a bit of support to keep them on the road—budgeting assistance, a free first oil change, a three-thousand-mile checkup, and in some cases financial help with unexpected repairs. Much of the nonprofit's service area is rural, with little public transport, though even clients who live in cities often cannot get to work without a car, said Operations Manager Bob Buckley.

"When I first started delivering cars, it was pretty emotional to me to see how we were changing people's lives," he said. A 2006 study found that 61 percent of people who received a donated car from the nonprofit reduced their dependence on Temporary Assistance for Needy Families; 60 percent said they were able to get a job because of the car, while 83 percent were able to keep a job because of it. A full 90 percent said that the car made them more hopeful.[17]

One of those clients was Stephanie LeBeau, the laid-off single mother described earlier. A sixteen-year-old Honda CRV from Good News Garage allowed her to take classes at a community college and work part-time. Three years later, she is a full-time administrative assistant at Good News Garage. "I came across an ad on Indeed.com," she said. "It sparked my interest. I thought it would be really nice if I was able to come back and kind of give back." She has transferred to a four-year university. That CRV is still running. Though LeBeau has traded up, she gave the car to a friend who relies on it now.

She believes that if she had not received a donated car, she might not be working full-time, studying toward a bachelor's degree, and watching her daughter blossom in a weekly dance class. "I think about it every day," she said.

Good News Garage got its start in 1994 when activist Hal Colston, who was working at a social services agency, had a client come to him in tears. The low-income single mother had purchased a used car that promptly broke down. The dealer refused to make repairs or refund her money. It's a story that is even more common today.

LOW-INCOME BUYER BEWARE

"Buy here, pay here" (BHPH) auto dealers combine the role of auto seller and financer. You've heard them on the radio: "Bad credit? No credit? No problem!" Iesha Marcelino, of Norwood, Massachusetts, bought a used Ford Escape from Auto Drive 1, which operates dealerships at a number of locations in the state. Immediately, Marcelino said, the car had problems, including an engine light that kept going on and "awful, awful noises" whenever the car was in reverse. She said that personnel at the car dealership would not take her calls and that, when they did, they sent her multiple times to a distant repair facility, which was making her odometer turn quickly. She believes the dealer was playing for time and mileage. "He was waiting for my warranty to run out," she said. She laughed, though not lightheartedly, when she described calling the dealership and being told that her contact was not there—while she was standing across the street staring at him through the dealership's big front window.

We were unable to reach Auto Drive 1 for comment.

The Massachusetts attorney general sued Auto Drive 1 on behalf of Marcelino and customers like her. The AG charged that Auto Drive 1 routinely sold defective and inoperable cars to consumers at above-market prices. The company agreed to make restitution to consumers, though seven months after the settlement Marcelino had yet to see a check. She is still paying off that Ford Escape, though she no longer has it, as well as the long-gone car that she'd bought before the Escape, also from Auto Drive 1. During periods when the car was unusable, she laid out cash to rent another vehicle and to pay a friend to pick her children up from school.

Marcelino describes the dealership as a "slumlord," an apt metaphor. BHPH customers, just like low-income renters, often have no other options. So they pay high prices for defective cars and sign predatory loans. With inadequate public transportation the norm in the country, they need cars to get their children to school and themselves to work. At this writing, a buyer with good credit will pay less than 5 percent interest on an auto loan. But BHPH customers will pay much higher rates. In Massachusetts, the interest rate on auto loans is capped at 21 percent. In some states, the cap is higher or nonexistent. In order to keep payments low, the length of the loan is extended. Marcelino's experience of paying off a dead car is not unusual. Terms of fifty months are common. With more regulations in mortgage lending, auto lending has become a new area of opportunity for subprime lenders. In fact, one of the major threats to the BHPH dealership industry is that outside lenders are aggressively marketing subprime auto loans as well.[18]

When you buy a house, the seller and the lender are generally not the same entity. That protects buyers. The bank will insist on an appraisal to make sure that the house you're buying is worth the price you're paying. After all, the house is securing the loan. It would be bad business for the bank to let you overpay. But in these auto sales, the seller is the bank.

So letting you overpay is advantageous. Letting you default is even better. The Massachusetts attorney general has sued a number of BHPH operations. One had repossession rates of 50 percent. After getting the original buyer's down payment and a series of monthly payments, the dealers simply resold the repossessed cars. That is part of the business model, as the National Independent Automobile Dealers Association advised its members: "More charge-offs on deep subprime auto securitization should be anticipated in the future. These customers will return to the BHPH market and their repossessed vehicles will be available at auction when they default. Profit opportunities for independent operators will improve as this occurs."[19]

That prediction of recycling customers who suffer repossession is probably accurate: most US Americans need a car, even if they cannot afford one. The Massachusetts attorney general's office found some BHPH dealers hired lead generators who targeted consumers with lower credit scores and incomes. "It's a complicated financial transaction that for most people is the biggest one they are ever going to make," said deputy division chief for consumer protection Shennan Kavanagh of the Massachusetts attorney general's office. "The person in the best position is the person who can walk away." Kavanagh said that BHPH dealers cater to customers who cannot walk away, because they don't have the time, money, or credit to seek out better deals. They are confronted with

> ## Bizarre Policy: An industry that uses the housing crisis as a template
>
> CAR OWNERSHIP HAS BEEN climbing among low-income people since the Great Recession. The rise in auto sales is being driven by the same thing that drove the housing bubble: subprime loans. The originators of these loans bundle and sell them off as securities, which also evokes a strong sense of housing crisis déjà vu.

high-pressure sales tactics on the front end—and when things go wrong, many like Marcelino are strung along as the remedy period expires.

DRIVING WHILE POOR

Sooner or later, most drivers will get a ticket. If you can pay it quickly, it's merely an inconvenience. Likewise, if you can keep current on your car registration and insurance, your driving life will probably go smoothly. But if you cannot do these things, the bills will mount up and can even push you toward being branded a criminal.

In a single year 230,000 Texans could not renew their driver's licenses because of unpaid fines or fees. One in eight of those people paid off their obligations through "jail credit," an allowance for every day spent behind bars.[20] The criminalization of "Driving While Poor" takes a terrible toll on families like the "Coras."

In a spiral notebook, "Isabelle Cora" has a budget written out in neat columns. No eating out, no cigarettes. Her goal is to be able to afford her own car before her mother reports to prison. Her mother, "Magaly," will be serving forty-five days for driving with a suspended license. Isabelle, twenty-one, has landed a job with an advocacy organization. It's an exciting opportunity, but it puts a strain on her arrangement of sharing a car with her mother. Isabelle's job calls for evening meetings and some travel. Public transportation is not an option. Though there is rail service, it does not run frequently. She would have to catch a 6:38 AM train to travel thirty miles to her office and arrive by 9 AM.

Buying a car is not nearly Isabelle's only financial hurdle. She also faces outstanding tickets—some dating back to before she ever got behind the wheel.

Magaly kept driving while her license was suspended. Like most people with suspended licenses, she still had a job to get to, children to drop at school, groceries to buy, and so on. When she'd get pulled over for various moving violations, she avoided arrest by pretending to be someone else—Isabelle.

More than $400 in tickets incurred by Magaly are charged to Isabelle in two different court jurisdictions. To apply to get them waived because of financial hardship, each court will charge Isabelle a $60 fee. She is working hard to pay off those tickets, so that she can get a license—something she has never done.

"When I was younger, before I turned eighteen I had tried really, really hard to get my permit. But under eighteen, you need your parent to come with you. My mom also has two other kids, so she was really never able to make it with me to go get my permit," Isabelle explained.

So she also drove without a license, which created new problems. "Once I turned eighteen, I tried. I tried but I was always getting pulled over right before I would go to get my permit . . . It was just horrible timing, but I drive myself to work. There's no other way for me to get around."

In Isabelle's glove box is what she describes as "fake insurance." Fraudulent insurance cards are widely available on the internet for a fee (Isabelle paid sixty dollars). Today, most police do not have the technology to verify the authenticity of an insurance card in a traffic stop, but the practice is under increasing scrutiny from law enforcement. Florida police, for example, have been running stings to catch sellers of these documents.[21] If Isabelle is found out, she'll face still more penalties.

Isabelle already has trouble getting to work on time because of her car-sharing arrangement. She has brothers, ages five and fifteen, who sometimes need transportation. But her supervisor is flexible about letting her make up work. Things will get more difficult when Magaly goes to prison, a consequence that both women believe is irrational.

"You're making her do forty-five days, and then she's good. Her license is reinstated. What is the forty-five days in there going to do for her that has to do with her driving?" Isabelle asked.

Magaly shared that she has suffered from depression all her life and has been in recovery from substance abuse disorder for two years. It is easy to paint Magaly as the villain in this story, but like most family stories things are more complicated than they seem. She described a childhood of enormous trauma. She witnessed her father shoot her brother; her sister died of a heroin overdose. She's made efforts. For example, she did the training to become a certified nursing assistant but cannot get work because of her criminal record. She was signed up for a course to become a medical transcriptionist—a job she could do from home—but her prison sentence meant she had to withdraw.

Her wood floors gleam; the Cora house is immaculate and decorated with fall leaves and pumpkins. She is trying, but she fears that the prison sentence will deal a blow to her whole family, one from which they might not recover. She is afraid that the fathers of her younger children will seek custody if they find out she's in prison. "I don't want to lose them because of those forty-five days that I'm gone. [My older son] goes over to the street so fast. It could happen. I've seen it."

We started out this chapter talking about how access to transportation is freedom. For the Cora family, that's particularly poignant as Magaly plans to begin her prison term.

We found that mothers especially struggled with transportation and that this became a barrier to work and to seeing that children were cared for and got to school and other activities. For example, Sarah, who asked to be identified by her first name only, worked at Taco Bell, and her shift ended at 3 AM. Buses stop running in Danbury, a small Connecticut city, at 6 PM on weekdays. She walked home two miles in the dark in an area with few sidewalks or streetlights. Asked if she felt safe, the mother of three replied, "You do what you've got to do."

Literally, it was what she had to do. There was no public transportation available to her, and she could not afford a car. Talk about poverty in this country often focuses on getting people in poverty jobs, but it generally fails to talk about how their access to jobs is limited by transportation and how a lack of transportation can even put workers like Sarah in hazardous situations. Undependable transportation robs workers of income when they get their pay docked for lateness. And it creates enormous stress for workers like Isabelle Cora, who is shining in her new career—and perpetually afraid of getting pulled over.

Limited access to transportation is stranding people in poverty.

What Can I Do?

1. **Ride public transportation.** Public transit systems run more frequently and have more extensive routes when they are widely used.

2. **Ask yourself: How will this work for someone without a car?** Then rethink how you do things. Maybe that means adjusting work hours so that employees can avoid full buses passing them by; doing parent-teacher conferences by Skype; sending clients or customers a checklist before an appointment so that they know every document they will need when they come in to meet with you and won't have to schedule repeat meetings.

3. **Ask corporations: How will your employees get to work?** Amazon is the most glaring example, but smaller corporations are also adept at getting governments to fork over tax breaks or

outright gifts in order to locate in a given city or state. Be an advocate (see the final chapter for the nuts and bolts of how) for employers to take responsibility for transportation. Publicly ask: How will people get to all these jobs you are promising? What will access be like from the neighborhoods with highest unemployment? What contribution will you make to upgrading infrastructure?

4. **Support transit-oriented development (TOD).** TOD places dense housing, along with commerce and recreation, in a walkable neighborhood with excellent access to public transportation. You can be in a position to support this kind of development by getting involved with local business groups, neighborhood associations, or your planning and zoning commission.

5. **Support free transportation for students.** Whether it's by yellow school bus or mass transit does not matter. No student should have to risk arrest to get to school.

6. **End arrests and fines for fare evasion.** Fining people in poverty because they cannot afford fares is absurd. Arresting them is even worse. Find out your community's policy and be an advocate for decriminalizing public transit.

CHAPTER 7

Hygiene

A Problem Swept Under the Rug

Rachel Alston had bundled up her newborn daughter and headed to the grocery store for milk and diapers. Doing the math in her head, she realized that she could not afford both. "I was standing in the middle of that aisle forever," she remembered. She started making a mental count of the diapers in her bag and on the changing table shelf. Could she make it another week? "I'm going to get the diapers. We don't really need milk," she decided. "It didn't really hit me until I was home, how sad it felt."

One in three moms cannot afford diapers,[1] but hygiene is different from other basic needs in that very few people argue that it is a right or work to supply it. In fact, it is often a struggle to even get people talking about it. There is no equivalent of food stamps that you can use to get soap, toothpaste, or detergent. While the National Diaper Bank Network and others are working to change this, few nonprofit providers offer these kinds of products for free. Hygiene is not recognized as essential—though if the average middle-class person found that the shower had stopped working after a sweaty workout on the morning of a job interview, they would rapidly come to appreciate just how essential hygiene is.

As we saw in chapter 4, too many US Americans are taking shelter in poverty housing. That can mean plumbing that does not work, infestation with pests, or other poverty-related factors that render a home too dirty to be a place where anyone would choose to prepare food, sleep, or simply live.

Lack of access to hygiene affects poverty in three ways:

- Not being clean can make you sick; and being sick makes it harder to climb out of poverty.
- It can be a barrier to work, school, and other positive activities.
- There is shame attached to being dirty.

We met time and again with people who lacked access to water or other hygiene essentials. "I don't buy my pads," "Janet Dennis" explained to us in her immaculate Bridgeport, Connecticut kitchen, where inspirational quotes and pictures of her son decorate the walls. She is committed to three things: keeping a roof over her son's head, making sure he is fed, and putting clean clothes on him every morning when he catches the school bus. She makes do when she's menstruating with rags and toilet paper. "Fred Hill," a Baltimore homeowner whose water has been shut off, relies on a friend's shower once a week. Young parents talk about waiting until a diaper is "heavy" to change it. These hardships affect not only health but also the ability to study and work—two things that are consistently described as the path out of poverty.

SKID ROW ADVOCATES FOR HYGIENE, BUT GETS MORE POLICING

Los Angeles' Skid Row is a disorienting mix of sensory deprivation and overload. There is far less car and foot traffic on these dusty streets than elsewhere in downtown L.A. This is a neighborhood of warehouses, social service agencies, and the lowest-rent units in the city.

There are not a lot of billboards or neon signs on Skid Row. Why advertise to people who don't have money? But there are flyers everywhere. Telephone poles are papered with notices from police telling people that they must move their property (which, of course, means their homes) for street cleaning.

The main thing that strikes you on Skid Row is the smell. About two thousand people live on these streets with almost no access to toilets. They use buckets—but where to dump them? On some streets, it smells so strongly of human excrement that you can taste it.

Skid Row has seventy-two security cameras, but few public toilets. An audit by advocates found that at any given time about a third of the toilets are out of order. According to the UN High Commissioner for Refugees, a minimum of one toilet should be available for every twenty occupants of a camp. Prior to additional facilities being added in response to the COVID-19 pandemic, the ratio on Skid Row was more than ten times that.

In 2017 Governor Jerry Brown declared a hepatitis A outbreak in California to be a "state of emergency." Brown's declaration was meant to obtain more vaccines, not the washing facilities advocates had demanded for three years as we described in chapter 4, for homeless people and those who are in frequent contact with them. By the time that the state declared the outbreak had ended a year later, 704 people had been reported infected, though the likelihood is that many people became only mildly ill and did not report it; 461 were hospitalized; and 21 died. Most of the cases, according to the state of California, were among people who were homeless or injecting drug users. The state would provide vaccines for 123,000 residents to battle the outbreak. But it would do almost nothing to increase access to toilets and hand-washing facilities.

To be blunt, hep A's normal mode of spread is through the inadvertent ingestion of fecal matter. That could mean sharing food with someone who did not adequately wash their hands after defecating, shaking hands with such a person and later wiping your own mouth, or drinking from water contaminated with stool—all highly possible in homeless encampments. It can also be spread through sex and other close personal contact, such as caring for an ill person. The cheapest form of hep A prevention is soap and water, something people on Skid Row had been consistently demanding. Instead, homeless people, who lack access to toilets, get arrested on charges like public urination.

From January 2017 to April 2018, the Centers for Disease Control received more than 2,500 reports of hepatitis A nationally, sometimes creating regional shortages of the adult vaccine. The majority of people with diagnosed cases report homelessness, drug use, or both. In addition to California, there were clusters reported in Utah, Missouri, Arkansas, Tennessee, Kentucky, Indiana, Ohio, Michigan, and West Virginia.

This represents a serious deterioration of the national public health. The United States has seen small outbreaks of hep A in the past, usually attributed to contaminated imported food. This is the first time since we've had public health authorities to track such things that there have been large outbreaks here because of poor sanitation. The US is a country with running water and sewers—not a country where people get hep A. Or at least, it didn't used to be. US children get the hep A vaccination as part of standard child wellness care. Adults in the past were only encouraged to get the vaccination if they were traveling to countries perceived to have much poorer infrastructure than the US.

We should care about this because every human being deserves to have their health and their dignity supported by facilities where they can relieve and clean themselves. But we obviously are not living in a world where this is recognized. So here is another reason: some of those homeless people are filling your drive-through orders. The media company Axios surveyed providers of homeless services and academics nationwide and found between 6 and 42 percent of homeless people were employed.[2]

Without a serious investment in hygiene for everyone, hep A will spread beyond high-risk groups.

The connection between hygiene, homelessness, and disease was again underlined more recently during the COVID-19 pandemic. The CDC directed communities with homeless encampments to "ensure nearby restroom facilities have functional water taps, are stocked with hand hygiene materials (soap, drying materials) and bath tissue, and remain open to people experiencing homelessness 24 hours per day."[3] During the pandemic, Los Angeles did deploy hundreds of washing stations and toilets around the city to serve the homeless population, but a report by Curbed found that the facilities were commonly lacking soap, water, and paper towels.[4]

CLEAN CLOTHES, AN ESSENTIAL SCHOOL SUPPLY

Every machine at Giant Laundry is working, and the warm dry air smells heavily of fabric softener. A shy little girl smiles and pulls the hood of her fuzzy sleeper down low over her face. She makes her way over to the table where the pizza, veggies, and fruit are spread. The nonprofit Laundry Love, which in partnership with local churches is paying for everyone's machine time and laundry supplies, puts out a meal as people wait—usually for multiple loads to be dried.

The girl's mother, Tasha, is happy that she's made it to the monthly free wash day. Sometimes she misses it because of work. Sometimes because she does not have the eighteen-dollar-round-trip cab fare to get to the laundry. There's no bus route that will get her here. Washing her eight-year-old's clothes is a priority. Without clean clothes, her daughter cannot go to school. Sometimes Tasha has cut back on food to make sure that does not happen.

The appliance maker Whirlpool began a program of putting washers and dryers in schools to see if it would affect attendance. They report that 86 percent of high-risk students had improved attendance after they were able to get their laundry done in school in the 2016–2017 school year. Teachers also report that the students participated more in class, were more motivated, and got involved in more extra-curricular activities.

Laundry is no small expense. Tasha's household of four includes a five-month-old granddaughter. Doing the laundry every other week costs her about $70, she said. That's not sustainable given her minimum wage job working at a dollar store—and she has no one else to rely on. "I grew up in the [foster care] system," she explained. "I can't pick up the phone and say, 'Mom?'"

Clean people are not only healthier; they are more likely to attend school and work, which produce higher skills and wages. Diaper banking—providing free diapers to families who cannot afford them—clearly illustrates this. As we mentioned, studies consistently show that one in three US families struggles to afford diapers.[5] One of the arguments for diaper banking is that it helps parents go to work. Most child-care providers require families to bring a supply of disposables for their babies. No diapers, no day care; no work, no pay. In 2017 the National Diaper Bank Network was able to document that. A study by the Center for Economic Analysis at University of Connecticut found that 57 percent of families who received diapers from the Diaper Bank of Connecticut had been unable to bring their babies to childcare at some point in the previous month because they did not have enough diapers.[6] Let's underline that—in most of the 2,679 households that researchers analyzed, people were pushed deeper into poverty because they could not afford diapers. These parents reported missing an average of four days of paid work or school per month.

That's a depressing finding, but there was great hope in the study as well. It revealed a stunningly simple way to help people rise out of poverty—give them diapers. The authors calculated that personal income increased eleven dollars for every dollar's worth of aid families received in the form of diapers. The gains came from more time on the job because of access to childcare. The economists also posited more paid work hours because parents would spend less time taking care of sick children, as children who get changed regularly are healthier. Finally, income rise was predicted because parents were able to complete educational programs that qualified them for higher-paying jobs. The analysis also found that 1.2 to 1.3 jobs are created for every $10,000 spent on diaper aid—a much better return on investment than the taxpayer-funded economic incentives that go to corporations for "job creation."

DIRTY SHAME

Not having enough diapers—or any other basic hygiene product, for that matter—does not just harm your health or your wallet. It harms you on the most fundamental level. Think of the meanings of the word *dirty*. Yes, it means "unclean," but it also means "dishonest or obscene." If cleanliness is next to godliness, what was Rachel Alston next to when she couldn't afford diapers for her baby?

At the time, she was living in Eugene, Oregon. She was able to find help to pay for utilities. Her husband found a job that came with housing. But no nonprofit or government agency provided help with diapers. With the help of a neighbor who sewed and some family assistance, she built up a supply of cloth diapers. By the time her second child was born, Alston and her husband were doing better financially. "I was able to focus on my children in a different way, without that stress," she reflected.

Not worrying about basic needs like diapers also gave her the chance to grow professionally. "It definitely gave me the bandwidth to start a business, to do the things I felt passionate about instead of just surviving."

She never forgot the feeling of standing in a grocery store and choosing between diapers and milk. After moving to Portland, she founded the PDX Diaper Bank, a nonprofit that distributes free diapers to families in need.

"It's not necessarily just about diaper need, but everybody needs help sometimes," she said. "In terms of diapers, I would encourage people to think about a diaper as not this material thing but about how this small thing can create this big effect and how I've seen those lives impacted long-term as parents are able to keep their jobs and finish their educations."

Access to hygiene reduces stress and also changes how people interact with the world, according to men we met at the free day at Giant Laundry. The world saw them differently when their clothes were consistently clean, they told us. Billy is living in a shelter in Norwalk, Connecticut. His roots in the city are deep. He remembers when this laundry facility was a drugstore, and he would go every Sunday to pick up Norwalk's daily, the *Hour,* with his father. The house he grew up in is a few blocks from here. "I get a lump in my throat whenever I go by," he said. He does not want to run into relatives and old classmates looking dirty. Having clean laundry makes him "feel like a new man."

Billy and Kevin, who is also staying in the same shelter, both talked about going to church, where the faith and fellowship are enormous positives in their lives. Neither of them wants to show up on Sunday morning in smelly clothes. "I need a haircut, but I don't have the money," Kevin commented as he folded a pair of jeans. "I'm tired of going to church with my hair looking all raggedy."

BEING TREATED LIKE A HUMAN BEING

About thirty people are waiting by the Lava Mae bus stationed by the park outside Los Angeles City Hall. The converted city bus is divided into individual showers, which people can use for twenty minutes. The water, they say, is hot the entire time, and the shower itself is immaculate.

Bizarre Policy: Cost $88, assistance $0

AN OBJECTIVE SOURCE ON the cost of keeping clean is the Internal Revenue Service's National Standards. This establishes the minimum amount a person needs to secure necessities and is used in calculating how much the government can demand of a person in payment of back taxes. According to the IRS, a single person must spend $43 monthly for personal care products and $45 on household supplies. For a family of four, it is $88 total on personal care products and $71 on household supplies. Though the government is willing to let you keep enough of your money to buy things like toothpaste as you pay off your debt, it will not provide assistance with these products for people in poverty.

Person after person says that the experience offered by this nonprofit program is far better than any other opportunity homeless people in Los Angeles have to get clean, as well as to have some privacy. Some people report dancing during their twenty-minute shower, or praying, or thinking.

"They treat you like a human being," said twenty-one-year-old Ariel Rose as she waited for her shower. Ariel Rose is a street name she asked we use for her protection. Her father disapproves of her gender expression, which she described as "maybe gender fluid." She has been without housing since she left her family home, where she said she was verbally and physically abused.

She and her friend Angel (also a street name) talked about what products they might leave with that day. Lava Mae staff typically give away whatever hygiene items they've gotten donated: shampoo, toothpaste, clean socks. Angel was hoping for tampons. Her backpack got stolen, a common occurrence for people who live on the street, and her period supplies were inside. "I try to keep clean, but it's impossible in a tent," she said.

In hours of sitting by the trailer, every person walked out of the shower smiling. Michael comes to the shower once a week, for the same reason that most people who have the option step into the shower every day: "It makes everyone feel good, doesn't it?"

A Better Way: Period supplies in schools

SOME STATES AND INDIVIDUAL school districts are now providing free period supplies in schools so that menstruating students don't have to miss days because they don't have the products they need to manage their periods. This reform is getting bipartisan support. For example, a New Hampshire bill to provide period supplies in all public schools was signed by Republican governor Chris Sununu. Because these legislative changes are relatively new, impact measures are largely unavailable. However, early outcomes compiled by the Alliance for Period Supplies found that 31 percent of people who received these products from a nonprofit said that this allowed them to attend school.[7]

What Can I Do?

1. **Start or support a basic needs bank.** Members of the National Diaper Bank Network and the Alliance for Period Supplies distribute free hygiene products to people in need. You can connect to your local basic needs bank or find out how to start one in your community by visiting diaperbanknetwork.org.

2. **Advocate for sales tax fairness.** Most states exempt necessities like food and medicine from sales tax, but it is common to tax hygiene products. Find out what your state's policy is by visiting Diaperbanknetwork.org and going to the advocacy page. By working to eliminate sales tax, you can make these products more accessible for everyone.

3. **Advocate for hygiene supplies in public buildings.** In most schools you'll find a teacher who is buying tissues and a school nurse who has a drawer full of hotel shampoos to give out to students who need them. They are terrific role models, but they cannot do it alone. Schools should have supplies on hand for any student who needs them. Holding a drive to collect these things is great. Going to the board of education and demanding that hygiene items be a line item in the budget is even better because the latter recognizes that hygiene is essential to learning, just as we now recognize that nutritious breakfast and lunch are. Period supplies should also be available for free in schools and in any public building: libraries, the department of motor vehicles, and so forth.

4. **Budget for hygiene.** Public buildings are not the only institutions that should have budgets for hygiene supplies. The same should be true of health clinics, job training programs, soup kitchens, or any other agency that serves low-income people.

5. **Advocate for public toilets and washing stations in your community.** Ask yourself: If I were homeless and needed to use the toilet and wash up, where could I do that in my town? Shelters are typically closed during the daytime, and not all people will use a shelter. Businesses tend to keep their restrooms locked. There must be places where people can meet their basic needs.

CHAPTER 8

Health

Health ≠ Health Care

Middle- and upper-class US Americans make resolutions about their health all the time. Go to the gym three days a week; eat more whole grains; practice daily meditation. These resolutions tend to focus on personal behaviors, not on formal health care delivered by a clinician. On an individual level, people recognize that the stuff of daily life plays an enormous role in determining their health. When US Americans talk about health as a policy issue, we often ignore this truth. We equate health with health care. We talk about the barriers that too many people face to seeing a clinician, having necessary surgery, or obtaining prescription medication. Knocking down these barriers and assuring that everyone has access to optimal health care is a matter of national urgency. But to create real health equity, the US would need to do something more, something radical: build a society where everyone has sufficient time and resources to eat healthfully, live in a safe home, and engage in exercise and other stress-reducing activities.

The United States spends more on health care per capita than any other nation, yet we are sicker and die younger than people in other industrialized countries. In *The American Health Care Paradox: Why Spending More Is Getting Us Less*, Elizabeth H. Bradley and Lauren A. Taylor argue convincingly that the explanation for our poorer health lies in what we do not spend public funds on—things like decent housing and healthy foods. They point out that while the United States spends 10 percent of gross domestic product on social services, France, Sweden, Austria, Switzerland, Demark, and Italy spend about twice that.[1] This upside-down spending, they write, threatens the health of US Americans across the socioeconomic spectrum.

But, as with so many bad policies, the impact is greatest on people in poverty. They are in worse health than US Americans as a whole because their poverty makes the basic needs that support good health difficult, and sometimes impossible, to obtain. For example, the poorest counties in the US have much higher hypertension rates than the most affluent ones. Poverty also creates toxic stress, which is prolonged activation of the stress response systems that can disrupt the development of brain architecture and other organ systems and increase the risk for stress-related disease and cognitive impairment, well into the adult years. Illness and disability keep people out of work and school, which of course contributes to poverty. So people get sick because they are poor, and they stay poor because they are sick.

TWO MANHATTANS

East Harlem is a good place to explore US health inequities. Walk a few blocks downtown and you'll be on the Upper East Side, which is the Manhattan you've seen in films, with doormen, the occasional celebrity, and world-class museums. East Harlem is not that Manhattan.

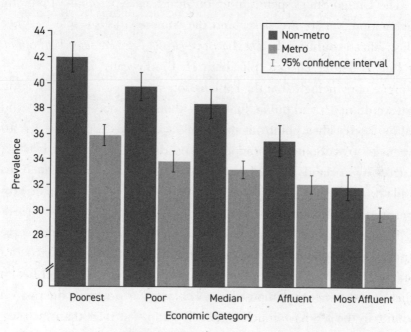

Prevalence of High Blood Pressure Among US Adults by County Economic Characteristics

Legend:
- Non-metro
- Metro
- I 95% confidence interval

Y-axis: Prevalence (0, 28, 30, 32, 34, 36, 38, 40, 42, 44)

X-axis: Economic Category (Poorest, Poor, Median, Affluent, Most Affluent)

Source: Centers for Disease Control and Prevention

New York City's largest Puerto Rican enclave is vibrant with historical sites and some great restaurants. But you're less likely to run into a one-percenter keeping a pied-à-terre here. Despite some gentrification, one-third of the neighborhood's rental apartments are public housing, and nearly half of East Harlem's children live in poverty.[2] Employment is generally found out of the neighborhood, meaning a commute that's hampered by crumbling sidewalks, a shortage of bus shelters, and unreliable subway service.

Residents of East Harlem live an average of 77.3 years, while life expectancy on the Upper East Side is 85.9 years.[3] East Harlem has an infant mortality rate of six per thousand live births. That number in the Upper East Side is one per thousand.[4] Remember, these are adjacent neighborhoods. The statistics make an excellent case that poverty can be fatal (emphasis as in the original source):

> One way to consider the effect of income on health is by comparing death rates among neighborhoods. "Avertable deaths" are those that could have been avoided if each neighborhood had the same death rate as the five wealthiest neighborhoods. **Using this measure, 42% of deaths could have been averted in East Harlem**.[5]

A person's own rating of physical health has proved to be an extremely accurate predictor of illness and even death. In East Harlem 79 percent of residents rank themselves as being in good, very good, or excellent health. On the Upper East Side, 92 percent of residents give themselves those ratings. Compared with Manhattan and New York City as a whole, East Harlem residents are less likely to exercise or to eat fruits and vegetables, and they are more likely to smoke tobacco and drink sugary beverages.[6]

Padmore John, a tall man in a broken-in corduroy sport coat, winds a visitor through the nooks and crannies of the East Harlem Neighborhood Health Action Center, which he directs. There are other similar centers in NYC, one in Brooklyn and one in the Bronx. Activities that could broadly be labeled public health have been going on here since the 1920s, when New York City and the Red Cross partnered to do maternal and child services here. After World War II the ethnic makeup of the neighborhood shifted from Italian to increasingly Puerto Rican. "Then the disinvestment started," John said, both in the neighborhood as a whole and in the health programs offered in the building, which is currently hosting an exhibit on redlining, a practice of race-based housing discrimination that drew money out of East Harlem. "These are communities that you've given no resources to and they are expected to . . ." He paused and looked for a word. "Exist!"

A few years ago, the building was due to be turned over to the police department for a substation in a neighborhood that many residents would call overpoliced already. Instead it went to the Department of Health, which has held community screenings here for *13th*, a documentary about the racist roots of mass incarceration, and *The Central Park Five*, which tells the story of a group of black and Latino youth wrongly convicted in a high-profile rape case. After the latter, lawyers from the Legal Aid Society talked about the city police's gang database. Being included on the database can lead to higher bail, longer sentences, and deportation. You don't need to have committed a crime to get in the database, and most people included are black or brown. Legal Aid is helping people file Freedom of Information Act requests to see if they are in the database.

It may seem odd for a health center to be focusing on incarceration along with more traditional offerings like exercise classes and vaccinations. But it makes perfect sense. Prison, a place generally reserved for the poorest among us, shortens lives. On average, every year of incarceration costs a person two years of life span.[7] Prisons serve high-fat, low-quality food, and the people who eat it are six times as likely to get a foodborne illness as the rest of the population, the Centers for Disease Control found.[8] Men in jail awaiting trial—most of whom stand accused of nonviolent crime—commit suicide at a rate of forty-three per hundred thousand, more than double the average rate for all US men.[9] So mass incarceration is, among other things, a public health crisis.

Upstairs at the Health Action Center is the Family Wellness Suite, where new mothers sit in a circle in the Baby Café, a room with all the artwork and trappings of a preschool class. Some of them are breastfeeding as they meet with a facilitator who is encouraging the practice. On other days, there is Zumba and a yoga class that aims to reduce the toxic stress of poverty. Reproductive health advocate Jessi Lopez is in his office fielding requests for cribs—a common ask, as the Health Action Center does a great deal of public education that encourages safe sleeping practices for new babies.

John points out that African American infants are more likely to die in their first year than white babies. (In the US, black babies from all socioeconomic statuses die at about twice the rate of white ones; and black mothers at three to four times the rate of white mothers.[10]) The center aims to prevent that in a variety of ways—everything from paying emergency rent for homeless mothers to giving information about how sleeping in an adult bed raises the risk of sudden infant death syndrome. But there is a "decent waiting list" to get a free crib, he said.

Space is going fast in the building, where long-unused sections are being renovated. It is the headquarters to nonprofits like Concrete Safari, an urban farming program for middle school youth. Families can also enroll for SNAP here. Undocumented residents can get city identification cards that increase their access to services. It is the home of SMART University, which stands for Sisterhood Mobilized for AIDS/HIV Research and Treatment.

SMART started in 1998, three years after Susan Rodriguez, a resident of the neighborhood, and one of her children were diagnosed with HIV. "There was little data regarding the treatment of women," she recalled. She began attending conferences and symposia to understand the options available to her and her daughter. She knew most women in her situation weren't getting access to that information and would need it broken down in lay terms to even be useful. She entered her daughter into a clinical trial that had a nutritional component and saw how diet dramatically improved the child's health. "I always thought there was more to it than just drugs," Rodriguez said.

HIV-positive women in East Harlem were facing educational hurdles, barriers to eating an optimal diet, and, Rodriguez told us, a general isolation even within the HIV/AIDS community, where women are a minority. Rodriguez started SMART by offering health education that began with teaching women how to turn on a computer. "That was monumental!" she remembered. She used her own fine arts background to start arts and crafts programs that would build community and give women an outlet to cope with stress. The organization lacked a stable home for years. Rodriguez said that in the early days landlords did not want positive women in their buildings. At one point, they were doing cooking classes in her apartment.

The definition of "healthy cooking" kept changing as the wasting that first characterized HIV/AIDS became less common. "People started getting obese and getting cardiovascular problems and high blood pressure," she said. At that point, it became clear that women who did not have HIV/AIDS could benefit from what SMART was offering, so the participation requirements changed. "You just have to be a self-identified woman, period," explained Rodriguez.

This afternoon, Rodriguez is struggling with a grant application and reflects that she is told no a lot. Teaching women to improve their health by giving them creative outlets or access to better food does not motivate funders the way, say, developing a new AIDS drug would. SMART is "a replicable model, but it takes a lot of blood, sweat, and tears," she said.

SPINACH SMOOTHIES AND SUPPORT

Tawnya Manion is perspiring a bit as she sprints around a huge multi-purpose room and stops to give instruction to women who are wearing plastic aprons and hairnets. The women talk, chop, and talk some more as they prepare a low-fat gumbo. Manion is the director of health and wellness programming for SMART. In addition to the gumbo, the women are making spinach smoothies and cauliflower "toasts," an appetizer where the titular vegetable substitutes for bread. Participants go home with a pantry bag filled with the ingredients to replicate the meal, implying that this kind of cuisine represents not a novelty but a plan. It also recognizes that brown rice, okra, and cauliflower can be pricey and consume a family's SNAP allotment all too quickly.

The gumbo is simmering on an induction cooktop on wheels. Though there is a kitchen upstairs here at the Health Action Center, it isn't large enough to accommodate the fifty or so women who typically attend these classes. That includes a table of older women who participate with the help of an interpreter translating the class into Mandarin. As rents increase in New York's Chinatown neighborhood, more Mandarin speakers are coming to live in East Harlem.

Manion talks about "mindful eating," inviting her students to pause and ask themselves if they are hungry before eating and then to say a prayer—or for those who do not pray, to express thankfulness for their food and the people sharing it. Many women report weight loss approaching and even exceeding a hundred pounds that they attribute to the cooking class. After class Manion talks about how premeal exercise is critical in East Harlem: "I think that mindfulness is so important, especially if you have a lot of stressors." She added that there are women in the room facing unemployment, housing insecurity, and a host of other challenges. "Sometimes this is a problem with eating, because it's such a great stress release." The trick is to savor delicious food while avoiding eating in excess, which can lead to "even more stressful events, such as chronic disease developing because of their diet."

The women in the class describe dramatic weight loss with broad smiles. Perhaps even more dramatically, they talk about serious illnesses that are being managed through the lifestyle changes they've made and through coming to a group that they describe using words like *family*, *safe*, and *uplifted*.

Bernadette was living with polycystic ovarian syndrome, an endocrine disorder that's linked to infertility and causes women to have irregular periods. In Bernadette's case, she had stopped menstruating entirely. Since she has been taking healthy cooking classes at SMART, Bernadette has lost sixty pounds. She is menstruating again and has seen her other symptoms improve.

Debbie's diet has changed, and so has her children's and grandchildren's. "Nobody in the house is doing soda no more." She lost 150 pounds in two years at SMART. Being able to take home healthy food is important to her: "I didn't have the money to buy these fruits and vegetables." Her cholesterol level has decreased, and her anxiety and depression are much better. "All that's gone because I'm getting out of the house." Yoga classes at SMART are helping manage her fibromyalgia, Debbie added.

Maxita has lost weight and brought her blood pressure and cholesterol levels down in the three years she has been attending the cooking classes. Her favorite breakfast now is egg whites with cilantro and just a touch of ham—a far cry from her old high-fat favorites.

She had been a cafeteria aide at a nearby nursing home, where she watched a very different kind of cooking for fourteen years. She had to retire six years before she was eligible for a pension because a variety of orthopedic woes, including a knee replacement, made standing for hours on end unbearable. "I miss the job," she said, and recalled the great care she took to make sure residents with dietary restrictions got the right trays. But coming to SMART classes helps fill the day: "I love crafts. It helps lift me."

TOO SICK TO WORK

Maxita's story is not unusual. Time and again in researching this book we talked with people in poverty who had chronic illnesses or disabilities that limited their ability to work, sinking them deeper into poverty. Keep in mind that poverty-wage jobs are more likely to involve lifting, long periods of standing, and other requirements that may be difficult for a person in ill health to withstand.

So again, we see a catch-22. You get sick because you are poor, and you get poorer because you are sick.

Danya Keene, a Yale University researcher, set out to understand how people make decisions about taking out reverse mortgages, a type of loan ripe for unscrupulous practices. The US Department of Housing and Urban Development projects that 20 percent of these loans will end in foreclosure.[11] The popular narrative is that lenders deceive people about the terms. In interviewing people who had taken out the loans, though, Keene found that homeowners understood the risks—they just didn't see any other options.

"Foreclosure stories were precipitated by an illness that really interfered with people's ability to work, which was their safety net," she said.

She interviewed reverse mortgage holders in an African American neighborhood of a New England city. Many, like this fifty-five-year-old nurse, felt forced into the arrangements when illness made work impossible: "I couldn't get up in the morning, you know. Back and forth to the doctor, getting therapy on the back and everything, and still—then when I go back to work, 'Oh, we don't have light duty,' . . . I just couldn't take it. One night, I couldn't even move my back. Couldn't get up. So I said, you know what, it's time to go out on disability. It's time."[12]

Keene's research did not extend to whether the woman succeeded in qualifying for a disability payment. Supplemental Security Income, a federal disability program, covers only severe disabilities. At this writing, the typical SSI benefit is $750 a month for a single adult. Enrollment in the program has decreased since the 1980s with the standards to qualify becoming more stringent.

A number of the homeowners Keene interviewed also entered into reverse mortgages because caring for a sick relative caused them to cut back on work. Again, there is little help for a person in this situation. There is no national program of paid family leave, and the US is the only industrialized nation that does not offer universal paid parental leave. US Americans have no legal right to paid time off, in contrast to European Union workers, who get a minimum of four weeks a year.[13] Children in low-income families sometimes miss school because when adults in the family cannot afford a day off without pay, kids must take care of sick siblings.

The connection between poverty and poor health begins even before birth and will affect education and earnings over the course of a lifetime.

The tragedy is that it need not be this way. The United States spends $9,536 per capita on health care—more than double what the United Kingdom, Canada, France, and Japan do. Yet our residents have shorter lives that are more diminished by illness than people in other rich countries. Shifting resources toward guaranteeing access to a healthy lifestyle across socioeconomic groups would put more people in a position to contribute to the economy. It would save lives and money.

Bizarre Policy: Sickest US Americans get fewest sick days

EVEN GENERALLY HEALTHY PEOPLE get sick. Most middle-class workers will spend a few days a year recuperating from some kind of virus while they still receive a salary. Not so for many low-income workers. An analysis of US Department of Labor data by the Economic Policy Institute found that only 39 percent of the bottom quarter of wage earners have access to paid sick days.[14]

What Can I Do?

1. **Fight for safety net programs.** Food aid, like SNAP and WIC, and housing assistance keep people healthy. Keeping people healthy is almost always cheaper than treating illness. Yet basic needs programs are historically underfunded and must fight every year for their meager slice of the pie. Let your members of Congress know that these things matter to you.

2. **Talk about racial and economic health disparities.** Health statistics are commonly broken down by income, race, and other demographics. But that information should be much

more widely shared. For example, you frequently hear that one in eight women will be diagnosed with breast cancer. But you do not hear that African Americans are 40 percent more likely to die than white women when they get the disease.[15] Lack of awareness about health justice leads to a poor distribution of resources.

3. **Invest your time and money in health over health care.** Research and clinical institutions tend to have large development departments and often large endowments. Organizations that promote prevention generally do not. If heart disease has struck your family and you want to do something about it, don't help build a new hospital wing or finance research. Chip in toward an exercise program in a low-income community or get yourself elected to a city board or commission and commit to making every neighborhood walkable. You'll save more lives—and you'll certainly start improving lives immediately.

4. **Prioritize children.** Growing up in poverty increases the lifetime risk of a slew of chronic diseases. In part, that's because of how toxic stress affects the development of the immune and other systems. Improving the conditions in which children grow up will make them healthier for a lifetime. Support public and private safety net programs, including diaper banks, of course. There are many programs that will help you mentor a young mother. Consider volunteering for one of them.

5. **Get involved at school.** Schools can be a hub to provide basic needs. Through your parent-teacher association, you can advocate for supports for children in poverty. Every school should offer a healthy breakfast and lunch. Some schools now also offer supper and send children home for the weekend with backpacks full of food. Some have showers—not just for after physical education but for children who do not have access to

running water at home—and washing machines. School-based health clinics can provide primary care and also work in health promotion. Even if you live in an affluent community, there will be some children enrolled who need help.

6. **Fight for sick time.** As we said, there is no federal law guaranteeing US Americans paid time off for any reason. Find out what the law is in your state and municipality. If there is no requirement for sick time, ask your state legislator to sponsor a bill changing that. Find out what the policy is where you work— and at places where you spend money. Paid sick time should not just be for management. Decent sick time policies benefit us all, as we have seen during the coronavirus pandemic.

A Better Way: Doulas in Brooklyn

THE INFANT MORTALITY RATE in the Brooklyn neighborhood of Brownsville (5.4 per 1,000 births) is the highest in New York City, while in the borough's Bedford Stuyvesant neighborhood, 4.9 children per 1,000 die before their first birthday. In contrast, the rate is 1.8 per 1,000 on the Upper East Side.[16] But for low-income women in those higher-risk neighborhoods supported by a doula, two risk factors—preterm labor and low birthweight—were reduced by 40 to 50 percent, according to Gabriela Ammann, who runs a doula program based out of Healthy Start Brooklyn. Mothers can opt into the program free of charge.

The professional organization DONA International (formerly Doulas of North America) defines a doula as "a trained professional who provides continuous physical, emotional and informational support to a mother before, during and shortly after childbirth to help her achieve the healthiest, most satisfying experience possible."

Ammann was inspired to begin By My Side Birth Support when she was teaching Lamaze classes at Healthy Start and met pregnant women who were uncertain whether they would have a support person during labor because there was no one among their partners, family, and friends who had a job where they could get paid time off to be present at the birth. That was one stressor among many.

"Pregnancy has its own set of challenges," said Ammann. "A lot of our clients have additional stresses that likely preceded the pregnancy and likely will continue after the pregnancy." She began a list: Housing insecurity, food insecurity, racism. "The doulas in that sense can help a lot to decrease the impacts of the daily stress."

A first meeting with a pregnant woman might involve the doula connecting her to services like WIC that help meet basic needs. But resources are not always adequate, especially when it comes to affordable, safe housing. "NYC is having a housing crisis," she said. "Our ability to assist with that is pretty limited."

Managing stress is important for a mother's comfort and for the outcomes of the pregnancy. "Stress hormones can slow labor, increase pain and lead to more medical interventions," she said.

During the birth, a doula will help a woman advocate for herself, which often means rejecting unnecessary interventions. Facing institutional racism, women can find it difficult to assert themselves in the hospital, though Ammann marvels at her clients' "incredible resourcefulness amidst all the challenges they are facing."

By My Side is working to recruit and train more women to work as doulas who come from similar backgrounds as the mothers it serves. Two former clients are now practicing as doulas. By My Side is one of a number of doula programs around the country serving mothers in poverty. Ammann has published about the program in hopes of helping more communities institute these services.

PART II

FORMS OF
OPPRESSION

CHAPTER 9

Racism

Stealing Homes

A s we said earlier, poverty and racism are each other's evil twin. It can be hard to know which you are witnessing. Yet while they often work in concert, they are distinct forces. Throughout part I, we talked about how access to basic needs like water and housing were particularly limited for racial and ethnic minorities. In this chapter we focus on just one area where racism harms economic wellbeing—housing foreclosure. High foreclosure rates wrest wealth away from people of color.

For working-class people, home ownership is nearly synonymous with wealth. Equity in a primary residence is the source of most asset wealth held by US families.[1] Becoming a homeowner is more difficult for buyers who are not white, which is tantamount to saying that it is more difficult for people who are not white to accumulate wealth. Tremendous work by Ta-Nehisi Coates and Richard Rothstein, among other writers, documents the long history of actions by government and the financial and real estate industries that have made it difficult for African Americans to finance and purchase homes.

When minority families manage to defy those forces and buy homes, they are vulnerable to foreclosure. During the Great Recession, African American and Hispanic owners lost their homes at nearly twice the rate that white owners did (8 percent versus 4.5 percent).[2] African American families lost 47.6 percent of their wealth during the financial crisis; Hispanic families lost 44.3 percent; and white families lost 26.2 percent.[3] The recovery has been weaker for minority households. Racial wealth inequities have actually widened since 2009 and are no better than when the Fair Housing Act was passed in 1968.[4]

Wealth is a lifeline in disasters: public catastrophes like hurricanes, and private ones like job loss, divorce, and cancer. Wealth tides you over when you cannot work or replaces your wrecked car so that you can keep going to work. Wealth can be leveraged to obtain things that create more wealth. Home equity commonly finances educations and business start-ups. A paid-up house can be sold to access skilled nursing care at the end of life, or it can be willed to family members, giving them an economic head start.

Foreclosure forces families to relocate away from schools, jobs, and social connections. Depending on their loan type, owners may lose the money they invested in the home. They may face bankruptcy and will certainly suffer poor credit. Bad credit is one of many injuries that make living in poverty so very expensive. The stress of losing a home is another devastating harm accompanying foreclosure. Indeed, suicides among former owners are high, leading some researchers to posit a causal connection. A five-year national study compared state-level foreclosure and suicide statistics and concluded that an uptick in foreclosures increases suicide, particularly among middle-aged homeowners.[5]

Average Family Wealth by Race and Ethnicity, 1983–2016

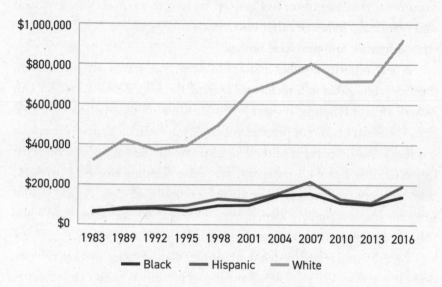

Homeownership Rate by Race and Ethnicity, 1983–2016

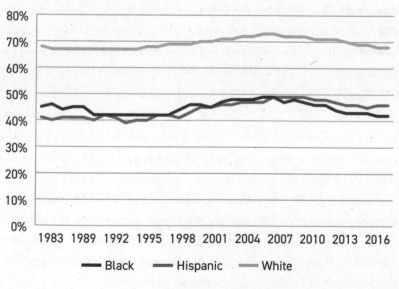

Source: The Urban Institute

WHY ARE RACE AND FORECLOSURE LINKED?

Some of our first interviews for this chapter were with nonprofits or government agencies that help people avoid foreclosure. Several professionals at these organizations talked a lot about budgeting, discipline, and realism. They spoke about their own thrifty habits and the necessity of teaching distressed homeowners to adopt similar ones. Their clients were facing foreclosure because of irresponsible spending, they believed.

In every single instance where we investigated economic hardship throughout this work and were told that people had made "bad choices," we found that people in poverty were making the only choices available to them. We found more than a thousand examples of African American and Hispanic homeowners at risk of losing their homes, not because they were profligate with money but because their lender was unethical. They were low-income people living in communities where conventional lenders seldom make loans, neighborhoods that were once called (and may as well still be called) "redlined." They took out bad loans because those were the only loans available to them. Their plight is not the consequence of irresponsible spending on their part. It is not an accident. It is not bad luck. It is the direct result of government policy and of malfeasance by a financial industry that continues to discriminate against people of color without fear that anemic regulators will exact any meaningful punishment.

THE HERRONS HOLD ON

The late Mack Herron's NFL career was brief, troubled, and sometimes glorious. Mack did manage to get something out of his glory days—enough money to help his mother, Effie, purchase the family home in Chicago's North Lawndale neighborhood. Mack's football money put the family over the top, but there was plenty of long-term sacrifice that went into buying the house. Effie, who has since passed, worked multiple jobs, and the budget was always tight. "I actually remember when I only had one meal a day, one pair of shoes, one skirt, one blouse that you wore on Sunday. I remember all these things," recalls Effie's oldest daughter, Barbara.

Barbara Herron, her one surviving brother, and a great-nephew now live in the home. They are at risk of losing it to foreclosure. Selling is out of the question because their debt on the place is so high and its condition is so poor. Barbara has about 125 neighbors who are in the same predicament, all African American. They've joined in a class-action suit against the mortgage giant Ditech, which they say misled homeowners into signing predatory loans. The company that has since bought Ditech, New Rez, did not respond to a request for comment.

North Lawndale is an African American neighborhood where a well-documented real estate scam prevented residents from owning their own homes in the 1950s and '60s. But for the Herron family, North Lawndale's tree-lined streets offered an oasis in the city. Like many of the houses on the street, the Herron home is topped with crenellations, making it a diminutive fortress squeezed into a city lot. It really did seem like a castle in 1958 when the family moved in. There were no rats or roaches, unlike the Northside apartment where they'd lived previously, remembers Barbara. She and her siblings ran all over the neighborhood. They loved to run, a talent that would take Mack to the NFL and put Barbara on the track team. She doesn't run anymore. At sixty-eight, Barbara is a slight, stooped woman with severe asthma.

Hand-painted billboards pop up in North Lawndale yards and issue brightly colored reminders to keep music volume low, respect neighbors, and be aware that "This block calls 911." But nobody thought to call the police when the real threat to their homes emerged. In 2010 a friend told the Herron family that a man was offering government grants to North Lawndale homeowners so that they could perform repairs and upgrades. You simply needed to be a senior citizen. Pretty soon that money man was sitting in the Herron living room—a man named Mark Diamond. Three years earlier Diamond had entered into a consent decree with the Federal Trade Commission and the state of Illinois in which he agreed not to conduct mortgage closings, as the state had accused him of deceptive practices. Diamond is today awaiting trial on wire fraud charges. We attempted to contact him through his attorney, who did not return phone calls.

"You know, he came off as a friendly type," Barbara recalled. Diamond had a lawyer with him. The Herrons did not. The signing was done late at night, which according to the family's attorney, J. Samuel Tenenbaum, was a common underhanded ploy to make sure elderly homeowners did not call a relative or a lawyer to help them in the process.

What Effie Herron was actually signing was not receipt of a government grant but a reverse mortgage for $180,000. She then turned the proceeds over to Diamond, with the understanding that he would make repairs on her home.

Tenenbaum is director of the Complex Civil Litigation and Investor Protection Center at the Pritzker School of Law at Northwestern University. He is representing plaintiffs like the Herrons who are trying to recover some of their losses, which are estimated at about $10 million. The mortgages were held by Reverse Mortgage Solutions, a company that the mortgage giant Ditech sold off during its Chapter 11 proceedings, leaving the petitioners with another legal hurdle to surmount. "There was no due diligence to make sure that people really knew what they were doing," Tenenbaum said. Court filings allege that Diamond took signed documents "back to the office to make copies" and would not return them until after the seventy-two-hour "cooling off period," when consumers can back out of a contract, had passed.

The Herrons got involved with Diamond because they wanted to make repairs to their home. Those repairs never happened, according to Barbara Herron, or were botched. Diamond was supposed to solve a water problem in the basement. But the day we visited there was black mold climbing the cellar walls. The exterior door was so badly fitted that sunlight streamed through underneath it. The sheetrock in the stairwell had holes that Barbara said were the result of the contractor moving ladders without proper care. Diamond also promised to renovate a bathroom, which Barbara complains is full of bugs because she cannot close the window. The work that was done took three years, with her repeatedly calling the contractor to insist he return and work, she said. He'd show up late at night, according to Barbara, and work only a short time before leaving.

The Herrons were nearly evicted from their home because they were not making payments on the reverse mortgage. In court, they won the right to stay, at least temporarily. But whether they will regain equity in the house remains a question mark.

"We've stopped taking other cases," Tenenbaum said of the clinic. "It's going to be years of litigation." At seventy, he worries that he won't be working long enough to get his clients justice. "Where are these people going to go?" he asked.

RACISM AND HOUSING: A BRIEF AND ONGOING HISTORY

In the early days of the United States blacks were more likely to work the land as slaves than to own it. After the Civil War, most land stayed in the hands of former slaveholders, as economist Richard Edwards explains:

> The Southern Homestead Act, passed in 1866, promised recently freed slaves and others the opportunity to homestead on public lands in five southern states. For freedpeople who were defeated in their efforts to gain ownership of plantation lands, the Southern Homestead Act seemed to be a possible avenue to Black landownership. Although some African Americans succeeded in gaining homesteaded land, most were unable to take advantage of the Southern Homestead Act because of their extreme poverty; the unsuitability of the lands available and difficulty of finding them; and the extreme hostility and violence that whites directed against them.[6]

Throughout the United States, law, custom, and criminal intimidation conspired to keep African Americans from owning land during the Reconstruction era.

In the twentieth century, efforts to deny land to black potential buyers were no less real, albeit somewhat more subtle. In 1934 Congress established the Federal Housing Administration, a New Deal agency that would set standards for construction and insure private mortgages. Because the FHA insurance protects lenders against losses, banks greatly expanded their mortgage offerings and improved affordability—for whites. Racism was baked into the agency. It would only underwrite mortgages in neighborhoods deemed a good risk. The FHA *Underwriting Manual* was quite clear about what that meant: "If a neighborhood is to retain stability it is necessary that properties shall continue to be occupied by the same social and racial classes. A change in social or racial occupancy generally leads to instability and a reduction of values."[7]

The FHA used color-coded maps to identify places that were bad risks—that is, neighborhoods with people of color in them. Later, the Veterans Administration would use those same maps to determine which vets should get subsidized mortgages. Areas with nonwhite homes were shaded red, hence the term "redlining." African American buyers were relegated to those enclaves because the *Underwriting Manual* warned of mixing races. So the FHA would not insure mortgages in African American neighborhoods and would not insure mortgages for African Americans buying in white neighborhoods. In summary, it would not insure mortgages for African Americans.

This policy reigned through an era when buying a home was enormously advantageous, as Robert Kuttner explains: "Homeownership became the single most important source of asset accumulation over the life cycle. For the first two postwar generations, housing values rose faster than inflation. For tens of millions of lucky homeowners of that era, the 'equity' created by the windfall of increasing real estate prices exceeded the equity created by paying off the mortgage."[8]

Redlining is not a thing of the past. In 2019 Liberty Bank settled a redlining lawsuit by pledging an additional $15 million in home financing and promising to open a branch in Hartford. Liberty did business in central Connecticut but did not have a branch in the state's minority-majority capital city. Indeed, its branches were heavily concentrated in white, suburban communities. The lawsuit alleged only 3.34 percent of the bank's mortgage lending went to African Americans and Latinos, though those groups make up more than 28 percent of the state's population. When the housing advocacy group Connecticut Fair Housing sent in testers with similar incomes and circumstances to apply for loans, black and Hispanic testers experienced less helpful service and in some cases were actively discouraged, according to the nonprofit's complaint. One tester minority buyer seeking financing for a house in suburban Southington was advised by a loan officer to instead look in a nearby city, Bristol, where she was told taxes would be lower. They are, in fact, higher.

The dream of home ownership is powerful, even for people denied conventional loans. So potential minority buyers may opt for nonstandard and disadvantageous loans, such as land contracts. Land contracts go by other names as well, including "contract for deed" and "land installment." In a conventional mortgage, buyers acquire the title to the property at closing and earn more equity in their home with each payment. Land contracts, on the other hand, are seller-financed arrangements, in which the seller retains the title. The buyer pays in installments and gets no equity until the loan is paid off in its entirety. When the loan is paid off, the buyer gets the title. But there are typically barriers to payment. For example, the contract may require the buyer to perform expensive maintenance on the property. If the buyer misses a single payment, or falls behind in their tax or insurance bills, they lose the home—and all the payments they've made.

Land contracts declined after the passage of the Fair Housing Act (1968) and Community Reinvestment Act (1977), which encouraged banks to invest in lower-income communities. But they made a comeback after the financial crisis of 2007–2008, when banks began writing fewer conventional mortgages.

There is not national data to prove African Americans are being targeted by these predatory loans, but there are piles of lawsuits in communities nationwide that show a pattern. For example, in 2017 a group of seventeen families from Atlanta—all African American—sued Texas-based Harbour Portfolio, which had bought up foreclosed properties in the city and was doling them out through land contracts. The plaintiffs noted that the company concentrated its Atlanta activities in census tracts that were 86 percent African American and alleged that it used deceptive practices. Harbour settled with the Atlanta plaintiffs, who came away with damages, equity in their homes, and loans restructured into conventional mortgages. Harbour faced similar lawsuits around the country.

DREAM HOMES TO NIGHTMARES

Bernadette Martinez, of Lumberton, Mississippi, is one of about a thousand African American and Latino owners suing Jim Walter Homes (aka Ditech) over land contract deals that they say left them with houses too overpriced to afford and too shoddy to sell. They are also seeking restitution through Ditech's bankruptcy proceedings.

Here is what happened, according to court documents filed by Martinez:

Martinez and her sister visited Jim Walter Homes to inquire about getting a home built on some family land. A sales representative told Martinez that she could get her "dream home" by getting financing using her land as security. The land was co-owned by the sisters, but the salesperson convinced Martinez's sister to give up her claim in order for the deal to go through. In 2005 Martinez closed on the deal in her front yard, without an attorney or a notary public present. She did not receive a closing disclosure, HUD settlement statement, or truth-in-lending disclosure.

The note she signed was for $230,277.60, in exchange for which she was supposed to get a 1,167-square-foot home built on land she already owned. Her house was appraised for $50,000 after it was built. A number of add-ons inflated Martinez's obligation, including a $6,000 homeowner's insurance charge from Best Insurors, a Ditech-affiliated company, a premium she was obliged to pay even though she'd gotten homeowner's insurance on her own—and much more affordably.

She was told that Best Insurors had such respect for the quality of Jim Walter Homes' work that they did not need to inspect the property to write insurance. But Martinez alleges that the work was of incredibly low quality. Concrete piers meant to support the house were not properly constructed. The electrical system is faulty, which resulted in a house fire. Sparks continue to fly out of outlets. The shingles slide off the roof because they were not nailed down.

She couldn't make the loan payments, nor could she sell the house. She said that her builder, who was also her lender, was sending men to her front door to yell abuse at her. This embarrassed her in front of her family, who all live close by. In 2013 she made a suicide attempt, which she attributes to harassment and cruelty on the part of collection agents.

If Martinez cannot make her payments, how does the lender profit? Again, according to the same court documents:

> The Respondents' pattern and practice is to create these notes without care to whether the purchasers can afford to pay back these high interest rate loans. The loan was more valuable as part of the resulting securitization that they sold to downstream investors than it was as an interest-making loan on a low-value property.
>
> Meanwhile, the victim cannot sell the house because it was so shoddily-made, and unable to keep up with the payments, because the price was inflated and greater than the victim can afford. As a result, the Respondents usually simply foreclose on the house and sell it on to the next unwitting victim. Or, in the rare instances in

which the victim can pay off the house, the Respondents reap many multiples of the house's value.[9]

The only one in a position to lose was Martinez.

We were able to find multiple cases of homeowners making allegations that Jim Walter Homes deceived them into signing bad loans for bad houses dating back to the 1970s. Sometimes the buyers won, but the business model was able to remain profitable for half a century. Likewise, Mark Diamond had a long run taking the homes of African Americans in Chicago before he was finally arrested. Both schemes rely on locals who do the legwork. But they ultimately profit a large corporation, one the US government deemed "too big to fail" and bailed out after the financial crisis that companies like Ditech helped cause. Ditech drew on nearly $300 million in federal bailout money after the financial crisis, not a penny of which has been repaid.

There was a time when African Americans were barred from home ownership and the wealth accumulation that accompanied it by explicit government policy. Today a lack of policy to ensure transparent and equitable lending is making it difficult even for those people of color who do achieve home ownership to sustain it. Foreclosure comes with a host of difficulties, ranging from Barbara Herron's constant worry about keeping a roof over her great-nephew's head to Bernadette Martinez's suicidal despair over harassment from collection agents. Without stronger laws and stronger enforcement, these stories will multiply.

Conventional wisdom says that hard work is the way to get ahead. But for those who could participate, a robust housing market from World War II through the early part of this century created a way to make money *without working*. You got more than a free place to live when the mortgage was paid off. You got a bigger asset than you purchased. It was a massive societal payday to which nonwhites were by and large not invited. And by the way, the federal government extends considerable tax benefits to the (predominantly white) people who can afford to buy homes. The mortgage interest deduction is the single-largest government investment that the United States makes in housing. It dwarfs programs such as Section 8, designed to make housing accessible for low-income people.

Decades after legal reform that was supposed to end racial discrimination in real estate lending, that discrimination clearly persists. Enforcement is too weak and too slow to make owners cheated out of their homes whole. Barbara Herron and Bernadette Martinez have already waited for years in substandard homes hoping for some justice. Restitution, if it ever comes, is likely to be many years in the future. These are two African American women who should be richer than they are. Stories like theirs play out across the country every day. Racism contributes to poverty in many ways—some subtle, some not. Government action and inaction have both made it harder for minority families to gain wealth through home ownership, and there has never been anything subtle about it.

What Can I Do?

1. **Support better financial oversight.** The Consumer Financial Protection Bureau has real potential to protect homeowners from unscrupulous lenders. But from 2016 the bureau's power has progressively eroded. You can tell your members of Congress that you want the CFPB to strongly police lenders, particularly in the area of home-financing discrimination.
2. **Reparations.** African Americans face financial hardship that springs from centuries of policies that have made and continue to make it difficult to own property. Congress should at the very least create a body to explore the possibility of reparations.
3. **Invest in communities of color.** As detailed in chapter 8, the city of New York consciously invested in public health programs

in neighborhoods where redlining and other discriminatory practices caused historical disinvestment. States and counties around the US should follow this example.

4. **Support affordable housing.** Affordable housing often gets held up at the local level. Consider running for your town's planning and zoning commission. In many communities, it is hard to fill these seats and volunteers can easily find themselves elected. If you don't want to join the zoning commission, you can show up at their meetings and be a voice for inclusive communities.

5. **Change credit.** The way credit scores are compiled tends to penalize people of color and does not accurately reflect the likelihood that someone will repay a loan. That is one reason that minority applicants are turned down for conventional mortgages at higher rates than whites. Credit scores should reflect consistent payment of rent and cell phone bills and other monthly charges, but they currently don't. The Credit Score Competition Act would even the playing field a bit, but the bill has sat in Congress for years without moving. You could call your members of Congress and ask them to give it some life.

A Better Way: Boosting home ownership by supporting savings

FROM 1997 TO 2002, the American Dream Policy Demonstration project tested a way to encourage savings among people with low incomes through Individual Development Accounts (IDAs). The program matched savings that individuals put into their accounts in the interest of supporting home ownership, education, and small business capitalization. Over thirteen sites throughout the US, these IDAs did indeed promote home ownership.[10] Of people who made withdrawals, 28 percent used the money to buy a home; 23 percent to support a small business; 21 percent to pay for education; and 18 percent for home repair. Of people who had not yet made withdrawals, 55 percent said they intended to use the money for a home purchase.

Even more interest seems to be directed toward Child Development Accounts or "baby bonds." These accounts are typically opened when a child is born or starts school. In some cases, governments seed the accounts, and in a few cases, philanthropists are doing it. Sometimes these arrangements encourage parents to contribute as well. When the accounts are tailored to low-income families, research shows that saving participation is high, that adults will work additional hours and cut back on spending to allow for saving, and that children who will one day benefit from the accounts perform better in school.[11]

Darrick Hamilton and William Darity Jr. have proposed a national program of baby bonds as a way to address the racial wealth gap and promote black home ownership.[12] They note that these accounts typically have bipartisan appeal. Given the racial wage and wealth gaps, any means-tested program would disproportionately benefit black families. They advocate a universal program but with higher contributions to accounts for children from less advantaged families. The authors estimate the cost of such a program would be $60 billion annually, less than the cost of TARP and less than the federal government currently spends on asset development incentives, such as those linked to home ownership or to savings for college or retirement. Those current incentives are most often taken advantage of by middle- and upper-class taxpayers.

CHAPTER 10

Sexism

Women's Work

Work is frequently prescribed as the way out of poverty. Yet most US adults living in poverty are employed. When we started writing this book, the unemployment rate was 3.7 percent. But people ages eighteen to sixty-four fell below the federal poverty guidelines at three times that rate. Certified nursing assistants like Chicago's Shatonia Jackson and Petra Salas work more than most US Americans. Salas calculated that she is on the job fifty-six hours in an average week and commutes an hour by bus each way. Jackson described herself as "worn out, exhausted, overwhelmed, burnt out." She added, "But I still have to get up and do it every single day."

Not every job puts food on the table, especially if you are doing "women's work." Women in the United States are 36 percent more likely to be in poverty than men and are more likely to live in extreme poverty, defined as subsisting on an income at or below 50 percent of the federal poverty guidelines.[1] While women of all races and ethnicities are more likely to be poor than men, the poverty rate is even higher among women who are black, Native American, Hispanic, or Asian.

There are many ways in which sexism compromises career and financial opportunities for women—too many for us to examine here. We will look at economic sexism through a single lens: the concentration of women in low-wage jobs. An analysis by the Institute for Women's Policy Research compared occupations where most workers are female with those where most workers are male. At every skill level, male-dominated occupations paid higher wages. The analysis also found that the occupations where women were breaking into traditionally male fields tended to be those requiring a college degree. In fields open to women with less education, gender segregation is nearly as stark today as it was in the 1960s.[2]

Women make up 93.8 percent of childcare workers, who are paid a median hourly wage of $11.65, according to the Bureau of Labor Statistics (BLS). Earning even less are restaurant waitstaff, at $11.00 per hour, with women making up 71.3 percent of the profession. Women are 89 percent of maids and housecleaners, with median weekly earnings of $490. Today only 30 percent of fast-food workers are teenagers, and 56.5 percent of fast-food workers over age twenty are women.[3] In other words, more of those low-wage jobs are held by people who are supporting themselves and even supporting families.

Nursing assistants like Jackson and Salas are in middle-skill occupations, jobs that require some training after high school but not a college degree. More than 89 percent of home health aides and nursing assistants are women, according to the BLS. A nursing assistant made a median hourly rate of $14.25 in 2019. Compare that with wages in the building trades, also generally middle-skill jobs. A carpenter's median wage for the same period was $23.24. Only 2.8 percent of carpenters are women, with the other building trades routinely coming in with single-digit representation for women.

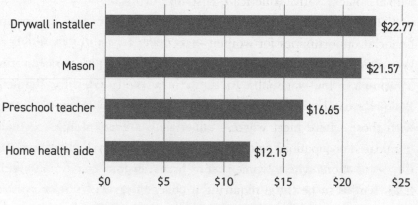

Median Hourly Wages for . . .

Drywall installer — $22.77
Mason — $21.57
Preschool teacher — $16.65
Home health aide — $12.15

$0 $5 $10 $15 $20 $25

Source: Bureau of Labor Statistics, May 2019

There are many reasons why women might end up providing care for the young, the old, and the sick, while men are more likely to be in construction or manufacturing. An ingrained cultural view of gender roles would need to be shifted on many levels to stop these assumptions from fueling gender segregation in employment. But something much more straightforward is also going on here: our government pays for training programs that steer women in poverty toward the long-term care industry, and it has decreased efforts to prepare them to compete in traditionally male fields where pay is higher.

TRAINING WOMEN FOR POVERTY JOBS

The federal Health Professions Opportunity Grants support programs that train people receiving Temporary Assistance for Needy Families (TANF) for careers in health-care professions. In the first round of the grant awards in 2010, 90 percent of those funds went to programs that trained people to be nursing assistants, among the worst-paying jobs in the industry.[4] Approximately 85 percent of the adults receiving TANF in 2018 were women.[5]

Federal dollars are also available through the Workforce Innovation and Opportunity Act for states to offer training to unemployed people. In some states, these resources are used to support nursing assistant courses. We also found at least one private foundation that funds the training.

A consultant for the federal government reviewed the feasibility of training TANF recipients as CNAs or home health aides. The resulting report noted that the jobs in question are low paying, typically offer poor or no benefits, and present workers with physical and emotional stress.[6] More than a decade later, these programs are still operating.

Why train people in poverty for a job that will keep them in poverty? The best route to getting out of poverty, a college degree, is difficult to achieve while on the program. (And even a college degree is not a guarantee of prosperity in the US today, of course, with 3.6 million bachelor's degree holders below the federal poverty guidelines.[7]) TANF considers vocational training as meeting its work requirement, but education that isn't strictly tied to employment is not supported by the program. TANF also does not provide for long-term support, which would generally be needed for someone to complete a bachelor's.

The real agenda of these programs may be filling a health-care workforce gap for the sake of an aging population who will need care, rather than helping people work their way out of poverty. There is a shortage of nursing assistants and similar direct-care workers. These high-turnover jobs are projected to grow as the population ages. The BLS projects 11 percent growth in demand between 2016 and 2026, ahead of the job sector as a whole.

Additionally, CNA and home health aide programs have a high success rate—if you measure success in women who complete the program and get a job. Training programs last between four and twelve weeks. High school graduates, even from low-performing schools, can do well in them. Many women will successfully complete their training. With health-care providers always in need of more nursing assistants, these women will quickly get jobs. A job, however, is not always a path out of poverty. For many workers, a low-wage job with little prospect for advancement is a near guarantee of poverty.

This is not to say that getting more women into traditionally male fields will magically end the wage gap. We found that even women who were making their way into male-dominated professions dealt with harassment and frequent layoffs that lowered their earnings. Rather, this is an argument that the current system of steering women toward low-wage, low-prospect jobs is bad policy. Without systemic improvement in the pay and working conditions for "women's work," people employed in these areas will not be able to achieve self-sufficiency and a reasonable standard of living. These essential fields will experience dangerous worker shortages because they provide such poor incentives for workers to enter and stay in them.

NO CAREER LADDER

The wage gap does not fully convey the economic disadvantage that goes along with professions deemed women's work. As we mentioned, a carpenter's median wage is $23.24. By definition, some make less, and some make more. Because the building trades have an apprenticeship system, workers can earn while they learn—generally at above-minimum wage. Throughout their careers, they can acquire additional skills that will qualify them for higher wages.

Salas twice changed jobs because her boss moved to a new nursing home and asked her to follow. That suggests that she's good at being a nursing assistant, a job she's held for thirty-three years. But the moves did not come with raises. No employer has ever offered her tuition support toward additional certifications or degrees. She believes it suits nursing homes to keep nursing assistants right where they are, performing the essential work of cleaning, feeding, and providing hands-on care.

"No, of course they're not going to have that encouragement, because they know that you're a good worker. They don't want to lose that good worker they have," she said.

A Better Way: Room to grow in home care

A NEW YORK NONPROFIT created a "care connections senior aide" role allowing home health aides with additional training to take on additional tasks, including monitoring patient symptoms and reporting them to a nurse remotely. The program is designed to prevent rehospitalization. The role comes with a 60 percent increase from a starting home health aide's pay.[8] According to the Paraprofessional Healthcare Institute, "Preliminary project outcomes show improvements in the rates of preventable hospitalizations, ER visits, and medication adherence. The project also helped reduce family caregiver strain."

There is no career ladder for women doing the hands-on work of health care.* After decades, most continue to make the base wage. Vocational programs, however, tout the ability of nursing assistants to continue their education to become licensed practical nurses (LPNs) or registered nurses (RNs). A review of five "model" training programs around the country for TANF recipients to become long-term care workers found that it was rare for women to go on to become LPNs or RNs.[9]

Amanda Kogut-Rosenau, a workforce development specialist, described women who progressed from middle-skill health-care jobs to nursing degrees as "unicorns." Any number of barriers, from high tuition to unavailable childcare, can derail a woman seeking nursing education, and that education will take years. "You don't have the life experience of

---

* In some states, people must become CNAs on the pathway to becoming registered nurses. We are talking not about women who become CNAs as part of their education to become a nurse but rather about the prospects of a CNA not already enrolled in a registered nursing program.

planning that far out," she said. Kogut-Rosenau used to recruit women for health-care job training. Now she steers them to construction.

While workers in the building trades can increase their skills on the job through working with more experienced tradespeople, nursing assistants cannot. They would need to be accepted in a program, pay for it, and attend classes. But women in these professions are obviously short on money—and perhaps even shorter on time. How do you go to school when you never have an evening off?

WORK, WORK, WORK

Jackson and Salas work in Chicago nursing homes, where they frequently put in double shifts. They both earn less than a living wage for a single person in Cook County, Illinois, and far less than a person with dependents requires. When Jackson's children were younger and living at home, the two girls shared a bedroom and her son slept on the couch because Jackson, a widow, could not afford an apartment big enough for the family. Today, she worries that she cannot provide health insurance for her younger daughter, a college student, during the summer when the university's health plan lapses.

With wages so low, nursing assistants must work much more than forty hours a week to make ends meet. That has enormous consequences for their families and for their own health. In chapter 3, we interviewed children who spent their evenings alone and eating fast food because their nursing assistant parents were working double shifts. Jackson blames herself for not being home with her son, who was arrested several times as a teenager: "I wasn't home to cook dinner. I wasn't home to make sure he not in trouble, because I had work, trying to make sure we got a roof over our head, food in our mouth . . . clothes on our back." At twenty-five, her son has left Chicago in search of a fresh start as a truck driver.

"You know, and he feel like he disappointed me," she said. "But I keep telling to him, 'Son, you can't feel that way because . . . when you're a teenager you don't know what to do. You don't have a clue. That's what you need your parent for—to guide you. I'm sorry I wasn't there, but this is what I had to do. I had to. We had to survive.'"

Salas also has too little time with her family. Because her husband is disabled, she is the sole breadwinner. After thirty-three years on the job, she is making $13.35 an hour. So Salas works double shifts and often comes in on her days off. Her kids complain that she does not spend enough time with them. "Well, I have to work so that we can survive," she tells them.

STRONG WOMEN, DIFFERENT PATHS

The MGM Springfield casino is faced with heavy panels of faux brick. Katurah Holness put them there. Holness, a second-year apprentice on her way to being a carpenter, remembers how exacting it was to lift the panels into place. This former Air Force mechanic is no stranger to heavy work. Her main concern was damaging an expensive panel. But there were journeyman carpenters on the job who helped her master the maneuver. "They were good guys," she said.

While there is no longer much federal support for helping women like Holness into construction, building trades unions seeking to diversify their ranks are offering pre-apprenticeship programs for women that include things like safety trainings and physical conditioning. Holness started her path to be a carpenter when she was driving for Uber and living in a veterans' homeless shelter. A fare who was a carpenter told her about the program. Holness dropped him off and then drove straight to the union hall.

Kogut-Rosenau said that there is a preconception that women cannot handle the physical demands of construction work—something she believes is absolutely false. Her organization, the New York City–based Nontraditional Employment for Women (NEW), offers a physical-conditioning boot camp where women carry heavy loads up and down stairs and do other exercises to build their strength and endurance. She has placed women as ironworkers, which she calls the most physically demanding of the building trades.

Nursing assistants do physical labor, including lifting patients. When Holness was faced with hoisting panels, her crew included more experienced workers who would instruct and, if necessary, help her. On short-staffed units, nursing assistants go the heavy work alone.

Every nursing assistant we spoke with talked about work-related injuries and a general weariness. Salas has had two knee replacements and shoulder surgery. Though she loves working with elderly nursing home residents, she is looking for hospital work that she believes will involve less lifting. "My whole body is in pain right now," she said.

Salas said she has not been compensated financially for her injuries, or even afforded respect for the sacrifices she's made for her job. "It's just like work, work, work, and yeah, they only laugh at you. They smile at you when they need a favor. Once you do them the favor, it's like *we don't need you no more*," she said.

Workers are more likely to be hurt lifting patients when they are rushed or do not have help, both conditions that can happen when they have responsibility for too many patients. Under Illinois law, a nursing assistant should only be responsible for ten patients per shift, but there is no penalty for nursing homes that exceed the number. The nursing assistants we spoke with say that they care for many times that number of patients on a routine basis, which makes their jobs harder and lowers the quality of care.

Jackson and Salas are part of a campaign organized by the Service Employees International Union to convince the state legislature to impose a fine for nursing homes that exceed the ten-patient ratio. Enforcing the ratio would change working conditions and, they hope, create more demand for nursing assistants that will lead to higher wages.

"I just want everybody to know that we not getting younger," said Jackson. "We getting older. And it could be you in this nursing home. Don't you want to be in the best care?"

DISRESPECT: THE COMMON DENOMINATOR

"We clean shit, and they think we are shit." We interviewed many direct-care workers for this book and repeatedly heard variations of that saying. Nursing assistants talked about employers who did not care about their financial struggles, did not listen to their suggestions, and failed to acknowledge their closeness to residents, as well as their grief when one of them died. Some also felt disrespected by nursing staff, though others reported that nurses valued CNA work.

Jackson has a dental crown that isn't affixed in her mouth and rocks up and down as she speaks. She cannot afford to go to the dentist on her wages of $11.65 an hour. When her supervisor tells her to smile during family member visits to the nursing home, the irony is not lost on Jackson. "How can I smile if I ain't got no teeth in my mouth?" she asked.

Women in building trades report a different variety of disrespect. Kathleen Klohe was on her knees nailing a wooden brace into concrete when she looked up to see a fellow carpenter mooning her. "What the hell are you doing?" she demanded.

"What are you doing here?" he replied. "You've got no place being here. Shouldn't you be home cooking somebody a meal?" The man was removed from the job when Klohe reported the incident to her shop steward. She doesn't know what happened to him after that.

The women in building trades we spoke with dealt with discrimination by working hard and having a thick skin. That means always being on time, never slacking off—even if male colleagues do—and not stepping back from the heaviest work.

"There's a very old-school mentality women can't cut it," said Holness. "I have seen women prove themselves as the better workers."

Maribel Colone worked on Wall Street for twenty-eight years reconciling accounts. Then came her layoff. "I'm going to reinvent my life," she decided and became a construction laborer. "We have to work fifty times harder than any male that works next to us. They don't want us there," she said. Harassment is but one example of that macho culture.

"The men in Wall Street, they were sneaky and shady. But the men in the trades, they tell you how they feel to your face," Colone said.

Support groups, formal or not, are common for women in the building trades. They can help women strategize on how to deal with discrimination or simply offer some emotional support. Colone makes sure to get together regularly with a woman she met when they were both apprentices. "She feels my pain. I feel her pain. We can't vent to a man," she said.

Nursing assistants may make low pay, but they rarely lack for work because of high turnover and high demand. Not so women in the building trades. When we met Holness, she had been laid off for months. She lives in Springfield, Massachusetts, a city that is not booming like Boston to the east, where building is active. Holness is working toward getting her commercial driver's license to give her other options when she does not have a construction job.

The building trades do not offer a guarantee of continued employment. A project takes as long as it takes, and layoffs start happening as workers complete various steps of putting up a building. A number of tradeswomen said that women were the first to be laid off. Research consistently shows that women and minorities experience layoffs at higher rates than white men in a variety of industries.[10]

Holness believes that she's not getting recommended for jobs because she does not have a working car: "It kills me, because for the first two years they never questioned it. I got there, no matter where they asked me to go." When Holness was in her pre-apprenticeship program, she managed to build a network of friends, relatives, and new union siblings who would give her a ride. She achieved perfect attendance.

Klohe said layoffs were frequent in her career. "People get laid off all the time, but you know that you're going to get laid off because you're the female. You're going to be the first to go," she said. She recalled a job at

New York's South Street Seaport where she and another coworker were laid off when things were shut down temporarily. They were both told they'd get called back soon when the project restarted. The coworker, a man, was called in a matter of weeks. Klohe never was.

"How much do you want to be on a job where they don't want you?" she asked.

Her solution was to "keep it moving," a constant refrain when she describes her career. That means putting her name in her union local's out-of-work list and calling up friends and old bosses to drum up work. Though women in the trades talk to each other about their high layoff rate, there's nothing that can be proved, according to Klohe. "Everybody gets laid off."

Despite all the demands of the profession, some women do manage to find their way in, like Holness. Her work as an apprentice carpenter allowed her to save money and get into an apartment. She is much better off than when she first arranged a patchwork of rides, put on her hardhat, and made the trek from the shelter to her pre-apprenticeship class. Holness is a person who moves forward. She's mourning the recent death of her father, but still beating the bushes for work and going to her truck driving course—one more job training that she hopes will give her an income stream. She still considers herself primarily a carpenter, though she's concerned about logging enough hours to maintain her union health insurance.

ESSENTIAL WORK

Every woman we spoke with had complaints about her job, but every woman loved what she was doing.

Klohe will travel around New York City pointing with pride to her handiwork. "I walk by the building and I will tell anybody within reach, 'See that building—I put that building up.'"

Holness has pictures on her phone of complex staircases that she built. She can also narrate a tour of her city and point out the buildings that she helped construct.

The nursing assistants we spoke with all expressed a deep satisfaction gleaned from working with patients. They used words like "family" and "love" to describe their interactions. Jackson's own adored grandparents died young, and now she sees her work as a way to recapture some of that relationship. "I love my elderly," she said repeatedly. These women complained about low pay, injuries they incurred lifting patients, and a general disrespect in the workplace. Nevertheless, not one of them wanted to leave the field.

The similarities between women in health care and women in construction were perhaps more striking than the differences. They were all doing essential and challenging work, and they all took pride in what they did. But they all experienced discrimination of some kind—either because they were doing women's work, or because they were women doing men's work.

In a society that invests work with so much moral rectitude and that prescribes work as an antidote to poverty, they all deserve better.

What Can I Do?

1. **Support a higher minimum wage.** For most women in traditionally female and low-paid professions, an increase in the minimum wage represents a pay raise.
2. **Support unions.** Women who belong to unions get higher wages, better benefits, and have advocates when they experience discrimination.
3. **Get active on the state level.** There are almost certainly bills active in your state legislature that concern pay and working conditions for home health aides, nursing assistants, childcare providers, and other women-dominated occupations. Nursing homes and home care agencies rely heavily on federal and state reimbursements. Activists can work to raise rates, provided they

are tied to increased compensation for workers. Contact your legislators and let them know that these issues are important to you.

4. **Advocate for childcare.** Childcare is a barrier for women who want to continue their education to qualify for better-paying jobs. In the case of low-wage workers, the cost of childcare often forces them to leave their children home alone or in low-quality care. Subsidies for childcare help parents work; and because women assume more than their fair share of responsibility for childcare, such subsidies are important tools to promote equity.

5. **Support paid family leave.** Paid family leave allows women to care for their families when outside care is not available. When women do not have access to paid family leave and they need to take time to care for family—they can be seen as unreliable by employers.

6. **Give preference to companies that hire women and minority workers in nontraditional and well-paid roles.** Companies claim to make efforts to recruit a diverse workforce, but those measures are often lackluster—like sending out a letter to women-serving organizations advertising opportunities but offering no return address or phone number. If your business or community has construction work to give out, ask to see actual numbers of women and people of color that the company employed on its last job.

7. **Support career exploration for girls.** The Girl Scouts and other organizations offer programs introducing girls to nontraditional occupations.

8. **Mentor a girl.** If you are in a traditionally male profession, provide opportunities for girls to shadow you.

Bizarre Policy: Training cut
for higher-paying jobs

THE AMOUNT OF PUBLIC money going to train women in traditionally male careers has declined. The Carl D. Perkins Act is the primary source of federal funding for career and technical education.
With its enactment in 1984, the law required that states spend at
least 3 percent of their federal funding in the area for the promotion of workplace gender equity, but that provision was lost in a
1998 reauthorization. Researchers Ariane Hegewisch and Heidi
Hartmann linked that to a shortage of programs to help women
enter traditionally male fields. "While the Perkins Act continues to
include participation in nontraditional career and technical education among its performance measures, the change from funded
mandates to unfunded voluntary efforts resulted in a dramatic
decline in the number and size of programs designed to improve
access to nontraditional careers."[11]

CHAPTER 11

Denial of Political Power

Government Not of, by, or for Poor People

Philosopher John Locke held that human beings have certain natural rights, including rights to life, liberty, and property. We consent to be governed with the understanding that the government has a duty to protect these rights. The Founding Fathers were deeply influenced by Locke, so this way of thinking about the relationship between people and government will resonate for many US Americans.

But not poor ones. Government in the United States is more likely to take rights away from low-income people than to protect their rights. The idea of consent is absurd, as people at the bottom of the economic ladder, or even closer to its middle, face significant barriers to winning elected office or even to influencing the governing class. Their contacts with their government are often in the form of a parole officer sending them back to jail for missing a meeting, an intake worker who decides they don't qualify for aid, or a child welfare worker who questions their parenting—not a legislator earnestly listening to their opinions. They probably have more interaction with government than wealthier residents, but those interactions are too often penalizing or negative, indicating that government does not exist to protect or serve them. No matter where they are from or what their immigration status is, poor US residents are not treated like beneficiaries of the noble principles upon which the nation was supposed to be founded.

POLITICAL OFFICE DOESN'T COME CHEAPLY

So long as they meet age and residency requirements, any citizen should be able to run for office. But electoral politics are generally a sport for the wealthy, meaning that eventual office holders can be oblivious to working-class concerns.

Mike Michaud, who represented Maine's Second Congressional District from 2003 to 2015, remembers talking to a federal trade representative who could not understand why the employees of a closed mill did not just seek jobs in another Maine city where the paper business was still booming. Michaud told him that the mills were three hours apart. People would need to move—and houses in cities where the mills have closed quickly become close to worthless and extremely difficult to sell. People were trapped.

Michaud knew this because he, his family, and most of his friends had worked for the Great Northern Paper Company. He said that he often provided a "reality check" as a Member of Congress. "It's not normal for a working person to run for Congress," he said.

Michaud ran as a Democrat for a vacant seat. He was already a member of the state legislature, a part-time commitment. Thanks to his union contract, he could get unpaid time off to serve in Augusta. Being a politician paid less than driving a forklift. He made a stipend of about $1,500 a year for his legislative service. So he tried to pick up overnight shifts at the mill when he could.

He stayed rent-free in an apartment building he owned with a brother. "I was very frugal and made sure I paid as I go," he said, attributing his debt-free life to his upbringing in a blue-collar Franco-American family of eight. When he ran for Congress, he convinced his campaign manager and other consultants to work for low pay with a bonus should Michaud win. "We had a lot of pizza parties. People gave five, ten dollars," Michaud said. He raised $1 million in his first Congressional run and beat a Republican opponent who spent double that. "I was the right fit for that district," he said. He believes it is still possible for a candidate with deep roots in a constituency to win, but admits that it is much harder today.

The Congressional freshman class of 2019 was exceptional in that 30 percent had a net worth of under $100,000, according to an analysis by the *Los Angeles Times*.[1] The median net worth of the new members was $412,011, while the average wealth of members of Congress is over $500,000, with many millionaires in the mix. For the sake of comparison, the US Census estimates that the national median assets for a household total just over $94,670, with most of that in home equity.[2] Bear in mind that unlike members of Congress, the average US American does not have a pension. Members of Congress become eligible for a pension after five years of service.

Congress is full of rich people because the price of admission is so high. The average incumbent senator raised more than $15 million in 2018, compared to just over $2 million per challenger, according to the Center for Responsive Politics.[3] The nonprofit also found that the average congressional race cost $5.7 million.[4]

Since the landmark Supreme Court case *Citizens United v. Federal Election Commission*, there has been much coverage of the role that big-dollar special interests play in funding campaigns. But not as much attention has been paid to where that money goes—overwhelmingly to incumbents. Incumbents almost always win; for decades reelection rates have exceeded 80 percent, no matter how much dissatisfaction voters may express. Thus is born a vicious circle: special interests fund incumbents because incumbents win, and incumbents are better positioned to win because special interests fund them.

So if you are not an incumbent, how do you break in? As with many things, it helps to be rich. Self-financed campaigns are increasingly common. Yet a series of millionaire challengers have lost to incumbents because, no matter how deep your own pockets are, chances are the incumbent can draw bigger donations.

This makes Congress mostly a closed system, with members who can keep a tight grasp on their seats with the help of moneyed interests. There are exceptions, to be sure: Alexandria Ocasio-Cortez began her congressional service with a total of $7,000 in her savings account.[5] But Congress is not a working place enclave. Michaud remembers that one of his pages seemed to always be at the center of things when congressional pages got together. "They all want to know what it's like to go to public school," the young man told him. Michaud had given the job to the son of mill workers, he explained, while most pages were the children of wealthy donors. They got a priceless introduction to politics that will advance their careers.

POOR AND MINORITY VOTERS STILL TURNED AWAY

While service at the highest level of government is largely the purview of wealthier citizens, voting is supposed to be more, well, democratic. The United States is a democracy (or a constitutional republic, if you want to get technical) because people can vote. It follows that the United States has never fully been a democracy for African Americans. First they could not vote because they were not considered people. Following the passage of the Fifteenth Amendment, which mandated, "The right of citizens of the United States to vote shall not be denied or abridged by the United

States or by any State on account of race, color, or previous condition of servitude," states rushed to get laws on the books that did just that.

Despite the gains made throughout the Civil Rights Movement, gains that activists sacrificed their lives for, there remain significant barriers in place that keep people of color away from the polls. Disenfranchisement is often aimed at black and Hispanic voters, but the tactics of suppression are effective against low-income US Americans of all races and ethnicities. When you are poor, everything is harder. It's harder to get time off from work, to get childcare, to get transportation. So any additional barrier you put between an eligible person and a voting booth will be higher for people in poverty. In the 2016 election more than half the eligible citizens who did not vote had family incomes below $30,000, while only 28 percent of people who did vote had incomes that low.[6]

In 1965 the United States enacted the National Voting Rights Act (NVRA) to combat the voter suppression that black citizens routinely faced. President Lyndon Johnson called on Congress to enact federal guarantees of voting access, which had previously been a matter left largely to the states, after civil rights demonstrators were met with extreme violence in Selma, Alabama. But the NVRA was not the last word on access to the polls. Efforts to disenfranchise specific groups have continued. Sometimes the courts have upheld the rights of voters. Sometimes not.

A major voting rights case based in Ohio demonstrates all too clearly the failure of courts to protect access to the polls. *Husted v. A. Philip Randolph Institute* came before the US Supreme Court to address Ohio's purge of voter rolls leading up to the 2016 election. To retain their franchise, voters who had not participated in the last two elections had to reregister in response to a mailing. Studies show that mail delivery is less reliable in minority neighborhoods and in neighborhoods where average income is below $35,000.[7] If your aim were to disenfranchise minority and poor voters, a mail-in requirement would be an excellent strategy.

The plaintiffs argued that missing an election was not cause to interfere with someone's constitutional right to vote—particularly since the state had long been actively trying to induce minority voters to miss elections. In African American neighborhoods, they said, many would-be voters were confronted with long lines at polling places, where workers were making significant errors. Some left after hours in line because they needed to go to school or work or to care for family members. The state had also done away with Golden Week, a promising program that offered same-day registration, early voting, and evening and weekend polling hours—accommodations for working people. Black Ohioans took advantage of Golden Week at higher rates than whites.

"I guess I really actually feel we shouldn't contort the voting process to accommodate the urban—read African-American—voter turnout machine," one member of the Franklin County Election Board commented.[8]

In 2016 Ohio and other states made it more difficult for many US Americans to cast their ballots. There were purges and decreased hours in many states, as well as onerous ID requirements. Keep in mind that in most democracies, voter registration is automatic, polling more user friendly, and turnout much higher. What happened in Ohio and other states was not reasonable or usual administrative changes. States, it appears, were purposely limiting voting rights.[9]

In 2018 the Supreme Court ruled 5–4 in the state of Ohio's favor in *Husted v. A. Philip Randolph Institute*. In her dissent, Justice Sonia Sotomayor wrote:

> Congress enacted the NVRA [National Voting Rights Act] against the backdrop of substantial efforts by States to disenfranchise low-income and minority voters, including programs that purged eligible voters from registration lists because they failed to vote in prior elections. The Court errs in ignoring this history and distorting the statutory text to arrive at a conclusion that not only is

contrary to the plain language of the NVRA but also contradicts the essential purposes of the statute, ultimately sanctioning the very purging that Congress expressly sought to protect against.

In response to the ruling, the House of Representatives passed the Voting Rights Advancement Act in 2019 to restore key provisions of the 1965 Voting Rights Act. However, the bill is unlikely to receive a vote in the Senate, and President Trump vowed to veto it should it reach his desk.

GOVERNMENT NOT AT YOUR SERVICE

Government officials are supposed to represent the people who send them to office, but those people are going to be whiter and wealthier

---

Bizarre Policy: Making the electorate crueler

BARRIERS TO VOTING MAKE for an electorate that is less sympathetic to economic struggles and more supportive of policies that punish poverty. A Pew Survey looking at financial security, which in addition to income included measures like having savings and not requiring public assistance, found that less financially secure US Americans participate less in government on a number of measures beyond voting, including contacting elected officials and even following who wins or loses elections. This lack of engagement translates to a national political philosophy that favors haves over have-nots. For example, 62 percent of the most secure said that "government can't afford to do more for the needy." Only 37 percent of the least secure held that view. While 65 percent of the least secure said that corporate profits were too high, only 46 percent of the most secure agreed.[10]

---

than the nation as a whole. People in poverty repeatedly recounted to us ways in which they felt government was nonresponsive and sometimes actively hostile to them.

Michael, forty-four, has spent the past year alternating between shelters and the streets of Los Angeles. Michael, whom we introduced in chapter 4, expects to be homeless for the rest of his life.

"Every time I call, Section 8 is closed for two years.* I give up trying. It's always a runaround," he said.

Michael's sources of income are a disability check (he has schizophrenia) and occasional panhandling. There are a variety of programs that he might qualify for, but he has had it with waiting hours in offices to be told that he doesn't have the right ID, which is often the case among people who are homeless. His backpack was stolen five times in the recent past, he said.

A startlingly large percentage of people in poverty do not get the government aid for which they are qualified. They may not know they qualify, may have been turned down wrongly, or they may, like Michael, have given up on the "runaround." Why is inconvenience and disrespect such a common experience when people ask for help that they need to stay afloat?

We would argue that intentional and unintentional barriers are at work. The intentional barrier is simple economics. Aid to the poor costs money, so there is a disincentive for the government to go out of its way to make applying easier. Furthermore, there is no competitor for this "business." The unintentional barrier is more insidious. People are not

---

* At the time we spoke with Michael in 2018, Section 8 in Los Angeles has not been taking applications since October 2017, when it was open for a two-week period. Before that, the nearest window of availability was a two-week period in 2004. The Los Angeles Housing Authority is not projecting when the program will next be taking applications.

respected when they go to get aid because we as a society disrespect people in poverty. The consequences are severe.

We should be clear that the people who provide these services are overworked and underpaid. The offices they work in are understaffed. In order to make real change, we need to make the system less complicated for both the client and the worker trying to provide the service.

WIC provides food to pregnant and nursing women and their children up to their fifth birthday. A University of New Hampshire study found that less than half of eligible families in the state were enrolled in the program. Author Kristen Smith noted that "there are a number of hurdles to participation in government assistance programs such as WIC, including psychological barriers (social stigma), structural barriers (lack of transportation), bureaucratic complications (arduous application processes), and financial costs (missed work when applying for the program)."[11]

The national research consortium Children's HealthWatch interviewed families in five cities who were eligible for but not receiving SNAP and found the following barriers:

- Lack of information about the program
- Head of household too young to apply
- Bureaucratic obstacles
- Disrespectful treatment at SNAP office or concern about stigma
- Administrative issues like reporting deadlines
- Immigration concerns

Children's HealthWatch found that children in these families that were not accessing food stamps were more likely to be underweight than their peers.[12]

In Connecticut residents access benefits through the state Department of Social Services (DSS). In 2013 DSS installed a new phone system that led to long waiting periods for years afterward. In July 2014 the average wait time at a DSS call center was eighty-seven minutes.[13] Some were calling on Lifeline phones, subsidized by the federal government for public aid recipients. Depending on the carrier, Lifeline gives the user between 250 and 1,000 free minutes a month. Just three calls with DSS in July 2014 could have left a user with no minutes to job hunt, call a doctor, or talk with a child's teacher.

Lifeline enrollment, by the way, has been declining since the Federal Communications Commission began instituting more restrictive rules and administrative hurdles around the program.[14] Some suspect that the administrative barriers were in fact designed to make sure that the benefit of a phone is available to fewer people. "This does not add up, unless the real goal is to further restrict participation in the program," commissioner Jessica Rosenworcel said as she dissented from the new rules.[15]

One of the greatest governmental insults to US residents came when TANF replaced Aid to Families with Dependent Children as the nation's primary cash assistance to people in poverty—what is commonly called welfare. TANF became law in 1996, with a stated goal of moving people off welfare rolls and promoting "personal responsibility." In more than two decades, funding for the program has not even been adjusted for inflation. People must meet stringent requirements to receive smaller benefits for shorter periods—and states have the freedom to spend federal TANF dollars in ways that have nothing to do with giving indigent families cash aid, including college tuition support for middle-class students. In thirteen states TANF recipients are required to take drug tests, which revealed less than 1 percent testing positive.[16] Many states have "family caps" that prevent increases to benefits when new children are born, the assumption being that a meager raise to a time-limited benefit could be an incentive for women to get pregnant. It is Ronald Reagan's famous racist creation of the "welfare queen," being used to guide federal policy. US society disapproves of many things that people in poverty do, but the thing that it disapproves of most vehemently is when poor people have children.

CHILD WELFARE SYSTEM PUNISHES POVERTY

Frank stands on his back porch, which is crammed with toys and broken-down furniture. He's trying to finish the attic to make more room for his family of seven. He's held back by his fibromyalgia and the cost of materials. He works until he's in too much pain or simply out of lumber. Today he's greeting Charlie Mulholland of Covenant to Care for Children, an organization that delivers various goods to families in poverty—beds being the most popular item. The waiting list is easily three years long, Mulholland said. By the time their turn comes, families have often moved, as poor people so frequently do, and cannot be found. But you can move up the waiting list if your family is involved with the Connecticut Department of Children and Families (DCF), as Frank's is.

The family's DCF worker does not like that several of the kids are sleeping in beds that are falling apart—and that Frank's eight-year-old son and seven-year-old daughter are sharing a bed. There was no way the family could afford even the beds Mulholland is delivering, twins from a discount house. Frank and his wife, who has uncontrolled seizures, are both unemployed.

Frank could have gotten those beds even quicker if DCF had actually threatened to remove his children. Families advance to the very front of Covenant to Care's list if it's a question of preventing a foster placement or helping a family reunite. Sometimes, a new bed can be the difference in keeping a family together—in other words, material poverty can lead the state to take custody of children it believes are otherwise safe with their parents.

Researchers will tell you that poverty is the single greatest predictor of child maltreatment, since that's what case files at state child welfare agencies show. However, those case files only represent families brought to the attention of the state. There are all sorts of reasons that low-income families come under more scrutiny: they live in close quarters where neighbors are likely to hear or see things they find suspicious;

their neighborhoods are highly policed; mandated reporters like teachers and pediatricians may simply be less likely to give them the benefit of the doubt.

While poverty in itself should never be a reason for the state to remove a child, families risk the state taking custody of a child if they cannot provide necessities, such as housing. These lapses legally constitute neglect rather than abuse. Neglect allegations make up the vast majority of the millions of child welfare cases that states handle each year.

Any involvement in the child welfare system is expensive for government, particularly foster care. Children who are in foster placement, of course, also pay a high price: the trauma of family separation and an increased risk of involvement in the juvenile justice system, long-term poverty, and homelessness. So providing supports that will keep children safe within their own families makes sense, wherever it's possible to do so. Most every state child welfare agency will talk about their commitment to doing just that. However, nationally preventive services and family support made up only 8 percent of state child welfare spending in 2017, according to the Administration for Children and Families. There are still families kept apart because of poverty—even though it would cost taxpayers less to simply provide them with some basic needs.

Oregon did a massive project looking at ten years of data from various state agencies to find predictors that a child would enter the state system. Chris Kelleher, then-coordinator of the Pay for Prevention initiative, said that poverty was far and away the greatest risk factor. The task of getting massive systems to talk with each other while preserving privacy rights is enormous and ongoing. The project's ultimate goal is to use that data to identify children at risk, provide help to their families, and by so doing prevent maltreatment while saving the state money. That isn't happening yet, said Kelleher, who explained that the project is still looking for ways to incorporate more robust data.

"There is a huge disconnect between research and what actually happens," he admitted. The plan is to recruit agency heads onto a steering committee that would be well positioned to make sure that the project's findings drive policy.

In the state of Connecticut, where Frank is trying to use his amateur carpentry skills to make his house habitable for his large family, there is some housing assistance for families in the child welfare system and the state provides some funding to Covenant to Care to deliver things like beds and school uniforms in the hopes of keeping families together, but that aid has been consistently cut. A federal monitor overseeing the state's embattled DCF has cited it for not providing enough material assistance for families. So Charlie Mulholland knows that he will never get very far down his waiting list. "Have you ever heard of the myth of Sisyphus?" he asked.

INCARCERATION: A CAUSE AND CONSEQUENCE OF POVERTY

Government separates some impoverished families through its child welfare systems and others through its prison systems. Eric Lee has worked hard to free himself from both.

Lee talked about the day a few years back when he returned to his old elementary school in Newark, Ohio, a small industrial city that had pretty much been home except for the twenty years he'd spent in prison, mostly for felony drug convictions. Lee was in his fifties, finally clean, sober, and determined to make an honest living to support his two youngest children. But things weren't going his way. He was at the elementary school because that's where the emergency food pantry is.

Sitting on a bench outside his second-grade classroom and waiting his turn, he remembered the corporal punishment that he says was commonplace when he was a student: "All those years ago, they told me I wasn't going to be shit. And there I was sitting in that same seat, going to get some canned goods that were donated. In that moment, I didn't know what to think . . . No wonder at thirteen, I was full of so much anger, hate, and stuff. They taught me how to hate."

Lee is now sixty and on the verge of getting a master's degree that will qualify him to be a substance abuse counselor. But the education that he hopes will secure his future has put him in debt and prolonged his poverty. Despite some grim reflection on his teachers and his father—who abandoned Lee's mother with eight children to care for—he is an apostle of self-reliance. According to Lee, his incarceration is ultimately the result of his own bad choices. "Jesus saved your soul. He didn't save your ass," he proclaimed.

Despite his insistence that people need to save their own asses, Lee spends a lot of time lending a hand. He chairs the Newark Think Tank on Poverty's Reentry Committee, which is designed to help men and women returning to the city from prison get established. Much of the talk at their meeting is about barriers to housing, mental health care, and jobs. But Lee wants to focus more on addressing the root causes of behavior—something that he says does not happen in prison and that parolees are de facto discouraged from doing because it may compromise their release.

Men come into his Tuesday support group saying, "Life is good. I am spiritually refreshed and just happy to be alive. I'm living the dream!" Lee, who was beat after a long day juggling family crises and community organizing, brightened, threw back his head and laughed, "I said, 'Bullshit!'"

The odds are not good for the men and women whom Lee helps. If they weren't poor when they went to prison, they will almost certainly be poor when they come out. And poverty itself is a threat to their freedom.

Of course, incarceration is not solely an outgrowth of poverty. Race may loom larger here than in any other social problem facing the United States. Lee is African American, like an extraordinary proportion of the US Americans living behind bars right now. In federal prisons, about 40 percent of inmates are African American, though the group makes up only about 13 percent of the US population.[17] Latinos and Hispanics make up about a third of the federal prison population and less than a fifth of the US population. In Michelle Alexander's *The New Jim Crow*, she argues, with a clarity and a volume of evidence that speaks for itself, that racism is not an ugly by-product of our prison system.[18] Denying men of color their freedom is the system's *purpose*, Alexander holds. The system could not possibly be more efficiently designed for this purpose. Rather than parrot the excellent work of Alexander and others on this topic, however, we will examine the economic causes and consequences of incarceration.

For children growing up in poverty, arrest is a common rite of passage. Research shows that one in three US Americans will be arrested for something more serious than a traffic violation by the time they are twenty-three.[19] In some communities, the rate is much higher. In most cases, those arrests will take place before their eighteenth birthday. The study only surveyed families of children eight or older. In many states, however, there is no minimum age at which a child can be handcuffed and taken away by police. Children younger than eight can and frequently do get arrested.

A juvenile arrest is a strong predictor of academic failure and of adult arrest down the road—both setups for long-term poverty. A single court appearance quadruples the chances that a student will leave high school before graduating.[20] Though most juvenile offenders will desist from lawbreaking in their mid-twenties,[21] a juvenile arrest does place a youth at greater risk of involvement in the adult system. Youth who have satisfied the court's conditions may still face challenges reenrolling in school or obtaining housing. Entire families can become homeless because one member's conviction makes them ineligible for public housing. Youth may find themselves on a sex offender registry, even for consensual sex with a peer, which will limit their educational and housing options forever.

High arrest rates of young people are not entirely surprising. A wealth of research on adolescent brain development shows that young people are inclined to be risk-takers but are not particularly adept at thinking through the consequences of their actions, especially when in a group of peers.[22] "All gas and no brakes" is the shorthand researchers often use to explain this stage of development.

Most of us will break the law at some point in our adolescence.* Until relatively recently, law enforcement did not involve itself in adolescent development unless serious crimes were committed. Families and educators largely worked together to shape and sometimes punish teen behavior. But this changed in the 1990s. More police became "resource officers" stationed in schools. For many, mission creep led them to become enforcers of school discipline. Children are arrested for simple schoolyard scuffles and even for dress code violations. Get-tough-on-crime policies led to longer sentences for youth and to their more frequent prosecution in adult court and even incarceration in adult jails and prisons. There has been some rollback in these harsh policies—however, they remain in force to some degree in every state. Poor children are less protected within the system, because they often do not get lawyers. The National Juvenile Defender Center found that most states provide no public defense or inadequate defense for youth (though a 1967 US Supreme Court decision affirmed the right to representation in juvenile courts).[23] The American Civil Liberties Union has alleged similar deficiencies in adult defense.†

Most people who run juvenile justice systems or attempt to reform them see adolescent brain development as centrally important in understanding juvenile crime. But there is a growing body of research that shows poverty, not age, is key.

---

* If you are shaking your head at this, remember that in some states children can get arrested for drinking, smoking cigarettes, or even making out with a peer.

† For example, in 2016, the ACLU sued the New Orleans Office of the Public Defender for refusing to represent clients because it does not have the funding to hire sufficient staff. In 2017 a federal judge dismissed the lawsuit, even while he acknowledged "It is clear that the Louisiana legislature is failing miserably at upholding its obligations."

"Within every race and community, adolescents suffer poverty rates two to three times higher than older adults do," according to Mike Males, senior research fellow at the Center on Juvenile and Criminal Justice, San Francisco. His research, the first of its kind in the field, shows that teens' impulsivity is associated with wealth. More money equals more restraint. "It is astonishing that researchers have compiled decades of theories and claims about teenagers' supposed risk-taking, impulsiveness, brain deficiencies, and crime-proneness without examining whether these are due to young people's low socioeconomic status, not young age," Males said.[24]

Regardless of poverty's effect on cognition and behavior, poor children are at greater risk of arrest for a number of reasons. Their communities—including their schools—are more heavily policed. They have fewer opportunities for positive recreational activities. They may feel pressure to earn money to contribute to their family's support. They are more likely to be diagnosed with mental illness and substance abuse, which are largely criminalized for poor children and adults.

At a listening session in Bridgeport, Connecticut, adults asked teens who had been through the juvenile justice system what would prevent reoffending. "Help me make money in a positive way," one young man answered.[25]

A study in Wilmington, Delaware, showed the residents of its poorest neighborhoods strongly desired employment, though 64 percent of them were jobless. Wilmington was—to great local resentment— dubbed "Murder Town" by *Newsweek* magazine because of the small city's homicide rate. Young men, in particular, spoke about "street life," mainly drug sales, as their primary opportunity to earn money for their families. The study's author, Yasser Arafat Payne, said that street life is such a pervasive source of income in some neighborhoods that the stigma of arrest and prison have diminished. Young men involved in these practices, as Payne once was himself, may be seen as leaders in the community, people who make sure that children have backpacks for the school year and essentially provide a safety net that government and other institutions have not maintained. Crime as employment is normalized across generations:

> Richard, like several other participants, suspected that in communities like Southbridge [a Wilmington neighborhood], structural conditions perpetuated economic poverty from one generation to the next. He explained, how he and others were, "born into (economic) poverty," and how the lack of quality employment leads most youth in Southbridge to the streets. He even argued that as structural inequality is passed on from generation to the next, so are the ideologies and activities of the streets—passed on, one generation to the next—as a strategy for low-income, Black men to cope with persistent and profound structural or economic violence.

Payne's work included an interview with Richard, a nineteen-year-old looking for a job, who said,

> You know, it's [employment] crazy! . . . I don't really got no friends in the city that got a job, 'cept my white friend . . . Even some of the older people, man, don't even got jobs . . . 'Cause like I said, we born into poverty, dog. We born into this game [of poverty & the streets], dog. I wasn't in this game for fun. It was just passed down from father to son . . .[26]

Richard went on to explain that people in his community do not have the tools to find lawful employment, nor do they have transportation to "good-paying jobs" that are usually outside his neighborhood:

> And Southbridge . . . I could name . . . two people got computers in they crib . . . have working internet . . . It's hard to look for a job when you ain't got no money, you gotta get on a bus, you gotta go here and there to fill out applications . . . You gotta leave Southbridge . . . When I lived in Southbridge, I never left Southbridge . . .

No real good payin' jobs unless it's in the middle of the city where you workin' in a big building or whatever, or construction.[27]

Payne's work documents how crime becomes a rational choice in the absence of other employment opportunities. Once someone has acquired a criminal record, even limited legitimate employment opportunities may disappear.

Back in Newark, Ohio, Eric Lee struggled to find some way to support his family while staying away from anything that could send him back to jail or reactivate his drug habit. "I was going to make a life for them kids. And I did," he remembered.

He showed up at a temp agency. "This lady, there was something about me she wouldn't like," he said. The woman kept telling Lee that there were no jobs for him, but he kept coming back, every morning arriving before the office even opened. Eventually, she offered him a three-day job pulling weeds at seven dollars an hour. Lee ended up staying with that landscaping company for nine years. It just about destroyed his back, but it did not pay the rent.

He ended up $200 short one month and got a money order from the St. Vincent de Paul Society to cover the gap. His landlord said that Lee had to pay the rent with "his own money" and threatened to call child protective services and report that the family was about to become homeless. Lee feared he would lose his kids and so sent them to a friend. He started living in an abandoned car.

He went to the Licking County Housing Coalition and got help to support rent in a new apartment. The family had long ago applied for Social Security for his youngest son, who had serious health issues. That finally came through, and it looked like the Lees were moving up.

Lee saw an ad: WHY RENT WHEN YOU CAN BUY? He found that he could purchase a house with a $400 monthly mortgage. The thought of never being at the mercy of a landlord again appealed to him mightily. He was featured in the local newspaper: "Homeless to homeowner in a month."

But the story didn't end happily. His payment soon ballooned to $900 a month. Even with some restructuring, he ended up losing the house. "I paid all that money in to that program and they still foreclosed on me," he said.

The physical labor of landscaping was getting harder and harder. "I lived in a lot of pain for a long time," he recalled. He recently had back surgery. At fifty-four, he went back to school to qualify himself to work as a counselor. Six years later, he's nearly done. He wants to work as many years in his new career as he possibly can. The twenty years he spent behind bars coupled with low-wage jobs on the outside mean that he is not in line for much Social Security—a common problem for people released from prison after long sentences.

While Lee may struggle in many ways, he is a leader in the community—a board member at the local St. Vincent de Paul Society and a member of the Newark Think Tank on Poverty, which we'll discuss more later. One of his Think Tank colleagues, Jim Otto, is tracking him down.

A retired chemical engineer, Otto is a fit-looking seventy-nine, a man who might seem at home on the golf course—except for the thick twine around his neck holding a rough-hewn wood cross. He is a deeply committed Roman Catholic who believes that his work with people before and after their release from prison is a calling. At a charismatic prayer meeting in 1975, the group leader talked about doing ministry at the United States Penitentiary, Leavenworth.

"I didn't do anything for thirty-five years," Otto admitted. He was working, raising a family, bringing Holy Communion to the elderly. But prison work kept coming up in one way or another. Finally, a prison chaplain convinced Otto to volunteer inside.

"Lord, I don't want to talk to these people," he prayed before he went in. "I'm not one that is an easy talker." The difficulty of reentry, however, moved him and kept him coming back. "I got to see how hard it was for them to get back on their feet."

He tells stories of men who cannot rent rooms or get jobs because of their records. He talks about men released with seventy bucks, which might pay for a night at a run-down motel but won't leave anything left over for a decent set of clothes for a job interview.

Men are released with serious mental health issues, but there are currently no psychiatrists in Newark, Ohio, seeing Medicaid patients. The growth in US population is outpacing the number of new psychiatrists entering practice.[28] Meanwhile, increasing insurance coverage for mental health care and efforts to reduce stigma are leading more people to seek help. Locals say that psychiatrists have too many choices to stay for long in the public clinic, where a crushing workload and a clientele living with a host of problems can wear clinicians down. Keep in mind: people are facing enormous stress upon release. Many literally have no idea where their next meal is coming from. If they use drugs or alcohol to cope, they go back to prison. If they want to work on healthier ways of dealing with stress, they are out of luck.

Mostly, Otto talks about how easy it is for the people he helps to land back in jail—often for technical parole violations, like missing an appointment, failing a drug test, or associating with a "felon." In one case we were involved in recently, that included a man getting a violation for staying with his mother, who had a criminal record.

There's the man he's been working with for six years, who keeps missing required reports to his parole officer. Reporting is especially strict for "Stephen" because he is a sex offender. One morning, Otto and Stephen were supposed to meet at 10 AM at the library. At 9 AM Stephen had a meeting with his parole officer. Stephen stood up Otto, which almost certainly meant he'd stood up the parole officer, too—and could very well go back to prison for it.

Otto pounded on Stephen's motel door until he answered. "He had no idea. He makes all the same stupid mistakes," Otto said with weary frustration. "I can tell him, but he doesn't hear."

He is hoping that Eric Lee can speak to Stephen more convincingly.

Otto brought Stephen to the parole officer and resolved the situation. But there have been other lapses—in reporting and in work. Some of it is Stephen's doing—some of it is the lack of public transportation in the city. "He doesn't know how to work," said Otto. Stephen's mother lives in a car. There is not much history of employment either in Stephen's family or in his wife's. The couple has a new baby, who sleeps at his maternal grandmother's because the house Stephen rents is filled with fleas and bed bugs. The wife does factory work. Stephen has two low-paying jobs and commutes long distances at night by bicycle. Otto both worries about that and delights that Stephen is clearly making a huge effort.

When Stephen does step up, it often doesn't matter. He'd been working one job for a week and a half. He made sure his "residence" was registered—even though at the time it was simply a space under a bridge. When Stephen asked for time off to check in with his parole officer, he was fired.

"He's trying," said Otto. "If they send him back to prison now, he will completely lose it."

About 45 percent of admissions to state prisons are for parole violations, such as missing a meeting or failing to register, rather than for actual crimes.[29] For men like Stephen, who lack reliable transportation and stable housing, it is easy to get caught in that cycle.

Increasingly, people are charged fees to pay for their own probation and parole supervision.* Likewise, they are charged for things like public defender representation, court administration, and jail operations.[30] People who cannot pay these fees—including penalties for late payments—may be incarcerated, which of course can lead to job loss, making payment even more difficult.

---

* Probation is community supervision in lieu of incarceration. Parole is supervision after incarceration.

In Benton County, Washington, people convicted of crimes were charged fees and restitution that could amount to more than $1,000, without any consideration of ability to pay. Jayne Fuentes, Gina Taggart, and Reese Groves, all of whom were incarcerated and forced to perform manual labor because they could not pay their fines, sued the county. The class action suit was settled to offer more protection to the indebted—but the county can still impose fees and incarcerate people for nonpayment. The ACLU, which represented the trio, describes their situations in a prepared statement:

> **Jayne Fuentes** was ordered to toil on a county work crew in 2013 when she was unemployed and unable to pay her court-imposed debts. At present she is working, but her salary isn't enough to enable her to pay court fines, fees, and costs and meet her basic needs for living. She recently was unable to work for three weeks while hospitalized with pneumonia and borrowed money from family members to avoid jail for nonpayment of court-imposed debts.

> **Gina Taggart** is a single mother with a minor child. She was jailed for nonpayment of court fines, fees, and costs in 2013 after being homeless and unemployed. At present she is working full-time for minimum wage at a fast food restaurant and sometimes has been unable to pay for basic necessities when her hours are reduced due to work being slow during the winter season.

> **Reese Groves** is a single father with sole custody of his children. He has made payments on imposed debt while working, but this year he lost his job and was then jailed for nonpayment of these court fines, fees, and costs.[31]

Forced labor for nonpayment—nonpayment that was entirely predictable—is quite simply slavery. Imprisonment for nonpayment is debtors' prison. We may have drones and microwavable pad thai, but for people in poverty, it is still the nineteenth century.

These practices are even imposed on children. The Juvenile Law Center found youth incarcerated around the country for nonpayment of court-levied fees. In Arkansas, a thirteen-year-old spent three months in a juvenile facility, some of it in solitary, because his family could not pay a $500 truancy fee.[32] Recently, activists have had success in ending some juvenile system fees. For example, they have been eliminated in California and Nevada.

Perhaps the most damaging effect of mass incarceration in poor communities is the destruction of families. Chris Wills has hands covered in tattoos and paint from his construction job. Across one hand is written "Daddy's Boy." On the other is his son's name. Wills is currently homeless, though he feels lucky to have landed a job as a laborer for a contractor who is sympathetic to people with records. Drugs led to his legal problems. He smoked his first joint when he was . . . five? Maybe eight? He's not sure. His aunt and uncle gave it to him to cheer him up because he had not been invited to a birthday party. He's got a teardrop tattoo that he acquired in juvenile hall in tribute to an uncle who had died of AIDS. Wills was eleven.

He talked endlessly about his son. He very much wants an apartment so that he'll have some place to take the boy during his visitation. On this sunny Sunday afternoon, they will play football in a park.

He had little contact with the boy during his incarceration and is trying to build a relationship with him now, even though the boy's mother is with another partner. Wills said at first he was resentful. Now he's focused on being grateful that his son has one more caring adult in his life. Wills glows when he talks about things like parent-teacher conferences.

He wants so much to get an apartment for his son's sake. He handed his pay envelope over to a friend to hold for him so that he cannot buy drugs. He can't go back there. He can't squander a cent that should go for a security deposit.

He left to pick up his son, but soon called to clarify something in the interview.

"Hey, I just wanted to make sure that I didn't come off as a victim. I'm not a victim. I'm not sorry for myself," he said.

Wills needs to keep asserting that he is "a good person," since he lives in a society that does not treat him like one. That's not just a matter of individual prejudice. It's government policy. Whether a person is facing the criminal legal system or simply trying to get involved in the political process, poverty creates huge disadvantages. That contradicts pretty much every civics lesson one might hear delivered in a US classroom. The problems recounted by the people in this chapter are the problems of everyone in the US, because we'd all like to believe that we live in a democracy. So long as rights are afforded on a pay-to-play basis, we do not. A government with a foundational duty to protect the liberty of the governed routinely robs people in poverty of theirs.

What Can I Do?

1. **Ban the box.** The Newark Poverty Think Tank convinced their city council to "Ban the Box" for public employers. That means applications would no longer have a checkoff box asking if applicants have ever been convicted of a felony. Employers may ask about criminal history and run background checks later in the hiring process. But it allows people to get initial consideration without being ruled out because of a criminal history.

   Ban the Box movements are growing in cities around the country. To learn how to start a campaign in your community, visit Bantheboxcampaign.org.

2. **Hire a returning member of your community.** If you are in a hiring position, consider offering an opportunity to someone with a record. Register at Jailtojob.com or Jobsthathirefelons .org. There may be organizations that offer job training and support in your community. They will help you make a good match.

3. **Don't be a NIMBY.** Finding places for housing or services for people returning from prison is extremely difficult because neighborhood (remember NIMBY—not in my backyard) opposition is common. If a facility is proposed in your neighborhood, be a leader and steer the conversation away from fear and stereotypes. Organize neighborhood discussion groups. Read books like this and others together to deepen understanding.

4. **Stop the school-to-prison pipeline.** Too many young people enter the prison system through arrests at school. But some communities have changed this by rethinking discipline. Police, parents, and schools can work together to make sure that schools are safe, productive environments without arresting large numbers of students. Visit Safequalityschools.org to learn more.

5. **Support public financing of elections.** Public financing levels the playing field and gives candidates who are not wealthy an opportunity to run. Find out where your state stands on public financing by visiting Ncsl.org and searching for "public financing."

6. **Volunteer on or before Election Day.** You can help people overcome voting barriers by offering rides to the polls or by participating in voter registration drives. Check with organizations like the League of Women Voters and the American Civil

Liberties Union for trainings that will allow you to be a poll watcher who can intervene if voting rights are violated.

7. **Work to allow those with a criminal record to vote.** People on probation and parole are often not allowed to vote. In many states and municipalities, there are fines and fees that need to be paid before release from probation, so many people in poverty remain on probation—and unable to vote—because they cannot pay. Working to change the law is the ultimate way to solve this problem. Fundraising to pay off fees is an interim step.

A Better Way: "Putting people in a situation where they demand respect"

THE NEWARK THINK TANK on Poverty was founded with support of the St. Vincent de Paul Society, a Roman Catholic group that involves lay people in service to alleviate poverty. Its home is a less famous Newark, a small city in Ohio at the edge of the Appalachians where more than 20 percent of the residents are living in poverty. Lesha Farias had been making home visits to people getting some kind of material assistance from the society. Along with helping people pay the rent, get dental care, and so on, she wanted to change the way that power structures interacted with people in poverty.

Farias, who spent much of her career helping college students become engaged in social justice work, cofounded the think tank with her partner, Allen Schwartz, a teacher, organizer, artist, and musician. They both come at the enterprise with deep convictions formed over decades of thinking about and working for justice. But they are committed to taking all that history and using it to support—not lead—the think tank.

The think tank's first initiative was driven by members who were having difficulty finding employment because of criminal records. They successfully got the city council to pass a ban-the-box resolution. Now Newark will not ask about criminal records on city job applications, though they can inquire later in the process. It's a chance for people to get a foot in the door.

They researched the issue, held forums, and educated elected officials. "Taking this box off this application is giving us the chance to sit in front of an employer and tell our story, not the story that society has already put upon us, to show who we've become and to show what we can do," Tina Cole, a think tank member, testified before the city council.

In addition to legislative advocacy, think tank members are taking up positions of leadership at organizations that serve people in poverty. Eric Lee and another think tank expert joined Farias on the local St. Vincent de Paul board of directors before she stepped off. On one Sunday afternoon, he leaves a think tank committee meeting to sit with the diners eating at the Salvation Army. That level of engagement has made him an incredibly valuable and insightful addition to the St. Vincent de Paul board, according to Farias.

"The Salvation Army is just my stomping grounds where I find myself sometimes, and a lot of our clients go there and eat lunch and eat dinner," said Lee. "And we find ourselves there just hanging out getting to know people, seeing where we can help out."

He joined the think tank after a faith-based group he was active in disbanded. The think tank "wanted more participation from people that actually experienced the poverty, experienced the homelessness, experienced that you can't get a job. Whereas the church, you know, there was a lot of church members involved. You didn't quite have the freedom to express yourself like you would in the think tank," Lee said.

It's a struggle, to be sure. One of the experts who was a driving force of the ban-the-box victory hasn't been to meetings in a long while. "I think we lost her temporarily to meth," Schwartz said. But Lee and others remain in it, doing the hard work of pushing the systems to treat people in poverty more fairly. "I think that is really one of our victories," said Schwartz, "is we are putting more people in that situation where they demand that respect."

CHAPTER 12

Mental Health Discrimination

Poverty Is Trauma

Mental illness is more common among people in economic hardship.[1] Is mental illness causing poverty or is poverty causing mental illness? The answer is both. Some people are at economic risk as a result of their psychiatric diagnosis because it can interfere with career and relationships. On the other hand, poverty itself is so stressful that it can harm mental health.

In this chapter, however, we concern ourselves with the latter. There is a great deal of research that demonstrates the chronic and toxic stress that is brought on by poverty is associated with higher rates of depression and other psychiatric illnesses. This doesn't mean that all low-income people are depressed any more than every soldier who sees combat has posttraumatic stress disorder (PTSD). But it does mean that if we reduce poverty, we will reduce mental illness.

Increasingly, clinicians and scholars are recognizing that societal oppression has implications for mental health diagnoses and treatment. For example, some professionals are calling for the traumatizing effects of racism to be acknowledged in the bible of psychiatry, *The Diagnostic and Statistical Manual of Mental Disorders'* diagnostic criteria for PTSD.[2]

The landmark CDC–Kaiser Permanente ACE (adverse childhood experiences) study linked traumatic early events, such as the incarceration of a parent, being abused, or living in a home with substance abuse, to a number of risks in adulthood, including cancer, heart disease, alcoholism, and suicide.[3] The total number of these experiences that a child endures make up the ACE score, with a higher score being widely accepted as predictive of the aforementioned risks. In 2018 two authors in the *North Carolina Medical Journal* suggested that "research demonstrates the correlation between childhood adversities linked to poverty and negative outcomes in adulthood, indicating that poverty may itself be considered an adverse childhood experience."[4]

California surgeon general Nadine Burke Harris said that the relationship between poverty and mental health creates a clear call to action: "All in all, this convergence of basic science, clinical research, and public health is reframing a problem so common that it was hidden in plain sight: Chronic stress and trauma are toxic to our children."[5]

Brain development does not happen in a lab. It happens in everyday life. Changing the daily experience of children living in poverty can have a profound impact. It is essential to look at common stressors faced by low-income families.

For example, in 2013 Joanne was one of the authors of a paper with colleagues at Yale School of Medicine and the National Diaper Bank Network that established a link between diaper need and maternal depression.[6] Our findings were everywhere—newspapers, television, radio. This was new evidence with critical implications. Maternal depression is enormously dangerous for mothers and for their children. The mother suffers from the misery that is depression, along with the significant toll on physical health that goes with it. Because mothers are such an important source of interaction in babies' lives, children are at risk of not getting the attention and response that they need to develop social and communication skills, and those deficits can have lifelong effects because they affect brain architecture and a child's stress response system.[7] That said, since mother-blaming is so much in vogue, let's be clear: this is not about mothers not caring enough, not trying hard enough, or any other kind of personal failure. This is the quite predictable result of a very real illness that no one would choose for herself.

Three years after that paper was published, the US Preventive Services Task Force recommended universal screening for depression in pregnant and postpartum women. This is a smart and long-overdue move, given the dangers associated with maternal depression that we just described. The goal of the screening is to move mothers experiencing depression into treatment.

But what about the mom whose depression is linked to the concrete reality that she cannot afford diapers? Perhaps she would benefit from therapy. Certainly, she would benefit from receiving diapers and thus being relieved of a major stressor. Mothers in the study ranked diaper need as more stressful than food insecurity. That's not surprising. WIC and SNAP can help people in poverty obtain food, though as we discussed, that help needs to be more accessible and extensive. There is no federal assistance with diapers. Though nonprofit diaper banks distribute seventy-two million diapers a year in the United States, we know that we are reaching only 4 percent of the families who need help.[8] It's like expecting nonprofits to provide universal education or maintain roads. Work of this magnitude requires government action.

For some women, a supply of diapers, which costs about $900 per year, could protect them and their children against the effects of maternal depression. Keep in mind that US spending on treating depressive disorders is $71 billion, more than we spend treating cancer.[9] But there is no line item in most government budgets for diapers. Far too often the professionals who serve low-income people are not trained to ask about things like diapers, laundry detergent, winter boots, or any of the myriad and mundane things it takes to simply live.

Poverty itself puts people at risk for mental health problems, which in turn make it difficult to do the things that help one escape poverty. As we demonstrated throughout the Basic Needs section of the book, low-wage jobs and public assistance are insufficient to support the bare necessities. That is stressful. But the systems that are in place to serve people in poverty rarely grasp the basic needs–mental health connection and almost never have the appropriate resources to provide material necessities.

Everyone who needs mental health care should get it—quickly, affordably, and respectfully. Mental health care needs to be more readily available for people of all economic levels—and particularly for people in poverty, who have especially limited access to high-quality care.[10]

Throughout the history of the United States, and likely going back further than that, oppressed people have been labeled "disordered" for their responses to hardship.[11] For example, a ship's doctor noted a "fixed melancholy" among Africans who had been kidnapped and were enduring the Middle Passage. A nineteenth-century physician would write that enslaved blacks were susceptible to a mental illness termed "drapetomania," an uncontrollable urge to run away.[12] Similarly, psychiatric diagnoses have historically been aimed at women seeking independence.

POVERTY MAY BE THE REAL DIAGNOSIS

While leaders in the field are recognizing the role of societal inequity in mental health diagnosis and treatment, professional development in the area lags. Thus, people are often encountering mental health and other professionals with little training about this critical relationship. The National Diaper Bank Network and MOMS Partnership program at the Yale School of Medicine developed the Basic Needs–Informed Care

Curriculum that trains people in the helping professions to recognize how material poverty affects people's lives and behavior. For example, when people are late for or miss appointments, they are too often presumed to be unmotivated or perhaps depressed or substance abusing. We encourage social workers, teachers, and health-care providers to ask the following questions: Is there a way for you to get to my office by public transportation? Can you afford a bus pass? How difficult is it for you to get time off from work within my office hours? Do you have childcare?

We knew we were onto something when a psychiatrist said after the training, "I've been prescribing Prozac for poverty, and it hasn't been working."

We have frequently seen people in poverty behave in ways that violate middle-class norms yet make perfect sense in the context of their lives. That point was acutely driven home by "Angel." Angel had been an administrator for an arts organization before a layoff and a rent increase rendered her homeless on the streets of Los Angeles, where we met her. She said that every woman who sleeps on the street is bound to be sexually assaulted, though she didn't want to discuss her own experience.

Every so often during our conversation, she'd use the serious vocal power that came from her theater experience and loudly pronounce some profanity. Activity on the busy street would briefly stop as people stared at her. Angel smiled. "They all think I'm a crazy bitch, so they don't mess with me," she whispered.

Angel's outburst made sense given her circumstances. She didn't have a door to lock—she had a voice, and she was using it. Angel was living with a toxic amount of stress. She might benefit from mental health care. But that care would be more effective if she had a safe and stable home.

Fortunately, some clinicians are leading the way in recognizing the connection between mental health and basic needs. The children that psychologist Cristina Muñiz de la Peña cares for by definition do not have a stable home. She is the cofounder and mental health director of Terra Firma, a Bronx-based health care and advocacy organization serving unaccompanied immigrant children. Though Terra Firma sees children from all over the world, most clients come from Central America. Many have experienced violence, been kidnapped by gangs, or spent time in US detention facilities.

"When we were designing the program, everybody would say, 'Well, these kids are going to have so much trauma. What trauma-focused interventions do we need to implement?' . . . From very early on, I had the clinical intuition that addressing trauma or focusing on it as a goal and fixing the trauma was not safe, was not appropriate, didn't feel ethical even," Muñiz said.

She likens doing trauma therapy with many of her clients to bandaging a patient in a burning building. You must first get the patient to safety. The fire is poverty.

"You can't open the emotional wounds of somebody, if they are leaving your office and going to an environment where they cannot take care of those wounds and feel safe and feel supported and feel at ease," she said.

The mental health care that Muñiz provides also has her working in tandem with attorneys to strengthen immigration cases so that children will not again be separated from a caregiver. "Collaborating with the attorney on an ongoing basis is a way of addressing that social need," she said. "We have a case management team that helps us with the most basic needs of food, water, shelter."

This awareness also changes the conversations that Muñiz has with her patients. She's likely to ask: "Are you going to school? How did you sleep last night? Do you have a coat for the winter?" The answers to these questions inform her assessment of the child's stress level: "A lot of that stress is kind of unconscious to them because they learned to live with it. So for people that live in a shelter, after a while, they just—all of us would do it—they do kind of just get used to it and ignore, but the body's still feeling the stress and the subconscious is still feeling the stress. You're just functioning in it."

In the stress of poverty, people may not function optimally. Financial stress causes a loss of cognitive functioning akin to losing a night's sleep. The proof of this comes from a 2013 study in which researchers asked people to answer questions involving spatial relationships and reasoning.[13] The researchers also asked volunteers to contemplate how they would pay for an expensive hypothetical car repair. After pondering the car repair challenge, affluent test takers' scores on these IQ-like questions remained stable. But people in poverty's performance suffered. The change in cognitive function was equivalent to what other studies had measured in people who had lost a night's sleep or who were chronic alcoholics. They conducted analogous experiments with farmers in India and found a similar variation in performance between a time of scarcity and harvest season.

The authors hypothesize that, for people without financial resources, these challenges take up more cognitive "bandwidth." Affluent people simply pay for car repairs. People without means must weigh the cost of payment plans, doing without a car, asking a relative for help, and on and on. In other words, for a person in poverty, the mind can be forever occupied with the problems of daily living. Being poor requires a lot of mental work.

The study makes an interesting proposal: "First, policy-makers should beware of imposing cognitive taxes on the poor just as they avoid monetary taxes on the poor. Filling out long forms, preparing for a lengthy interview, deciphering new rules, or responding to complex incentives all consume cognitive resources. Policy-makers rarely recognize these cognitive taxes; yet, our results suggest that they should focus on reducing them."[14]

Looking at "bandwidth" is one way to approach the cognitive consequences of being poor. There are decades of research related to poverty-related stress (PRS). "In addition to the increased volume of stressors created by poverty's context of stress, poverty amplifies the negative effects of all types of stress, such that PRS impairs an individual's ability to mount a response to new threats and challenges," according to Martha E. Wadsworth and Shauna L. Rienks.[15]

Put more simply, poverty makes everything harder. That harder cognitive work is often done under a weight of anxiety and depression:

> Compared with children and adolescents from higher-SES [socioeconomic status] backgrounds, children and adolescents from low-SES backgrounds show higher rates of depression, anxiety, attention problems and conduct disorders, and a higher prevalence of internalizing (that is, depression- or anxiety-like) and externalizing (that is, aggressive and impulsive) behaviours, all of which increase with the duration of impoverishment. In addition, childhood SES influences cognitive development; it is positively correlated with intelligence and academic achievement from early childhood and through adolescence.
>
> These effects are likely to account, at least in part, for the persistence of poverty across generations: individuals of low childhood SES face various social and economic barriers to success and well-being, and do so with the added disadvantage of worse health, reduced emotional resilience and impaired cognitive skills.[16]

MAINSTREAM IRRATIONAL BELIEFS THAT BLAME VICTIMS

It is more self-reassuring for people to believe that the man sleeping in their doorway has a mental illness or abuses drugs and alcohol than to believe he simply does not have the money to make rent. For one thing, discrimination against people with substance abuse disorder of all income levels is common despite clear proof that addiction is a disease. Discrimination against people with mental illness is also common. As long as poverty is caused by some internal factor, it is easy to think it is beyond our control—or even to cast blame.

A Better Way: Facing poverty and mental illness head-on

THE DESTRESS PROJECT LOOKED at the effect of government austerity programs on the mental health of people in poverty. This project of University of Exeter, University of Plymouth, and City, University of London, explored "the medicalisation of poverty-related distress,"[17] noting with concern that prescriptions for antidepressants and other psychoactive drugs were increasing sharply in Great Britain's low-income communities. One doctor interviewed in the study said of prescribing antidepressants, "You know by doing that you feel that at least you have tried to give something when you can't change their . . . you can't get their, you can't give them a roof over their heads, you can't change the fact that they don't have any support or family around."[18]

The project developed resources to help physicians address problems directly related to poverty, an area where British—and by and large US—health-care providers do not generally receive training: "A key aspect of this work involves enabling GPs [general practitioners] to feel better able to play a supportive and empathic role that encourages patients to reflect on their situation and identify positive ways forward, rather than feeling that they necessarily need to 'fix' patients through diagnosis and rapid prescriptions for treatment."[19]

But what if he is sleeping in that doorway because wages are unacceptably low, or rents are unreasonably high? Or no one will rent to him because of his delinquent utility bills? Or he has decided to spend his limited resources on food and medicine rather than housing? All of those are problems with policy solutions. They are things that we can change, and therefore things for which we have responsibility.

But what if the man sleeping in the doorway has a drug addiction or is suffering from mental illness, or both? What then? An all too likely possibility is that he did not have a mental illness or drug problem until the trauma inherent in his situation—sleeping in the cold, exposed to violence, hunger, and the threat of arrest—made him vulnerable to it.

Are there people who were pushed into poverty because they have mental illness or substance abuse issues? Yes, and so there is also an imperative to provide them with accessible, high-quality care. But there is also a straightforward and largely ignored policy solution that will drastically reduce the mental health burden among people in poverty— providing basic needs. At present, many systems are ill equipped to figure out which response is appropriate.

What Can I Do?

1. **Be basic needs informed.** As mentioned earlier, there is a curriculum available that will give people in the helping professions the skills to start differentiating between behaviors linked to mental health and those resulting from poverty. Contact the National Diaper Bank Network to learn more.

2. **Oppose adding work requirements to entitlement programs.** Recent years have seen a spate of federal administrative regulation limiting people's rights to access SNAP and other federal benefits. Work requirements in other programs have generated little or no long-term increase in earnings and employment and have caused many families—often those with the greatest disadvantages—to lose assistance, leaving them in

deep poverty.[20] The requirement is particularly burdensome for someone living with a mental illness that interferes with work.

3. **Never refer to a person by a diagnosis.** One of us worked for an organization that would refer to clients with labels like "a schizophrenic." Language matters—such labels make it appear that a person's life is defined by disease. In addition to neglecting other needs, they overshadow that person's strengths.

CHAPTER 13

High-Poverty Schools

Class Matters

Lytle, Texas, was in mourning. A young mother had died from asthma, leaving six children and a husband who works sporadically setting trailers on foundations. The family home is also a trailer, run-down even for Twin Lakes, an impoverished section of Lytle. Discarded furniture and tools sat out front, with one floppy-eared dog lying proudly in the middle. Because the home had no tub, running water, or electricity, the last bath the mother gave her youngest was in an ice chest. That's the image that broke everyone's heart. Nearly every teacher in Lytle spoke about the boy bathing in the ice chest and was visibly moved by it. In this small town, everybody knows everybody.

The mother died just after midnight. That day, several of her children arrived at Lytle Elementary School, to the surprise of all the adults there. "This is our favorite safe place," one of the children explained.

The school system and the churches form the social safety net in Lytle, which is a half hour from San Antonio and the kinds of government and nonprofit programs that provide assistance in more populous areas. For example, when a child came to school with a foul-smelling backpack, a teacher discovered that the boy was regularly using it to take cafeteria food home to get his family through the weekend. The school appealed to local businesses and churches to provide backpacks full of packaged food that go home with students in need every Friday—something similar to programs generally run by food banks.

The major bridge between the school system and faith communities is Mae Flores, the children's pastor at Prevailing Word Church and a member of the school board. She eased her SUV along rutted dirt roads of Twin Lakes, roads an administrator told us tear up even school buses. The developer who started the subdivision went bankrupt, leaving things half-finished. There were some well-tended small homes, but they were outnumbered by trailers expanded through tarps, bits of fencing, and old paneling. Sometimes an extension cord could be seen stretching from one trailer to another, as a neighbor provided power for someone who had a shutoff. Flores had been collecting all manner of things for the family that lost a wife and mother. She had raised money to send all the children to summer camp. She had started picking the kids up every Sunday for church. Usually, she needs to take the church van through Twin Lakes twice to pick up all the children in the neighborhood who come to church without parents. There is always a meal afterward. "Some of the kids come hungry," Flores said.

In a compound of sorts, an extended family's trailers huddled on an acre of land owned by its matriarch, "Gabby Obrador," a woman who would throw back her head and laugh at the slightest provocation. Her words were punctuated by sweeping gestures that showed off her hot-pink nails. An above-ground swimming pool sat in a clearing between the trailers and was the hot spot for her grandchildren and their friends. Gabby joked that the neighborhood children shouldn't expect to be fed because the pool set her back so much. But she ordered them three pizzas on the first swim day.

Flores and Gabby Obrador embraced. They were warm and easy together, despite the older woman's refusal to heed Flores's oft-repeated advice that she and her partner of twenty years become officially married, that she give up cigarettes, and so on. This forty-six-year-old grandmother could not afford to fix her Toyota Camry, which had mysteriously stopped running, but she was donating a microwave for the family who lost their mother. "We have to go out of our way for each other," Flores said.

The Obrador family is committed to all their children excelling in school. Though the adults for the most part did not finish high school, they were convinced that education is a ticket out of poverty for their children.

Gabby has a third-grade education and became disabled after a series of heart attacks. She also described an incident of paralysis that sounded like a stroke. She volunteers at the primary school and frequently bakes for her grandchildren's classes. "I want them to have a lot of what I didn't have and what I couldn't give my kids," she said and pointed with pride to a grandson who is a schoolteacher in Japan.

Gabby's daughter, "Valeria Obrador," was wearing a T-shirt with the hashtag #momlife. She has four children in the local schools. All were taking the bus now that their grandmother's car was out of commission. Generations of this family have known their share of hardship. When Valeria was a child, the family lived in a rest area for three months after Gabby's marriage broke up. "I don't like to ask people for nothing," said Gabby, who is proud that she never sought assistance from her family and never used food stamps.

Valeria dropped out of school in the eighth grade when she had her first child. "She's smart!" Flores said of Valeria. The young mother waved off a suggestion that she could get her GED. But she wants her children to finish high school. "I want them to have a better life than I do now," she said. One son wants to be a football player, a goal she assured him that he could reach "because you're going to finish school, and you're going to do what you have to do."

STAY IN SCHOOL: EASIER SAID THAN DONE

Research consistently shows that income rises significantly with a high school diploma and again for people who complete college. Children in poverty are on the receiving end of admonitions from pro athletes and other luminaries to "Stay in school and study hard!" But they often find themselves in homes and school systems that make it difficult to do either. To be clear, children growing up in poverty can succeed academically. Yet their potential often goes unrecognized and unrealized.

Students come to school with experiences of material deprivation and other traumas that harm their ability to learn. Furthermore, they don't always come to school, or don't come on time because of flat tires, the need to care for younger siblings, unmanaged chronic illnesses, and more. In every school district, some students face big hurdles to learning. But in high-poverty school districts, *most* students face barriers of some kind.

Think what that means. In the districts with the least resources, there are always students—probably multiple students in every classroom—in some kind of crisis. Somewhere in between a beloved brother being incarcerated, a kid getting teased for coming to school with dirty clothes, a student missing a full week because of asthma flare-ups, homework that didn't get done because a parent was working a double shift and not home to supervise, a girl absent because she's gone to live with a grandmother in another town while her mother recovers from surgery . . . somewhere in there, a teacher is supposed to show the class how to multiply fractions. What are the odds of success? Even if everyone who is present for the lesson grasps it immediately, it will likely have to be repeated—once, twice, more—before moving on to a new concept, because high absenteeism will have caused students to miss any given lesson. The more children who are in crisis, the harder it is to teach anyone. This is one reason why high-poverty schools tend to have such poor outcomes.

In high-poverty schools nationally, about 68 percent of twelfth-graders graduate, compared with 91 percent in low-poverty schools, and the gap seems to be worsening.[1] The US Government Accountability Office did a review that found high-poverty schools less likely to offer courses such as Algebra I, Biology, Calculus, and Physics that prepare students for college.[2] An analysis of Virginia schools found that only about a third of schools in high-poverty districts qualified for state certification, while nearly all in low-poverty districts did.[3]

To complete the circle, these are the schools we are talking about when we tell kids, "Stay in school!" We hold out education as the path out of poverty. But in high-poverty schools, that path is steep and rocky, and many climb it barefoot.

We focus on Lytle, Texas, in this chapter because its school district at least tries to provide shoes, sometimes literally. Lytle takes a unique approach, inspired in part by the fact that 70 percent of the student body lives in poverty. Lytle Independent School District places a strong focus on developmental stages and social and emotional learning. They train teachers—at $500 a head, which is no small expense for the town—in a program called Capturing Kids' Hearts designed to build strong relationships with students. It is one of several curricula focused on social development that the district embraces. Every student in the lower grades is greeted at the classroom door by their teacher with a hug, high five, or handshake, according to the student's choice. Kids smile and introduce themselves to visitors. They make short films about subjects like kindness. If you get people talking long enough, they'll have something to say about the Robotics Club or kids who have gotten scholarships to top universities. But everybody leads with talking about things like character, social development, and even love.

As mentioned earlier, Lytle schools often serve as the source of basic needs to families. "I think we've always had an attitude here that if they couldn't take care of it at home, we were going to take care of it here," said superintendent Michelle Carroll Smith. For example, there are showers in the elementary school and a laundry facility in the primary school. Teachers walk kids between the buildings if they need help getting themselves and their clothes clean. Parents and other siblings are welcome to use the facilities, too.

The district has decided not to teach to standardized tests—where nationally children in poverty get low scores. The state's assessment of the school district is predictably unfavorable. Using various standards, the state of Texas gave the Lytle Independent School District an overall grade of C in 2020.[4] "The test-based accountability system has really forced school districts, if they're going to chase that, into having a very narrow curriculum and a very narrowed sense of what is true learning. And we've never really bought into that," Smith said. The scores have consequences. Schools that score badly for five consecutive years risk a state takeover, but the district is also part of a consortium that's working to develop objective ways to quantify how successful it is in alternative measures, such as student engagement, a process that starts in students' earliest years.

LITTLE LEARNERS: BIG CHALLENGES

The voices of four-year-olds filled Carol Ketron's Head Start classroom in Lytle Primary School, which houses preschool through grade one. Closing in on lunch, she hadn't had a moment all day to get to the restroom. "My eyeballs are floating," she said with her unwavering broad smile. It seemed that she was always talking to the children; and several were talking to her. She led the children through a video featuring letters and sounds—*U, umbrella, ukulele*—that the children enthusiastically sang and expressed in sign language. Next, she read them a storybook and invited students to identify the rhymes. When they got one right she told them to "kiss your brain!" and touched her lips to her hand and then her hand to her head.

Ketron's job is demanding. It takes enormous energy to manage a group of young children. But Ketron is trying to do something even more difficult—she is trying to prepare children who come from homes that lack working appliances or adequate food to be great students.

High-quality early childhood education can help kids be better prepared for school, but low-income families have significantly fewer choices than more affluent parents when choosing a childcare provider.[5] They are less likely to send their children to a preschool or childcare center.[6] That's not to say that children don't receive good care when left with relatives and neighbors. But more formalized arrangements are generally using evidence-based curricula proved to help children succeed in school. Yet a thoroughly vetted workbook isn't everything. Ketron, in fact, regrets that she is teaching academic content at the level she is, which includes pre-reading skills that she once worked on as a kindergarten teacher. Asked what her students need most, Ketron's eyes misted up. "Love," she said. "Oh God, they need love."

One by one, children left the circle to brush their teeth in the classroom sink with the help of an assistant teacher. "A couple of them don't want to give up that toothbrush," said Ketron. "They come here, and they scrub like there's no tomorrow." Those are the kids who do not have toothbrushes at home, she explained, adding that it's common for Head Start teachers to chip in to buy families food, clothing, and other necessities.

Head Start is a federal program instituted by Lyndon Johnson, who was himself a teacher in Cotulla, a rural south Texas town where most families' roots stretch to Mexico, not unlike Lytle. LBJ was so horrified by his students' living conditions that he wrote to his mother asking her to send toothpaste for the children. Head Start offers early childhood education for children in poverty, while also connecting families to medical and dental care and other community services. The program's aim is to prepare children living in poverty to learn on pace with their more affluent peers once they start elementary school. Decades of contradictory research give a variable picture of the success and long-term impact of the program.

Ketron said that the most critical thing she can do is teach her students to communicate. She believes that they haven't learned it at home because of too much screen time, a host of family relationship and health problems, and plain old poverty, which keeps adults stressed and often working long hours.

There were seventeen children in the room, but her attention was centered on "Logan," a little boy with close-cropped blond hair. Logan was wearing a T-shirt that read:

AWE

SOME

LIKE

DAD

He was moved from another classroom to hers in hope he'd be a better fit with the children here. "He's a screamer," explained Ketron, as Logan wailed nonverbally because other children had beat him to the toy kitchenette where he wanted to play in free time. "I promise you can go after lunch, if you make good choices," Ketron told him. She'd been working with him on talking things out with classmates rather than just letting out an "Aaagh!" at high volume. He has "really good days," she added, but he sometimes slips back. After some negotiation with his teacher, Logan sat silently, with a face like thunder that he rested on his fists.

Logan's parents are divorcing, a stressor that Ketron believed was triggering his behavior. Parents' separation is considered an adverse childhood experience (ACE). As discussed in chapter 12, high ACE scores are linked to a host of problems. Some, like difficulty focusing and self-regulating behavior, can be barriers to success in school. There are also protective factors, principally one or more adults a child can rely upon for help, which ameliorate the risks of a high ACE score. That's an area where schools can make a difference.

Poverty itself comes with an extraordinarily high stress level that has toxic consequences for brain development—this is true even in homes where no other stressors are present—no abuse, no incarceration, no separations. An NIH study found that the brains of children up to age four raised in poverty were actually smaller than those of their peers.[7] The size reduction came largely in the frontal and parietal regions associated with executive function: a range of cognitive abilities that includes impulse control and planning. The science suggests two key points:

- It is critical that we do everything we can to end child poverty. At the very least, we must help families with their material needs so that the household stress level drops to create a less toxic environment for brain development.
- Executive function can be improved throughout our lifetimes. A child who struggles behaviorally or academically early on can make great strides later. But as we'll discuss later, too many children are written off because of an overemphasis on standardized testing and exclusionary discipline.

Another hurdle facing young learners in poverty is a word deficit. Logan has language but lacks the self-control to use it in stressful situations. "Oscar," a student from a few years back, mainly grunted and used gestures to signal his needs. At four years old, he had almost no vocabulary. He'd make a sucking sound to indicate that he was thirsty and could manage to say, "shoe shoe" when he needed help tying his. Ketron connected him to a speech specialist. Fortunately, the intervention helped.

Recent research shows that children in poverty will have heard about four million fewer words than children from wealthier households by age four and will have had fewer adult-child interactions.[8] The "word gap" is far smaller than an earlier and influential study showed, and the concepts surrounding the work are laden with cultural assumptions. (The idea of a parent spending considerable time talking directly to a child is not a universal standard.) A 2018 study in five communities linked culture rather than income to a rich word environment for a young child.[9] Nevertheless, early childhood education places a heavy emphasis on language. Children who enter classrooms with more words have a tremendous advantage.

Helping children who enter school with fewer advantages than their classmates requires a district to consider how it's organized, how adults and children interact, and even what goes on the walls.

DESIGNING SCHOOLS FOR CHILDREN

Something is missing at Lytle Elementary School. There are some examples of student work on the walls. But the halls are not lined with posters peppering students with inspiring messages. Principal Wendy Carroll-Conover will not allow "worn-out words" to clutter her hallways or her students' brains. "They don't need that stimulus," she said.

The school is also unusual in that classrooms are all exposed to the hallways with glass walls, and children are frequently out in those hallways or in small breakout rooms working on group projects. "It's, to me, a window on the world," the principal said. "They are part of everything."

She stopped to chat with two boys working on a project about George Washington Carver. The boys told her a bit about Carver's life. Carroll-Conover shared that her dad farmed peanuts for a while and explained the drying process, which prompted the students to ask a barrage of questions about the making of peanut butter.

"It's amazing to me that this kind of school is built for children in poverty, because they don't usually get that," she said as she moved through the wide and gleaming hallways. During our tour, the townspeople were voting on a bonding initiative to invest $8.5 million in capital improvements to the schools. The measure ended up passing.

The school system is also active in applying for grants. Carroll-Conover shows off thousands of dollars' worth of Legos that she's gotten that way for the Lego Club. Teachers are encouraged to create clubs according to their own interests. There is now a newspaper club by student request, a quilting club, and more. The clubs meet before school starts and serve as an incentive for kids to come early. It's a way of combating tardiness with a carrot rather than a stick.

Nationally, tardiness, truancy, and other school rule violations frequently land kids in suspension and even expulsion, sanctions collectively known as "exclusionary discipline"—in other words, punishments that keep students out of the classroom. Research consistently shows that students of color and students in high-poverty schools face these punishments more frequently than their peers. Research also shows that racial and ethnic discrimination, intentional or implicit, plays a strong role in these inequities.

In 2014 the US Departments of Education and Justice issued a "Dear Colleague" letter noting the racial inequities it had tracked in US schools:

> An increasing number of students are losing important instructional time due to exclusionary discipline. The increasing use of disciplinary sanctions such as in-school and out-of-school suspensions, expulsions, or referrals to law enforcement authorities creates the potential for significant, negative educational and long-term outcomes, and can contribute to what has been termed the "school to prison pipeline." Studies have suggested a correlation between exclusionary discipline policies and practices and an array of serious educational, economic, and social problems, including school avoidance and diminished educational engagement; decreased academic achievement; increased behavior problems; increased

likelihood of dropping out; substance abuse; and involvement with juvenile justice systems.[10]

The Trump Administration retracted the letter.

Testing may play a part in exclusionary discipline as well. A study conducted after No Child Left Behind had raised the consequences of poor standardized test scores found that, while low-performing students always faced more exclusionary discipline, the rate increased during periods when standardized testing was being conducted.[11]

Not in Lytle. "I don't really care if we do well on the state test," said Carroll-Conover. "I want them to be safe, and be loved, and be successful."

Carroll-Conover and Smith are sisters. It's common to run into relatives in this town of three thousand people. They look alike, and they share a disdain for standardized tests, which they think label kids in poverty all too early as low-performing students. Smith wants to eliminate grade levels up to the third grade and instead track a series of developmental milestones, with the understanding that not everyone will reach a given language or math reasoning milestone at the same age.

"I think [the proposed system] can help with the poverty issue, because they just basically need more time. They haven't had as much time as our middle-class/affluent kids have had in academic-type learning," said Smith.

Smith's contention that kids need to be kids (she put a slide in the primary school library to make that very point) is at odds with the drive to let students earn college credits in high school—something that's increasingly popular in schools serving children of all income levels. "I have my own personal concerns about pushing this college down into the high school," she said. "My daughter graduated with twenty-one hours of college. She's okay with doing that. Not every kid is OK with that. They go to college, and they don't have that safety net of freshmen courses anymore, particularly if we send them off to the universities. I've seen several of our valedictorians struggle, and they can't make it, and they're back home after a year. Because they go up there to [Texas] A&M or [University of Texas] with twenty-four hours. They don't get many of those freshmen courses."

Students in poverty are less likely to go to college than their wealthier peers—but even those who go are less likely to finish. Students in the lowest family income quartile completed college within six years at a rate of 26 percent, compared with 59 percent of those in the highest quartile.[12] Low-income students who enroll in but do not complete college face the prospect of student loan repayment without the income boost that comes with a degree.

The struggles of students in poverty who go to college are considerable. A federal report about food insecurity on college campuses that reviewed thirty-one studies on the topic found that the majority concluded that more than 30 percent of college students experience hunger.[13] Additionally, students may have considerable family responsibilities and parents who object to them leaving their communities to study. Or they may come from low-performing schools that have not prepared them for college.

"Robert," a recent graduate of Lytle High School, was offered full scholarships at several universities—offers that he probably would not accept. "The scholarships don't cover everything," said Robert, who worked two twelve-hour shifts a week at a low-wage job, in addition to carrying a high school course load and competing in sports. Some of his family's ten children are out on their own, including a sister who graduated from an Ivy League school and a brother who is incarcerated. Yet there are younger ones that Robert feels responsible for. His mother has schizophrenia. His father "works very hard" but has an alcohol addiction.

"It's kept me from really studying more and trying to get ahead in school. But yeah, it is a sacrifice I'm willing to make for my family," says Robert, calmly and even proudly.

Robert will graduate high school ready to start his sophomore year of college because of all the dual-credit courses he has taken. He did not share the superintendent's misgivings about that. He thought the ability to do college work was the best thing about his high school experience.

Only, Robert won't be going to college, at least not right away. He is opting for the Air Force, in part because the Internal Revenue Service has charged his father with tax fraud, and that is putting Robert's financial aid in jeopardy. The father was living apart from the family after a stint in prison but thought, since he sent money home, he could still claim his wife and children as dependents, according to Robert. The IRS thought otherwise. Robert talked about how he is handling that disappointment: "Honestly, just introspection. I realize the way I feel, and then I'll look it up and there's a lot of helpful advice on the internet. There really is." He reads biographies of inspiring figures like Andrew Carnegie.

He is also concerned with setting an example for his four younger brothers. "I do feel like it's definitely way more responsibility than someone my age should have, but I think that I can handle it, and I was meant to handle it."

Robert was all confidence and resolve, while his classmate and friend, "Aaron," was tentative and teared up as he told his story.

Aaron had also gotten full scholarships to several schools. He wanted to study biochemistry to develop treatments for people who have experienced childhood traumas. "It's more of something I don't really tell a lot of people because I think it has a stigma to it," he said.

Since his father left, Aaron has shared a home with his mother, who does seasonal work. Local churches have helped them with food. He works part-time at an animal shelter.

The stress of choosing a college was bringing down this honor student. "Right now, I'm in a slump because I'm failing a class, and I need to catch up on the work," he said.

He had mixed feelings about going away and leaving a younger brother ("I had to become a father figure") and his mother: "She won't have anyone else around her, not even her own family because she's from Mexico . . . That's why I'm hesitant to go to Austin or Texas State—even though they're somewhat close, they're still far. That's why [University of Texas at San Antonio] is still a consideration for me . . . just because it's close to home."

Aaron also thinks a less competitive college may be best for him because he sees his education thus far as subpar. "I feel robbed because I'm going off to a good four-year university that I'm probably going to fail out of," he said.

Talking with Robert and Aaron we were struck by the weight of adult responsibility that had landed on them early. Aaron had some good advice for us on reporting how poverty affects students: "I think you should ask where students went for help [and] they couldn't get it. I think that's an important question, especially for people living in poverty because students just can't run to their family for help because they know they can't help them."

Later we saw Aaron at the Showcase, an end-of-year event where students display their work in the high school gym as parents and other supporters file by. He stood behind a mini Ferris wheel built by the robotics club. His calculus class did the computations for the design.

"I couldn't have done that," an adult said.

Aaron smiled slightly and shrugged.

A few rows over, elementary students had difficulty standing still around their models of the planets. "Would you like me to tell you about the solar system?" asked "Hector" in perfect English. We'd met his mother, "Hilda Sánchez," earlier. She was studying hard to learn English because she is working toward citizenship. Sánchez cleans houses for a living while her husband works at construction sites. It was an emotional interview, where she spoke about two attempted assaults, including a man, a pillar of the community, who cornered her while she was cleaning the bathroom.

She beamed at Hector. "Ella es de Connecticut," she told Hector, and he was full of questions. *Is it beautiful there? Does it snow all the time?*

Hector wanted to know everything.

What Can I Do?

1. **Support parents.** Parents in poverty want the best for their children, as all parents do, but they often lack the resources to deliver it. There are various mentoring programs that allow you to be a support for young mothers. Try calling your community information line, typically 211, to find one in your area. Support diaper banks and other nonprofits that help to relieve the material stress of poverty.

2. **Demand that your school district prioritize children in poverty.** You can do this by getting involved with your PTA or school board. School districts are often judged on how their most privileged students fare. Advocate for measures that show how struggling students are helped to make concrete gains. Attendance, as we discussed, is a particular struggle for children in poverty. Ask the board of education to report on it regularly; encourage your local newspaper to cover it *at least as often as they cover test scores.*

3. **Advocate for basic needs–informed schools.** To offer equal access to education, schools must make sure that poverty is not a barrier. That means having washing machines in schools, and making sure kids have weather-appropriate clothing and even alarm clocks if their parents are at work and cannot wake them in the morning.

4. **Fight to decouple schools from property taxes.** In most of the US, public schools are supported by municipal property taxes. That means wealthy towns have more to spend on education and poor towns—where the need is greater—have less. Hold a forum on the topic and invite your state legislator. Write a letter to the editor. This will be a long, uphill fight, but it's essential to take those first steps.

5. **Don't rely on individual actions.** We've met so many wonderful and caring teachers, administrators, and school nurses who dig into their pockets to meet kids' basic needs. That's great—and everyone who can afford to offer this kind of help should. But it's not a sustainable solution. Do some detective work in your community. What are the resources for basic needs, for covering the expenses of a field trip, for getting a family through an emergency like a fire or a hospitalization? Start some conversations in your community about the gap between what people need and what people have.

6. **Protect the rights of teen workers.** In some states, employers can pay high school students less than minimum wage. For families in poverty, teens contribute to the household finances—their wages are as essential to survival as any adult's. Many of these kids are already working so many hours that it harms their studies. Paying them less than minimum wage means they must work even more hours.

A Better Way: Talk

PROGRAMS ARE UNDERWAY IN Rhode Island, New York, Georgia, and elsewhere to coach parents and other caregivers in talking to their children from birth to three. Providence Talks sends trained home visitors to support parents for eight months with books and tips on talking with their children. The program has babies wear a "word pedometer" that tracks the number of words a baby is hearing and the number of adult interactions. It also supports community playgroups and professional development for child-care providers.

The National Diaper Bank Network partnered with Too Small to Fail and Penguin Books for Young Readers to create Diaper Time is Talk Time. We provided children's books to low-income parents along with information about talking, singing, and reading to babies. These resources, of course, came with diapers. We know that diaper need increases household stress and maternal depression—and that means fewer quality interactions between adults and children.

Talk is cheap—free even. But parents need to be aware of its importance and not so stressed by poverty itself that quality inter-actions suffer.

PART III

SOLUTIONS

CHAPTER 14

Possibilities

The Poor Don't Need to Be with You Always

People are poor because the money they have is insufficient to pay for the things they need. That's this book in a nutshell. The problem is straightforward, though that does not mean that the solution will be easy to achieve. As we have discussed, poverty was widespread in the United States even before the pandemic caused massive job loss. Many entrenched systems are perfectly designed to preserve inequality. There are two ways to start dismantling those systems: increase the amount of money people have or decrease the price of the things they need. Some combination of these strategies could also work.

There is a growing realization that major economic reform toward fairness and inclusion must happen. Mainstream thinkers and policymakers are now talking about programs like universal basic income and a national jobs guarantee. Particularly in light of predictions that automation will drastically reduce jobs, such programs are sounding less like a socialist pipedream.

Without endorsing any single one, we will review some macro policies in play that could address poverty in America. None of them is perfect. It is critical to acknowledge that up front, because getting lost in the weeds is the greatest threat to creating a rational economy. *But what about XYZ?* is the enemy of innovation. We must recognize that none of these policies is nearly as flawed as our present sink-or-swim economy where a significant proportion of the country is drowning. That drowning is not without cost—in incarceration, chronic illness, and other miseries that drive spending. Preventing them is as much a financial benefit as a moral imperative.

BANKING ON PEOPLE

A number of the policies we will review include no-strings-attached cash transfers. That may seem extreme, but proponents of such systems have included Martin Luther King Jr., Milton Friedman, and Richard Nixon, who largely delegated a pilot basic income program to a young Donald Rumsfeld. The idea of instituting a basic income gained traction during the previous administration of Lyndon Johnson. Rumsfeld and his aide, Dick Cheney, oversaw a number of basic income experiments. Figures on the right and left have seen these programs as a way to both trim down human services bureaucracies and eliminate poverty. In response to the COVID-19 pandemic, the US government made cash payments directly to citizens—something advocates for people in poverty have wanted for years. During that extreme circumstance, there was a clear recognition that the way to end economic hardship is with an infusion of resources. This most obvious of strategies, however, has rarely been employed in ordinary times to address poverty.

It is critical that any major economic reform take into account people who live in extreme poverty. Most cash transfer proposals set an income of around $12,000 a year, and many call for financing the program in part by dismantling the social safety net. While this might benefit many low-wage workers, it would leave people with no other source of income devoid of the resources that currently help them meet basic needs.

Three objections repeatedly are raised when people dismiss the idea of cash transfers: people will spend the money irresponsibly; people will stop working; and we cannot afford it. All of these assertions are false.

The money does get spent responsibly

It's interesting that there is a presumption that people will spend money they are given by the government differently than they spend money they receive as wages. Most of us use our paychecks to first keep the lights on and fill the refrigerator, with excess going to savings, discretionary but perfectly licit purchases, and charity. Why would a cash transfer be different? Presumably because it goes to poor people, whom we consider suspect.

Researchers have proved that cash transfers do not lead to the purchase of "temptation goods," like alcohol and tobacco. Reviewing multiple studies of cash transfers in Latin America, Africa, and Asia, the World Bank found:

> Almost without exception, studies find either no significant impact or a significant negative impact of transfers on temptation goods. In the only (two, non-experimental) studies with positive significant impacts, the magnitude is small. This result is supported by data from Latin America, Africa, and Asia. A growing number of studies from a range of contexts therefore indicate that concerns about the use of cash transfers for alcohol and tobacco consumption are unfounded.[1]

Let's focus on that "negative impact" for a moment. A number of studies show that people smoke or drink less when they receive a cash transfer. For example, participants in a Mexican program, Oportunidades, were less likely to have a habitual drinker in their household than peers who were not receiving payments.[2] It makes sense that reducing a household's financial stress would reduce—not increase—destructive means of coping with stress, like alcohol and tobacco.

Extra income does not make people stop working

Two decades of studies in the United States from the earned income tax credit show that hours worked rise when a family receives the EITC.[3] Transferring cash to families in poverty in the US has provided an incentive to work because it makes increased employment a path to greater prosperity—rather than simply a way to end up worse off because of the loss of public benefits. A study of the Mexican cash transfer program Progresa found that the program had no effect on labor market participation but a big effect on reducing poverty.[4] A series of 1970s experiments in cash transfers in the United States and Canada showed a 13 percent decrease in work hours, but that was connected to more school attendance and family childcare, both social goods:

> Female spouses reduced their hours and re-entered the workforce less quickly after a break. The general result found in all the experiments was that secondary earners tended to take some part of the increased family income in the form of more time for household production, particularly staying home with newborns. Effectively, married women used the GAI [guaranteed annual income] to finance longer maternity leaves. Tertiary earners, largely adolescent males, reduced their hours of work dramatically, but the largest decreases occurred because they began to enter the workforce later. This delay in taking a first job at an older age suggests that some of these adolescent males might be spending more years in school. The biggest effects, that is, could be seen as either an economic cost in the form of work disincentives or an economic benefit in the form of human capital accumulation.[5]

We can afford a significant increased benefit to poor US Americans

We already spend the money—just not on the people who need it most. Recall from chapter 3 that the single-greatest investment in housing made by the US government is the mortgage interest deduction, which benefits people in mansions more than people in bungalows and does not benefit renters at all.

A 2017 report by the Institute of Taxation and Economic Policy found that nearly 20 percent of US corporations operating at a profit had an effective tax rate of 19 percent or less. AT&T, Wells Fargo, JPMorgan Chase, Verizon, and IBM all enjoyed more than $130 billion in tax breaks during the eight-year period covered by the study. That alone is enough to nearly double SNAP for two years. A number of large companies, including General Electric, Pacific Gas and Electric, and Priceline .com, actually received more in breaks than they paid in.[6]

POLICIES TO HASTEN THE END OF POVERTY

Once we accept that poverty is a matter of resources, solutions begin to present themselves. The United States actually has a number of programs that are effective in connecting people and resources, but these programs have never been scaled to eliminate poverty. Around the globe there are tried-and-true as well as promising new policies that could easily be adapted here.

Expanding the social safety net

When the government gives resources to people in poverty, it decreases human misery, dramatically improves outcomes for children, and stimulates the economy. Only the thorough demonization of people in poverty could make these programs controversial or explain the annual rending of garments that happens around their funding. Programs such as SNAP, Section 8, and TANF are consistently under fire and have never been funded at anything approaching adequate levels. People who could benefit from them do not qualify; benefits are too low; and people get kicked off prematurely because of a fear of the dreaded "dependency."

Rather than begging for crumbs from the table, people who care about poverty might launch public campaigns to dramatically increase funding for these programs. For example, what if we launched a campaign to eradicate hunger in the United States? As of April 2018, the US Department of Agriculture reported 39.6 million people participated in SNAP with an average monthly benefit of $122.39. Both the benefit and the participation rate were lower than a year previous. New work requirements and other restrictions will lower participation further.

Meanwhile, forty-one million US Americans live with food insecurity, including thirteen million children, according to the nonprofit Feeding America. While child health is particularly at risk when nutrition is poor, it is important to remember that most childless adults will get thrown off the SNAP rolls after three months—regardless of whether their circumstances have changed. (Can't let them become dependent!)

The numbers tell us that approximately 1.4 million hungry US Americans are not receiving SNAP. As we discussed in detail in chapter 2, even those who are getting SNAP benefits are shortchanged. The "Thrifty Food Plan" that determines SNAP benefits is unrealistic and too low to support a healthy diet.

As with all the policy possibilities that we'll recount, there is a cost. In no case is that cost unbearable. It is simply a matter of priorities. In 2017 the US government spent $70 billion on SNAP and other domestic food assistance programs. By way of comparison, it spent $590 billion on defense.

We could easily double spending on nutritional programs, ensuring that everyone who needed the help got enough support. That money could conceivably come from defense or some other generously funded discretionary federal spending category, or by eliminating tax breaks that privilege corporations and the wealthiest individuals. What if instead of letting US Americans go hungry, we asked Amazon to pay taxes?

Another important change would be to require that cash payments from TANF be sufficient to raise people above 50 percent of poverty in every state. We also could require that at least 50 percent of state TANF dollars go directly to providing for the basic needs of families, rather than diverted to fund other state priorities.

Federal subsidies for basic needs

No matter how poor you are, there are roads that run through your town. There are schools where you can send your children free of charge. They may not be particularly good roads or good schools, but they still provide a benefit. They are universally available because we recognize that you cannot run a viable society without free movement and education.

It is increasingly clear that you cannot run a viable society where people do not have their basic needs met. Humanitarian considerations aside, people who lack basic needs cannot participate robustly in the economy, as workers, consumers, or taxpayers. There are plenty of examples of subsidy programs that work.

- In Sweden residents can apply for a housing allowance, or *bostadsbidrag*, if they need help making the rent or mortgage payment. This differs dramatically from Section 8, the US federal rental assistance program. Section 8 has caps. There are only so many slots available—and availability has nothing to do with need. As we saw in California, people may have to wait years before there is even an opening to apply for Section 8. While US Americans are increasingly spending more than the government-recommended 30 percent of income on housing, Swedes on average spend 21 percent, according to the Swedish government.[7]

- The Rand Corporation reviewed programs that subsidized the purchase of healthy foods. In almost all the twenty locations worldwide that the review addressed, the subsidies increased consumption of high-quality foods. The exception was the United States, where they reviewed an incentive program to get SNAP users eating more fruits and vegetables. The program failed, the cited study concluded, because the subsidy was too low to make a difference.[8] Suppose we started subsidizing the purchase of fruits and vegetables at the retail level? Diabetes cost the United States $327 billion annually, according to the American Diabetes Association, in health-care dollars and lost productivity. So we do have the money to spend subsidizing healthy diets—but now we spend it subsidizing the consequences of not having a healthy diet.

- Japan approaches basic needs in a fundamentally different way. Article 25 of the country's constitution states: "All people shall have the right to maintain the minimum standards of wholesome and cultured living.

   "In all spheres of life, the State shall use its endeavors for the promotion and extension of social welfare and security, and of public health."

   Japan is clearly a capitalist county, but it enshrines social welfare in its constitution. That has far-reaching consequences. For example, childcare at government-approved facilities is essentially free in the country for children up to age five, thanks to subsidies.

Guaranteed minimum income

A guaranteed minimum income provides a supplement to bring what a family makes up to the level of what they need—or at least closer to it. There are usually no work requirements, but GMI has tended to be so low in demonstration projects that additional income was extremely desirable. It is true that GMI will subsidize employers who fail to pay families a living wage. We do that already, of course, through SNAP, Section 8, the earned income tax credit, and other programs. Proponents of income transfers as opposed to aid that targets a single item argue that they make it possible for people to buy what they need. In some cases, yes, people need food. But in others, they may need a reliable used car to get them to a better-paying job. Cash provides that flexibility.

The 1970s saw a great deal of experimentation in guaranteed minimum income, both in the United States and abroad. Unfortunately, the benefits proved in these experiments have been hidden for decades. In several cases, outcomes research was either badly done or suppressed.

For example, in the summer of 1968, more than 1,200 economists signed a letter supporting basic income that was quoted on page one of the *New York Times*. It read, in part, "The country will not have met its responsibility until everyone in the nation is assured an income no less than the officially recognized definition of poverty . . . The costs of such plans are substantial but well within the nation's economic and fiscal capacity."[9]

President Richard Nixon, who for all his sins is referred to by Noam Chomsky as "the last New Deal president,"[10] listened. From 1968 to 1982 the United States conducted a number of basic income experiments in Colorado, Indiana, Iowa, New Jersey, North Carolina, Pennsylvania, and Washington. The subsidy was delivered through negative income tax—participants had to demonstrate need to receive aid, which came in the form of large income tax refunds exceeding what they had paid in during the year, similar to the earned income tax credit.

243

The experiments showed only a small decline in work hours, gains in health and education, and reduced crime. As noted earlier, much of that time subtracted from work was spent in caring for children and pursuing an education.

But the idea of basic income was largely torpedoed in the United States by a finding that it encouraged divorce, something seen quite dramatically in the Seattle sample, where evaluators said divorce rose 50 percent. Decades later, researchers discovered that basic income did not contribute to divorce at all, but that the finding was attributable to reporting and statistical errors—the evaluators got the numbers wrong.[11]

The largest guaranteed minimum income experiment so far took place in the Canadian province of Manitoba from 1974 to 1979. Like the US experiments, the Canadian model was based on negative income tax. Mincome hit a serious snag when the era's inflation called for payments to be substantially increased, though the government allotted no additional money to the project. The money came out of research and analysis. Data were collected and then for the most part simply archived.

The original idea was that Mincome could be scaled nationally, but the liberal government that instituted the pilot was replaced by a conservative one. Not only was the great experiment not expanded—it did not even get a final report. The only factor analyzed was participation in the labor market, which was seen as the key question of the experiment. As explained above, there was a dip, but it was largely attributable to maternity leaves and high school completion.

With considerable persistence, Evelyn L. Forget, a researcher at the University of Manitoba, obtained the data more than thirty years later. Forget looked at residents of Dauphin, a small town where all income-eligible residents were enrolled in Mincome. Hospitalizations fell 8.5 percent relative to a control group of similar Canadians. The drop in hospitalizations centered around accidents, injuries, and mental health. Also, more children in Dauphin families finished high school. These gains are particularly impressive, as only about a third of Dauphin's population was receiving Mincome—and in some cases, the payment for which they qualified was quite small. Forget wrote:

> Research has examined the relationship between health and each of the related concepts of mean family income, income distribution, and the incidence of poverty. Our focus is on a slightly different dimension of economic well-being: income security, which is a concept distinct from income or socio-economic status. Income security, the guarantee that all participants can expect a basic annual income whether or not they work, gives people a longer planning horizon, allowing them to get beyond just making ends meet.[12]

She theorizes that even families whose incomes exceeded the level where they would qualify for Mincome were affected by a sense of security. If they hit a rough patch, they would still have a cushion. That could have lowered stress levels throughout the community.

Today, a number of pilot programs are exploring the effect of guaranteed minimum income. For example, in 2017 the country of Finland launched a pilot in which some randomly selected unemployed people received a monthly unconditional payment of about $685. The government turned down a researcher's request to expand the experiment to some employed Finns. People who received the payments were happier and healthier than people who got standard unemployment insurance. Both groups found employment at about the same rate.[13] In Kenya, the nonprofit GiveDirectly is testing basic income among Kenyans in poverty living in rural Siaya County. The twelve-year trial began in 2017 after a one-year pilot and will eventually include twenty-one thousand people, most of whom will not receive cash transfers for the whole length of the study. Participants are paid the equivalent of twenty-two dollars per month, which about doubles the average income. Early outcomes included increases in assets and income, improvements in psychological well-being and food security, and a drop in domestic violence.[14]

Universal basic income

Unlike guaranteed minimum income, universal basic income goes to everyone—rich and poor. Proponents reason that more affluent people will end up returning their stipend through higher taxes. Administration is also more straightforward without means testing, though obviously the sum of the payouts is larger. Experiments in universal basic income include the following:

- **Y Combinator:** Funded by the startup incubator company, the plan is to pay one thousand people in two US states $1,000 monthly for three to five years and closely study the impact on them and their communities. Y Combinator researchers cite psychological reasons for considering a basic income: "Research points to negative economic, social, and psychological feedback loops that keep individuals without a steady income 'trapped' in poverty. A basic income seeks to break these feedback loops."[15] Y Combinator began a small pilot of UBI in Oakland, California, in 2016. The pilot's main purpose was to tease out logistics for the larger study. Outcomes data were not published.
- **Hawaii:** The first state in the US to study basic income, Hawaii is exploring UBI as a response to automation and globalization.
- **Stockton:** The California city began giving 130 low-income residents a $500 monthly payment in 2019. Outcomes researchers found that most used the payments to fund basic needs (40 percent spent it on food). Slated to end in the summer of 2020, at this writing Mayor Michael Tubbs is trying to extend the program. Tubbs, who grew up in poverty, told *California Magazine,* "It would've meant the world to my mother. It would've meant that she was less anxious and less stressed . . . It would've allowed her to have a more human experience."[16]

- **Scotland:** The national government will award grants to the local councils in Glasgow, Edinburgh, Fife, and North Ayrshire to develop basic income pilots.

Increased minimum wage and an end to subminimum tipped and piece wages

If you feel like you are working harder and harder and having an increasingly difficult time making ends meet, you are probably right. US American workers have been falling behind for decades, as cost of living has increased, but wages have not.

The current federal minimum wage is $7.25 per hour, though many states set a higher rate. Washington, DC, has the highest minimum wage in the country at $14.00. Adjusted for inflation, the federal minimum wage in 1968 would have been worth about $10.15 in 2018 dollars, according to the Economic Policy Institute.

Workers who receive tips can legally be paid as little as $2.13 an hour. Piece rate wages, where workers are paid a fixed "piece rate" for each unit they produce, can be even lower.

Several cities have acted to protect workers through higher minimum wages, including Seattle, which in 2015 began a gradual climb toward $15 an hour. While the left generally supports minimum wage increases as a way to offer workers security and better quality of life, conservatives argue that increased minimum wages will simply lead to layoffs. The experience in Seattle did not settle that argument.

A study of restaurant workers in the city found that hikes to $11 and $13 were connected with low-wage workers actually taking home less pay because their hours were cut.[17] Another study, also focusing on restaurant workers, found that real wages did increase and that employment did not decrease.[18] A paper by the Economic Policy Institute criticized the first study on the grounds of methodology: "The study may be biased toward finding job loss [because] it excludes about 40 percent of total employment in the state, making it very difficult to draw meaningful conclusions about what actually happened to low-wage employment in Seattle."[19]

As with all these economic experiments, a greater volume of high-quality research is needed to get at the truth. Significantly, the US has the lowest minimum wage relative to average wage of any country in the Organisation for Economic Development and Cooperation, whose members are nations with highly developed economies. If others can do better by minimum wage workers, why can't we?

National jobs guarantee

At this writing, several Senate proposals are pushing a program to provide a $15-an-hour job with benefits for any US American who wants one. As with FDR's New Deal, these jobs would support public infrastructure and services. The economy is generally considered at full employment when unemployment is between 4 and 6 percent, as was the case before the pandemic. But that does not account for people who have dropped out of the economy, discouraged that they will ever find a job, or the 20 percent of people who are in the gig economy, some as a last resort. Furthermore, some groups historically experience worse unemployment than others. The unemployment rate among African Americans, for example, tends to be roughly twice the national average. So just how good the job market is depends on who you are and where you live.

Proponents of a national job guarantee say that the strategy will approach true full employment. Conceivably, it would have the effect of raising the minimum wage—it's unlikely many people would agree to work for less than $15 an hour in the private sector if they had access to more lucrative guaranteed jobs.

A study by the Center for Budget and Policy Priorities put the cost of a national jobs program at $543 billion, with a wage lower than $15 but adjustable to keep families above the federal poverty level. Writing in The Intercept, David Dayen argued that directly creating jobs would be cheaper at that price than indirectly trying to create jobs through corporate subsidies:

> Combining economic development subsidies and corporate tax cuts comes out to an average annual total of $214 billion per year, spent chasing job creation by handing over money to corporations. And there's more. Nearly every state in America offers job creation tax credits, literally money paid per job. There are massive incentives in each state available for film and television production. Special "bonus depreciation" rules allow companies to write down equipment costs, deferring taxes for years on investments. And there are dozens of other ways in which corporations grab public money with the promise of delivering jobs.[20]

Dayen is right. We spend money on so-called job creation that amounts to tax breaks for corporations. We spend more on incarceration and community supervision, on special education, on treating preventable illnesses. We spend money on a host of things that would never occur, if only people had money in the first place.

It is time to bring bolder ideas to the forefront, whatever your venue to do that might be. It is time to ask your members of Congress and state legislators about them—frequently. If you are a student, it's time to write your dissertation about one of them. If you are a philanthropist, it's time to fund demonstration projects. If you are already involved in providing material assistance to people in poverty, it is time to speak out publicly about these ideas and—best-case scenario—put yourself out of business.

CHAPTER 15

Advocacy

Making Change

Since 2016 US Americans have become increasingly active in the political process—a hopeful first step toward economic justice. Yet while we would argue that poverty plays a role in almost every issue, it does not always get the attention it deserves in movements that are addressing myriad problems in an often-chaotic political environment.

We all need to make an issue out of poverty. There are lots of ways to do that. Most of this book has been about other people's stories and about policy. Our hope was to inspire individuals to get active. Now we're going to turn inward a bit and talk about how one of the authors did just that by focusing on the most basic thing imaginable—diapers.

JOANNE'S STORY

I, Joanne, was working with families who had been chronically homeless through my job as a social worker at the Yale Child Study Center.

The genesis for my career change—and this book—came when I saw an intellectually disabled mother of two reusing a disposable diaper that had been left out to dry. I explained to her that using a fresh diaper every time was essential for her baby's health. She told me that she could not afford diapers or toilet paper. The family was sharing a cloth towel to clean up after using the toilet.

I made an assumption—never a good idea. I assumed she did not understand the sources of help out there for her. I thought, surely, she could use her food stamps to buy these products or that she could get them from WIC. Wrong and wrong. If you want diapers in the United States, you'd best have cash—or even better, a credit card so that you can shop online and get the best deals. People without transportation or sufficient cash tend to buy diapers in small quantities at corner stores, where they are significantly more expensive.

My client was enrolled in a job-training program, which she had to attend in order to get TANF, the cash assistance that (barely) supported her family. She had access to subsidized childcare so that she could attend the training. But her provider, like most, required that she supply disposable diapers as a condition of the baby attending.

Because she could not afford diapers, she was subject to a domino effect. No diapers equals no childcare equals no work or school. And of course, there are the rashes, and sometimes more serious infections, that come with too few diaper changes, the fussiness, the crying, the feeling of failure because you cannot meet your child's most basic needs. I ended up buying diapers for the family out of my own pocket, a frequent strategy for social workers when they realize that there is no official channel prepared to give a client what they need. But I would not be her social worker forever. Plus, I knew that there would be millions of families around the country in exactly the same situation. What about them?

I started looking into hygiene supplies, what they cost and what help there was for families who could not afford them. It was nearly impossible for people short on money to get these essential products. We talked about it a lot as a family, and in 2004 we decided to just get started. That meant going to the warehouse club, the cheapest place to buy diapers, and loading up our minivan with cases of them. We got close friends to do the same. The diapers ended up at our house. I added another line to our family cell phone plan, and that became the virtual headquarters of the Diaper Bank.

Early on, I decided that the Diaper Bank would not have a physical presence where it handed out diapers. Even though its successor, the Diaper Bank of Connecticut, has a large warehouse space and office, this is still true. I knew that there were agencies throughout my community that already served poor and low-income families with young children. I partnered with them for a few reasons:

- It got us going faster—with less need for our own infrastructure.
- It allowed us to reach into corners of the community where our core group did not have connections.
- We were able to support, rather than compete with, nonprofits already doing important work.

Our diaper buyers and drivers became board members. We held diaper drives, raised money, and talked with the media about diaper need. Though I was living a diaper-centric life, it was never solely about diapers. I realized that the need for tampons, toothpaste, laundry detergent, and many other hygiene and household supplies was also urgent. But I chose to do one thing, and do it well, I hope, rather than split my focus.

Choosing diapers was designed to raise public support and also maximize impact. Babies are sympathetic. Yes, I did get calls and letters from people who demonized the parents—actually, almost exclusively the mothers—for "having babies they cannot afford." But far more people were horrified at the idea of babies spending days in dirty diapers. Those people tended to be thinking of what it would be like for their own children and grandchildren to be in such dire straits. That kind of empathy is what continues to drive the diaper bank movement.

In taking on partner agencies, we built ourselves a base in the community. Nonprofits that people already considered essential considered the Diaper Bank essential. That helped us make connections to people who would give money, diapers, and professional services to help us grow.

Soon we had some paid staff. While the growth was tremendous, we did not grow for the sake of growing. Staff spent most of their time ensuring that we were operating smoothly and providing as many diapers as possible to our partners—not doing marketing. Make no mistake: marketing is critical, but it is often the "fun part" to most people and can suck more energy than it should. Your first job is to build something that is worth marketing.

The Diaper Bank got a lot of attention, as I did personally. When national media covered our work, it created more opportunities. Eventually, a major diaper brand, Huggies, agreed to support me as I started the National Diaper Bank Network (NDBN). Today NDBN has more than two hundred member organizations in communities throughout the country. The national organization gives these local diaper banks access to huge diaper donations as well as technical assistance that helps them become strong and efficient nonprofits able to help their communities for the long haul. NDBN also does policy advocacy on behalf of families in poverty, particularly around hygiene needs. Some of the key players in the diaper bank movement have years of policy experience, advanced degrees, and connections to large organizations. Others have no real preparation for the work but draw on their own experience of poverty, or simply their good hearts, and they set up distribution programs run out of church basements or their own garages. They come from all religious and political persuasions. Together, we've given out more than two hundred million diapers since 2011. We recently started the Alliance for Period Supplies to get these essential products to the one in four menstruators who say they've had to do without them.

Diaper banking is what this entire book is about: the idea that there are necessities beyond the means of people in poverty and no public programming to help them bridge that gap. Without these necessities, people miss work and school. They get sick. They sink deeper into poverty.

We have proved that families who receive free diapers earn more money and have healthier children. Parents report that they and their children are "happier" as a result of the diapers. You can help people work their way out of poverty, just by giving them diapers. By taking away one of the stressors that comes with poverty, you can make a home a much more developmentally healthy place for a baby to grow up. Giving people diapers does not solve everything. But it solves quite a bit.

HOW TO CHANGE THE WORLD IN EIGHT STEPS

You could give people diapers, or tampons, or household cleaning products; NDBN would be glad to help you. Or you could find some similar leverage point where a small, simple form of assistance makes an outsized difference in people's lives. Or you can organize people in your community to support macroeconomic change, like a guaranteed minimum income, or essential local change, like making sure the bus system reliably gets lower-wage workers to the job on time.

The point is this: no matter who you are, you can play an important role in ending poverty in the United States, relieving poverty in your community, and affirming the rights of people who live in poverty.

And you can start today. Here are eight steps to take action:

1. Find your base

Where there is community, there is a greater ability to effect change. So what is your community? It might be a labor union, a congregation, a political party, a PTA, or an activist group. If you do not already belong to such a community, seriously think about joining and being active. These groups are usually run by people who are willing to do the work: serve on the committee, run the bake sale, provide the rides to the polls.

As you become a more integral member of the group, you get taken seriously when you ask these kinds of questions:

- Are our students missing school because they don't have clean uniforms—and should we be providing laundry facilities in the building?
- How does our faith require us to advocate for fair housing?
- Are the candidates we're supporting taking strong stands on economic justice?

2. Work directly with people in poverty

To advocate effectively for people, you need to understand the realities of their lives. Thank you for reading this book, but reading will only get you so far. There are two ways to work with people in poverty: by serving them and by partnering with them. Both are essential. Service would be giving material or intangible help, like food or tutoring. Partnership would be finding a way for a more affluent and a less affluent organization to work together toward a common goal. For example, suburban and urban faith communities could hold forums on affordable housing as a regional issue, rather than one that is contained by municipal borders, develop a plan to promote more units, and then make it happen.

3. Build a team

Start talking with people about poverty. Many will give you a wide berth. A few will be full of questions, or maybe full of stories of their own difficulties, past or present. You want these folks—all of them. You especially want people who bring a wide range of skills, experiences, and connections. Some people are great at direct service but cannot write a press release to save their lives. Others have their state representative on speed dial but are not the best at motivating volunteers. Your weakness is someone else's strength—together, you're perfect. The team can consist of individuals—it can also consist of organizations coming together to fight for an important reform.

4. Set a goal

Take your time on this one; you're going to be working on your goal for somewhere between six months and a lifetime. You need to make sure it's something for which you can sustain your own and others' enthusiasm. A great pitfall of activism is that we see so many wrongs that need righting, and we can find it difficult to exercise enough focus to be effective. Here are some important questions to ask yourself:

- **Will this action significantly improve the lives of people in poverty?**
- **Is someone else already doing it?** If the answer is yes, you can move on to another issue or see if you can partner with the organization that's already on the job. Either is a great option. Remember, in every community there is a limited amount of philanthropic funding and a limited number of people with the expertise and time to move an issue forward. Don't turn allies into competitors for those resources.
- **Am I the best person or are we the best group to do this?** Try to choose something that is in keeping with your collective expertise.
- **Where's the leverage point?** Poverty is a big problem. Providing diapers struck Joanne as a good place to start because diapers make families healthier and increase access to work and early childhood education. That's a lot of improvement from a simple thing. Think of a leverage point in policy issues as well. For example, ban-the-box laws prohibit employers from asking about criminal records on job applications—though they can

ask about records later in the process. This is a simple, straight-forward measure that can be passed on to the local or state level. It's zero cost (which legislators always love) and gets more people out of poverty and into jobs. Movements often focus on big things, but small things can make big changes.

- **Is this something that I can get people excited about?** Reform happens much more frequently when you can explain what you want and why in a few sentences that evoke an emotional response.

5. Set clear responsibilities

Best-case scenario? You take your work public, and you are inundated with people who want more info or want to help. You need to know who is going to return the calls, populate the database, do the trainings. The phrase "well-oiled machine" should spring to mind. If a prospective volunteer or donor tries to get involved but finds no one is ready to receive their help, they are unlikely to try a second time. The logistical part of activism is boring. Activists are passionate people. We tend not to like writing manuals and organizing phone trees. We have to do it anyway.

6. Go public

You might do this through the press, social media, an event, or all of the above. The important thing is to have a clear and consistent message that inspires an emotional response as well as action steps that you want leaders and/or the general public to take. Think about who your spokespeople should be. People with varied backgrounds and experience tend to make a more convincing case. If a formerly incarcerated person, a police chief, a preacher, and an entrepreneur are all on board, you are going to attract much more interest and support.

7. Move your government

This is a complex task that spawned an entire multibillion-dollar industry: lobbying. But ordinary people with no money have done it well and successfully. A great free resource is the Indivisible Guide, available at Indivisible.org.

Here are some general principles:

- Politicians always, always, always are thinking about the next election. You need to make it in their interest (or at least not contrary to their interest) to support your goal.

- Doing the right thing is almost always cost-effective. Find ways to demonstrate that.

- Show how alleviating poverty will help the whole community. For example, in supporting a bill to raise the minimum wage, be sure to stress that this reform will strengthen the tax base and reduce the need for taxpayer-funded services that people making poverty wages require to survive.

- Don't neglect your state or municipality. People get excited about national issues, but Congress passes far fewer significant bills than it once did. Many of the things that affect poverty in our communities are decided at the state or local level. You have more power closer to home than you do at the federal level. Your state legislators will take a personal meeting with average constituents. In most states, they will treat half a dozen calls from constituents as a groundswell. You can easily testify on behalf of bills in your state legislature. On the local level, you can access and influence your local elected officials. If they don't listen, consider running yourself.

- Large numbers of organized people taking action make change. Posting on social media helps a cause along, but it is important to move as many supporters as possible to more commitment. That could include contacting an elected official about a pending bill, asking a legislator to visit your program and talk with families, or encouraging and assisting members of the press to report on issues. Ask members of your group to do specific tasks like these—rather than just offer their support vaguely.

8. Refuse to accept poverty

Poverty is not natural. There is no reason why human societies cannot be organized without it. Poverty is a choice that the fortunate collectively make. Even within social justice circles, there is often resignation about poverty, an assumption that there will always be a group of people in this country who cannot meet their basic needs.

The single most important thing that anyone can do to end US poverty is to assert that it is a problem we can solve. Defeatism has expanded poverty and economic inequality. As we stated in the opening of this book, close to 40 percent of US Americans cannot afford to meet their basic needs. Most people would agree that is outrageous. But is 30 percent acceptable; 20 percent; 10 percent? No, there is no tolerable amount of economic suffering in the richest nation in human history. This shame ends when enough of us accept a simple truth:

No American should ever be poor.

Acknowledgments

All of this started with diapers. When Joanne became determined that no child should do without them, it crystallized the way that she thought about poverty. It also connected her to fiercely kind people whose influence echoes on every page. Joanne would particularly like to acknowledge the team at the National Diaper Bank Network, both the board of directors and the staff: Chris Blake, Lynn Comer, Tamara Killian, Mary Madoule, Hope Martin, Troy Moore, Sydney Phillips, Susan Van Ness, Phillip Vander Klay, and Rachel Segaloff. She is grateful to Janet Stolfi Alfano, executive director of the Diaper Bank of Connecticut, an early reader of this manuscript, and an invaluable friend and colleague. More broadly, everyone involved in the diaper banking movement contributed to the thinking and conviction that informs *Broke in America*.

Colleen is grateful to all her first coworkers, who pushed beyond exhaustion for less than minimum wage, including her mother, Mary Collins. These mighty women showed her what poverty is—and why it is. Tommie Shaddox put Colleen on the path that led to Carol Morgan and eventually to Lytle, Texas, an extraordinary place that figures so prominently in this volume. Martha Stone offered sound, passionate advice. Karen Schmidt provided a New York base of operations and much more.

The authors are grateful to our agent, Stacy Testa, who had unwavering belief in us and in this book and advocated for it with a winning combination of intelligence and zeal. The team at BenBella Books were wonderful partners from the start. They understood exactly what we were trying to do and adopted our mission of exposing and ending US poverty as their own. We are especially thankful to our wonderful editor, Claire Schulz. She made this book better, sharper, and more engaging.

We thank everyone who read early drafts of this work, challenged us, and offered suggestions, encouragement, and inspiration: Janet Stolfi Alfano, Jessica Bartholow, Mike Berman, Kathleen DiChiara, Kathy Flaherty, David Goldblum, Jesse Goldblum, Mollie Goldblum, Sherman Goldblum, Theresa Govert, Ellen Luger, Maxine Phillips, Mimi Samuel, Karen Schmidt, Charlie Shaddox, Russell Shaddox, and Megan V. Smith. They all improved *Broke in America*. Errors, of course, are our own. We are delighted and so grateful that Bomani Jones turned his fine hand to the foreword.

We thank our families endlessly, the ones who read drafts and the ones who patiently endured for the years we spent talking about what we had learned, much of which was hard to hear.

Most of all, we thank the people in these pages for letting us into their lives. Sources shared their pain and their resilience with us. It was an honor to record so much honesty and bravery. We can never repay their generosity.

Notes

Introduction

1. US Bureau of Labor Statistics, "Employees on Nonfarm Payrolls by Industry Sector and Selected Industry Detail," modified May 11, 2020, www.bls.gov/news.release/empsit.t17.htm.
2. Cameron Huddelston, "Survey: 69% of Americans Have Less Than $1,000 in Savings," GOBankingRates, December 16, 2019, www.gobankingrates.com/saving-money/savings-advice/americans-have-less-than-1000-in-savings.

Chapter 1

1. Stephen Pimpare, "The Poverty of American Film," *OUPblog*, February 25, 2017, blog.oup.com/2017/02/poverty-homeless-representation-american-film/.
2. Pimpare, "Poverty of American Film."
3. Bas W. van Doorn, "Pre- and Post-welfare Reform Media Portrayals of Poverty in the United States: The Continuing Importance of Race and Ethnicity," *Politics & Policy* 43, no. 1 (February 15, 2015): 142–62, doi.org/10.1111/polp.12107.
4. Kathryn Cronquist, "Characteristics of Supplemental Nutritional Assistance Households: Fiscal Year 2018," US Department of Agriculture, November 2019, fns-prod.azureedge.net/sites/default/files/resource-files/Characteristics2018.pdf.
5. Kaiser Family Foundation, "Distribution of the Nonelderly with Medicaid by Race/Ethnicity," accessed April 20, 2020, kff.org/medicaid/state-indicator/distribution-by-raceethnicity-4/.
6. Center for Medicaid and Medicare Services, "December 2019 Medicaid and CHIP Enrollment Highlights," accessed April 20, 2020, medicaid.gov/medicaid/program-information/medicaid-and-chip-enrollment-data/report-highlights/index.html.
7. Office of Family Assistance, "TANF: Total Number of Recipients Fiscal Year 2019," accessed April 20, 2020, www.acf.hhs.gov/sites/default/files/ofa/tanf_recipients_fy19.pdf.
8. Gordon M. Fisher, "The Development and History of Poverty Thresholds," *Social Security Bulletin* 55, no. 4 (1992), ssa.gov/history/fisheronpoverty.html.
9. Chris Salviati, "Apartment List National Rent Report," Rentonomics, March 31, 2020, apartmentlist.com/rentonomics/national-rent-data/.
10. Diana M. Pearce, "The Self-Sufficiency Standard for Connecticut 2019," Center for Women's Welfare, October 2019.

263

11. Michael Karpman, Stephen Zuckerman, and Dulce Gonzalez, "Material Hardship Among Non-elderly Adults and Their Families 2017: Implications for the Social Safety Net," The Urban Institute, August 2018, urban.org/research/publication/material-hardship-among -nonelderly-adults-and-their-families-2017.

12. Cameron Huddleston, "Survey: 69% of Americans Have Less Than $1000 in Savings," GoBankingRates.com, December 16, 2019, www.gobankingrates.com/saving-money/savings -advice/americans-have-less-than-1000-in-savings/#A.

13. Lawrence Mishel and Julia Wolfe, "CEO Compensation Has Grown 940% Since 1978," Economic Policy Institute, August 14, 2019, www.epi.org/publication/ceo-compensation-2018/.

14. Mishel and Wolfe, "CEO Compensation Has Grown 940% Since 1978."

15. Francesca Ortegren, "How US Health Policy Changes Have Affected Health Care Costs over Time," Clever, September 23, 2019, listwithclever.com/real-estate-blog/healthcare-costs -over-time/.

16. Bureau of Labor Statistics, "Contingent and Alternative Employment Arrangements," June 7, 2018, www.bls.gov/news.release/conemp.nr0.htm.

17. "Latest Massacre Drives Gun Control Support to New High, Quinnipiac University National Poll Finds; Voters Reject GOP Tax Plan 2-1," Quinnipiac University, November 15, 2017, poll.qu.edu/national/release-detail?ReleaseID=2501.

18. Tax Policy Center, "Briefing Book: Key Elements of the US Tax System," accessed April 23, 2020, www.taxpolicycenter.org/briefing-book/how-many-people-pay-estate-tax.

Chapter 2

1. Elizabeth A. Mack and Sarah Wrase, "A Burgeoning Crisis? A Nationwide Assessment of the Geography of Water Affordability in the United States," *PLOS One* 12, no. 1 (November 2017), doi.org/10.1371/journal.pone.0169488.

2. Environmental Protection Agency, "Drinking Water and Wastewater Utility Customer Assistance Programs," April 2016, www.epa.gov/sites/production/files/2016-04/documents/dw -ww_utilities_cap_combined_508-front2.pdf.

3. Erik Olson and Kristi Pullen Fedinick, "What's in Your Water? Flint and Beyond: Analysis of EPA Data Reveals Widespread Lead Crisis Potentially Affecting Millions of Americans," NRDC, June 2016, www.nrdc.org/sites/default/files/whats-in-your-water-flint-beyond-report .pdf.

4. Joel Kurth, "Contract for Detroit Water Shutoffs Doubles in One Year," *Detroit News*, October 13, 2013, www.detroitnews.com/story/news/local/detroit-city/2016/10/13/contract-detroit -water-shutoffs-doubles-one-year/92031538.

5. Center on Budget and Policy Priorities, "Capital Spending Had Fallen in the Vast Majority of States," accessed April 24, 2020, www.cbpp.org/capital-spending-has-fallen-in-the-vast -majority-of-states.

6. Office of the High Commissioner, United Nations Human Rights, "Detroit: Disconnecting Water from People Who Cannot Pay—an Affront to Human Rights, Say UN Experts," June 25, 2014, www.ohchr.org/EN/NewsEvents/Pages/DisplayNews.aspx?NewsID=14777.

7. Johns Hopkins Center for American Indian Health, "Water Quality Study (2010–2011)," accessed November 25, 2019, caih.jhu.edu/programs/water-and-air-quality/.

8. United States Census Bureau, "Plumbing Facilities for All Housing Units (Table B25047)," accessed June 17, 2020, data.census.gov/cedsci/table?q=indoor%20plumbing&hidePreview =false&table=B25047&tid=ACSDT1Y2017.B25047&lastDisplayedRow=14.

9. Alaska Native Tribal Health Consortium, "Portable Alternative Sanitation System: Kivalina Alaska. Final Report," accessed April 24, 2020, anthc.org/wp-content/uploads/2016/01 /Kivalina-Report-E-Version.pdf.

10. Alaska Native Tribal Health Consortium, "Portable Alternative Sanitation System: Kivalina Alaska. Final Report."

11. Personal communication with Mayor Elvadus Fields.

12. Pew Charitable Trusts. "Cutting Lead Poisoning and Public Costs," accessed April 24, 2020, www.pewtrusts.org/~/media/assets/2010/02/22/063_10_paes-costs-of-lead-poisoning-brief _web.pdf

13. World Health Organization, "Water, Health and Ecosystems," accessed April 24, 2020, www.who.int/heli/risks/water/water/en/.

14. Allie Gross, "Experts See Public Health Crisis in Detroit Water Shut-Offs," *Detroit Free Press*, July 26, 2017.

15. MDC, "The Metropolitan District Water Supply Facts," accessed April 24, 2020, themdc.org /assets/uploads/files/press%20releases/2016/WATER%20SUPPLY%20FACTS%202 _16_16(2).pdf.

16. Kate Aronoff, "Atlantic City Could Be the Next Flint—but Residents Are Fighting to Save Their Water," *In These Times*, June 12, 2017, inthesetimes.com/article/20209/privateers-on -the-jersey-shore-atlantic-city-water-chris-christie-naacp

17. Public Policy Institute of California, "Water for Farms," October 2016, www.ppic.org/content /pubs/report/R_1016EH4R.pdf.

18. Corey Williams, "The Demographics of Detroit Are Changing Rapidly," *Business Insider*, May 21, 2015, www.businessinsider.com/the-demographics-of-detroit-are-changing-rapidly -2015-5.

19. Live Midtown, "Incentives" (since deleted, accessed via web.archive.org), web.archive.org /web/20171222072152/www.livemidtown.org/incentives.

Chapter 3

1. US Congress, "Richard B. Russell National School Lunch Act (1 U.S.C. 112, 204) 79th Congress, June 4, 1946," accessed April 27, 2020, fns-prod.azureedge.net/sites/default/files /resource-files/COMPS-10333.pdf.

2. John Crawley and Johanna Catherine Maclean, "Unfit for Service: The Implications of Rising Obesity for U.S. Military Recruitment," National Bureau of Economic Research Working Papers, September 2010, www.nber.org/papers/w16408.pdf.

3. "Social Welfare Under Reagan," CQ Researcher, March 9, 1984, library.cqpress.com/cq researcher/document.php?id=cqresrre1984030900.

4. Christopher M. Bacon and Gregory A. Baker, "The Rise of Food Banks and the Challenge of Matching Food Assistance with Potential Need: Towards a Spatially Specific, Rapid Assessment Approach," *Agriculture and Human Values* 34 (April 10, 2017): 899–919, doi.org/10.1007 /s10460-017-9783-y.

5. World Bank, "Prevalence of Underweight Children for Age," accessed July 28, 2020, data .worldbank.org/indicator/SH.STA.MALN.ZS?most_recent_value_desc=false.

6. Heather C. Hamner, Cria G. Perrine, and Kelley S. Scanlon, "Usual Intake of Key Minerals Among Children in the Second Year of Life, NHANES 2003–2012," *Nutrients* 8, no. 8 (July 30, 2016): 468, doi.org/10.3390/nu8080468.

7. Anne Skalicky, Alan F. Meyers, William G. Adams, Zhaoyan Yang, John T. Cook, and Deborah A. Frank, "Child Food Insecurity and Iron Deficiency Anemia in Low-Income Infants and Toddlers in the United States," *Maternal and Child Health Journal* 10, no. 2 (November 19, 2005): 177–85, doi.org/10.1007/s10995-005-0036-0.

8. Betsy Lozoff, Julia B. Smith, Niko Kaciroti, Katy M. Clark, Sylvia Guevara, Elias Jimenez, "Functional Significance of Early Life Iron Deficiency: Outcomes at 25 Years," *Journal of Pediatrics* 165, no. 5 (November 2013): 1260–1266, doi.org/10.1016/j.jpeds.2013.05.015.

9. Janice Ke and Elizabeth Lee Ford-Jones, "Food Insecurity and Hunger: A Review of the Effects on Children's Health and Behaviour," *Paediatrics & Child Health* 20, no. 2 (March 2015): 89–91, doi.org/10.1093/pch/20.2.89.

10. Rachie Weisberg, "The Role of a Trauma-Informed Model in Addressing Food Insecurity," Drexel University Center for Hunger-Free Communities, September 5, 2018, www.center forhungerfreecommunities.org/our-projects/building-wealth-and-health-network/blog/role -trauma-informed-model-addressing-food.

11. Maryah Stella Fram, Edward A. Frongillo, Sonya J. Jones, Roger C. Williams, Michael P. Burke, Kendra P. DeLoach, and Christine E. Blake, "Children Are Aware of Food Insecurity and Take Responsibility for Managing Food Resources," *Journal of Nutrition* 141, no. 6 (June 2011): 1114–19, doi.org/10.3945/jn.110.135988.

12. Fram et al., "Children Are Aware of Food Insecurity and Take Responsibility for Managing Food Resources."

13. Grace Rasmusson, Janet A. Lydecker, Jaime A. Coffino, Marney A. White, and Carlos M. Grilo, "Household Food Insecurity Is Associated with Binge-Eating Disorder and Obesity," *International Journal of Eating Disorders* 52, no. 1 (January 2019): 28–35, doi.org/10.1002 /eat.22990.

14. Congress of the United States Congressional Budget Office, "Options to Reduce the Budgetary Costs of the Federal Crop Insurance Program," December 22, 2017, www.cbo.gov /system/files/115th-congress-2017-2018/reports/53375-federalcropinsuranceprogram.pdf.

15. Ed Yong "Corn Is Everywhere in American Fast Food," *National Geographic,* November 1, 2008, www.nationalgeographic.com/science/phenomena/2008/11/11/corn-is-everywhere-in -american-fast-food/.

16. USDA Economic Research Service, "Food Dollar Table, 2018," updated March 23, 2020, data.ers.usda.gov/reports.aspx?ID=17885.

17. David Eddy, "Mechanization Matters in Vegetable Production," Growing Produce, June 1, 2007, www.growingproduce.com/vegetables/mechanization-matters-in-vegetable -production/.

18. USDA Economic Research Service, "Loss-Adjusted Food Availability Documentation," updated January 9, 2020, www.ers.usda.gov/data-products/food-availability-per-capita-data-system /loss-adjusted-food-availability-documentation/.

19. Food Research & Action Center, "Research Brief, Breakfast for Learning," October 2016, frac.org/wp-content/uploads/breakfastforlearning-1.pdf.

20. Eddie Yoon, "The Grocery Industry Confronts A New Problem: Only 10% of Americans Love Cooking," *Harvard Business Review*, September 22, 2017, hbr.org/2017/09/the-grocery-industry-confronts-a-new-problem-only-10-of-americans-love-cooking.

21. Heather Hartline-Grafton and James Weill, "Replacing the Thrifty Food Plan in Order to Provide Adequate Allotments for SNAP Beneficiaries," Food Research & Action Center, December 2012, frac.org/wp-content/uploads/thrifty_food_plan_2012.pdf.

22. George C. Davis and Wen You, "The Thrifty Food Plan Is Not Thrifty When Labor Cost Is Considered," *Journal of Nutrition* 140, no. 4 (February 24 2010): 854–57, doi.org/10.3945/jn.109.119594.

23. Hartline-Grafton and Weill, "Replacing the Thrifty Food Plan in Order to Provide Adequate Allotments for SNAP Beneficiaries," 3.

24. Los Angeles Community Action Network, "The Paradox of Food in Skid Row: 2017 Community Food Assessment," January 9, 2018.

25. Los Angeles Community Action Network, "Paradox of Food in Skid Row."

Chapter 4

1. Jay Shambaugh, Ryan Nunn, Patrick Liu, and Gren Nantz, "Thirteen Facts About Wage Growth," Brookings Institute, September 25, 2017, www.brookings.edu/research/thirteen-facts-about-wage-growth/.

2. Patrick Bayer, Fernando Ferreira, and Stephen L. Ross, "What Drives Racial and Ethnic Differences in High-Cost Mortgages? The Role of High-Risk Lenders," *Review of Financial Studies* 31, no. 1 (January 2018): 175–205, doi.org/10.1093/rfs/hhx035.

3. Margery Austin Turner, Rob Santos, Diane K. Levy, Doug Wissoker, Claudia Aranda, and Rob Pitingolo, "Housing Discrimination Against Racial and Ethnic Minorities 2012," US Department of Housing and Urban Development, June 2013, www.huduser.gov/portal//Publications/pdf/HUD-514_HDS2012.pdf.

4. Institute of Medicine (US) Committee on Health Care for Homeless People, "Health Problems of Homeless People," in *Homelessness, Health, and Human Needs* (Washington, DC: National Academies Press, 1988), accessed April 28, 2020, www.ncbi.nlm.nih.gov/books/NBK218236.

5. Substance Abuse and Mental Health Services Administration, "Current Statistics on the Prevalence and Characteristics of People Experiencing Homelessness in the United States," updated July 2011, www.samhsa.gov/sites/default/files/programs_campaigns/homelessness_programs_resources/hrc-factsheet-current-statistics-prevalence-characteristics-homelessness.pdf.

6. Western Regional Advocacy Project, "Without Housing: Decades of Federal Housing Cutbacks, Massive Homelessness, and Policy Failures," 2010, wraphome.org/what/without-housing/.

7. Ben Casselman, "The Tax Deductions Economists Hate," FiveThirtyEight, April 3, 2015, fivethirtyeight.com/features/the-tax-deductions-economists-hate/.

8. Jim Tankersley and Ben Casselman, "As Mortgage Interest Deduction Vanishes, Housing Market Offers a Shrug," *New York Times*, August 4, 2019, www.nytimes.com/2019/08/04/business/economy/mortgage-interest-deduction-tax.html.

9. Matthew Desmond, "How Homeownership Became the Engine of American Inequality," *New York Times Magazine*, May 9, 2017, www.nytimes.com/2017/05/09/magazine/how-homeownership-became-the-engine-of-american-inequality.html.

10. White House, "Housing Development Toolkit," September 2016, www.whitehouse.gov/sites/whitehouse.gov/files/images/Housing_Development_Toolkit%20f.2.pdf.

11. Connecticut Fair Housing Center and State of Connecticut Department of Housing, "Analysis of Impediments to Fair Housing Choice 2015," 2015, portal.ct.gov/-/media/DOH/AnalysisofImpediments2015pdf.

12. SCOTUS, "City of Boise v. Robert Martin, et al.," December 16, 2019, www.supremecourt.gov/docket/docketfiles/html/public/19-247.html; Benjamin Oreskes, "Homeless People Could Lose the Right to Sleep on Sidewalks if Western Cities Have Their Way," *Los Angeles Times*, September 25, 2019, www.latimes.com/california/story/2019-09-25/boise-homeless-encampment-amicus-brief-supreme-court-appeal-cities.

13. Berkeley Law, University of California, "California's New Vagrancy Laws: The Growing Enactment and Enforcement of Anti-homeless Laws in the Golden State," June 2016, www.law.berkeley.edu/wp-content/uploads/2015/12/Californias-New-Vagrancy-Laws.pdf.

14. Priyanka Dayal McCluskey, "Boston Medical Center Has a New Prescription for Its Most Vulnerable Patients: Housing," *Boston Globe*, December 7, 2017, www3.bostonglobe.com/business/2017/12/07/boston-medical-center-launches-million-initiative-help-house-patients/LypiRr0F4ZxCBdDMTx7CvJ/story.html.

15. Nancy Gonzales, Ana Mari Cauce, Ruth J. Friedman, and Craig A. Mason, "Family, Peer, and Neighborhood Influences on Academic Achievement Among African-American Adolescents: One Year Prospective Effects," *American Journal of Community Psychology* 24, no. 3 (1996): 365–87.

16. Yasser Arafat Payne, "The People's Report: The Link Between Structural Violence and Crime in Wilmington, Delaware," People's Report, September 16, 2013, www.thepeoplesreport.com/images/pdf/The_Peoples_Report_final_draft_9-12-13.pdf.

17. Women's Task Force of the District of Columbia Interagency Council on Homelessness, "2017 DC Women's Needs Assessment Report," January 26, 2018, www.calvaryservices.org/wp-content/uploads/2018/01/2017dcwnafullreport.pdf.

18. Downtown Women's Action Coalition, "2016 Downtown Women's Needs Assessment," October 24, 2016, www.downtownwomenscenter.org/2016-needs-assessment/.

19. HUD Exchange, "Point in Time Count of Homeless Persons: Engaging with Domestic Violence Survivors; What CoCs Need to Know," accessed April 28, 2020, files.hudexchange.info/resources/documents/PIT-and-DV-What-CoCs-Need-To-Know.pdf.

20. Andrew Aurand, Dan Emmanuel, Daniel Threet, Ikra Rafi, and Diane Yentel, "The Gap: A Shortage of Affordable Homes," National Low Income Housing Coalition, March 2020, reports.nlihc.org/sites/default/files/gap/Gap-Report_2020.pdf.

21. Chad Aldeman, "NOLA, Hurricane Katrina and Teacher's Pensions," Teacher's Pension Blog, August 24, 2015, www.teacherpensions.org/blog/nola-hurricane-katrina-and-teacher-pensions.

22. Naomi Klein, *The Shock Doctrine: The Rise of Disaster Capitalism* (New York: Knopf, 2007), 3–8.

23. Gary Rivlin, "Why New Orleans's Black Residents Are Still Underwater After Katrina," *New York Times Magazine*, August 18, 2015, www.nytimes.com/2015/08/23/magazine/why-new-orleans-black-residents-are-still-under-water-after-katrina.html.

24. Furman Center for Real Estate & Urban Policy, New York University, "Searching for the Right Spot: Minimum Parking Requirements and Housing Affordability in New York City," Institute for Affordable Housing Policy, March 2012, furmancenter.org/files/publications /furman_parking_requirements_policy_brief_3_21_12_final.pdf.

Chapter 5

1. Tony G. Reams, "Improving the Effectiveness of Federal Energy Assistance for Low-Income Households," Scholars Strategy Network, January 1, 2017, scholars.org/contribution /improving-effectiveness-federal-energy-assistance-low-income-households.

2. Ahmad F. Alkhuzam, Jean Arlet, and Silvia Lopez Rocha, "Private Versus Public Electricity Distribution Utilities: Are Outcomes Different for End-Users?" World Bank Blogs, May 3, 2018, blogs.worldbank.org/developmenttalk/private-versus-public-electricity-distribution -utilities-are-outcomes-different-end-users.

3. Clayton Coleman and Emma Dietz, "Fact Sheet: Fossil Fuel Subsidies: A Closer Look at Tax Breaks and Societal Costs," Environmental and Energy Study Institute, July 29, 2019, www.eesi .org/papers/view/fact-sheet-fossil-fuel-subsidies-a-closer-look-at-tax-breaks-and-societal-costs.

4. Ariel Drebhol and Lauren Ross, "Lifting the High Energy Burden in America's Largest Cities: How Energy Efficiency Can Improve Low Income and Underserved Communities," American Council for an Energy-Efficient Economy, April 20, 2016, www.aceee.org/research -report/u1602.

5. Eugene M. Trisko, "Energy Cost Impacts on Mississippi Families, 2015," American Coalition for Clean Coal Electricity, January 2016, www.americaspower.org/wp-content/uploads /2016/02/MS-Energy-Cost-Analysis-116R.pdf.

6. Marcus Franklin, Caroline Kurtz, Mike Alksnis, Lorah Steichen, and Chiquita Younger, "Lights Out in the Cold: Reforming Utility Shut-Off Policies as If Human Rights Matter," NAACP, March 2017, www.naacp.org/wp-content/uploads/2017/12/Lights-Out-in-the-Cold _NAACP.pdf.

7. Diana Hernández, "Understanding 'Energy Insecurity' and Why It Matters to Health," *Social Science & Medicine* 167 (October 2016): 1–10. doi.org/10.1016/j.socscimed.2016.08.029.

8. Libby Perl, "LIHEAP: Program and Funding," Congressional Research Office, June 22, 2018, fas.org/sgp/crs/misc/RL31865.pdf.

9. Unsent letter, June 24, 2018. Obtained and published by Itai Vardi, DeSmog, accessed April 29, 2020, www.desmogblog.com/2019/03/11/rhode-island-governor-raimondo-silenced -critique-national-grid-lng-health-justice.

10. Food and Water Watch, "Pernicious Placement of Pennsylvania Power Plants: National Gas-Fired Power Plant Boom Reinforces Environmental Injustice," June 20, 2018, www.foodand waterwatch.org/sites/default/files/rpt_1806_pagasplants_web3.pdf.

Chapter 6

1. Congressional Research Service, "Funding and Financing Highways and Public Transportation," updated June 7, 2019, fas.org/sgp/crs/misc/R45350.pdf.

2. Richard Ezike, "Transportation, Sustainability, and Equity, and the Effect on the African-American Community," Congressional Black Caucus Foundation, 2016, www.cbcfinc.org /wp-content/uploads/2016/10/CBCFTransportationBriefing.pdf.

3. Shira Offer, "Barriers to Social Support Among Low-Income Mothers," *International Journal of Sociology and Social Policy* 32, nos. 3–4 (April 20, 2012): 120–33, doi.org/10 .1108/01443331211214712.

4. New York Times Editorial Board, "M.T.A. Delays: How Did the Subway Get So Bad?" *New York Times*, February 20, 2018.

5. Arlene Weintraub, "An Unhealthy Commute: The Transit Challenges Facing New York's Health Care Sector," Center for an Urban Future, January 2018, 14, nycfuture.org/pdf/CUF _An_Unhealthy_Commute.pdf.

6. Arlene Weintraub, "Unhealthy Commute," 13.

7. US Department of Transportation, "Status of the Nation's Highways, Bridges, and Transit: Conditions and Performance," 23rd ed., November 21, 2019, www.fhwa.dot.gov/policy /23cpr/pdfs/23cpr.pdf.

8. Hugh M. Clark, "Who Rides Public Transportation," American Public Transportation Association, January 2017, www.apta.com/wp-content/uploads/Resources/resources/reportsand publications/Documents/APTA-Who-Rides-Public-Transportation-2017.pdf.

9. Hugh M. Clark, "Who Rides Public Transportation."

10. Amanda Hess, "Race, Class and the Stigma of Riding the Bus in America," CityLab, July 10, 2012, www.citylab.com/solutions/2012/07/race-class-and-stigma-riding-bus-america/2510/.

11. Examples are from "Transportation Toolkit for the Business Community" created with funding from the Office of Disability Employment Policy, U.S. Department of Labor, through a cooperative agreement between the Community Transportation Association of America and the Federal Transit Administration, January 2012.

12. Vincent Barone, "MTA Board Approves Hiring 500 New Police Officers Amid Controversy," amNewYork, December 2019, www.amny.com/news/mta-board-approves-hiring-500 -new-police-officers-amid-controversy/.

13. Alexandria Ocasio-Cortez, Jose E. Serrano, Jerrold Nadler, Michael Gianaris, Luis R. Sepulveda, Jessica Ramos, Julia Salazar, and Alessandra Biaggi, "Letter to Andrew Cuomo," December 17, 2019, twitter.com/RepAOC/status/1206993080156602371/photo/1.

14. Angie Schmitt, "Why Cities Are Starting to Decriminalize Fare Evasion," Streetsblog USA, March 8, 2017, usa.streetsblog.org/2017/03/08/why-cities-are-starting-to-decriminalize-fare -evasion/.

15. Andy Mannix, "Internal Review Shows Major Racial Disparities in Metro Transit Arrest and Citation Rates," MinnPost, December 17, 2015, www.minnpost.com/politics-policy/2015/12 /internal-review-shows-major-racial-disparities-metro-transit-arrest-and-cita/.

16. Anna Flagg and Ashley Nerbovig, "New York City Still Has a Race Problem," The Marshall Project, September 12, 2018, www.themarshallproject.org/2018/09/12/subway-policing -in-new-york-city-still-has-a-race-problem; Heidi Groover, "Black Passengers Cited, Punished Disproportionately by Sound Transit Fare Enforcement," *Seattle Times*, October 4, 2019, www.seattletimes.com/seattle-news/transportation/faced-with-racial-disparities-sound -transit-debates-changes-to-fare-enforcement/.

17. Good News Garage, "Impact," accessed May 5, 2020, www.goodnewsgarage.org/Impact.

18. Kenneth Shilson, "Buy Here–Pay Here: 2016 Industry Benchmarks," in *2017 Used Car Industry Report* (National Independent Automobile Dealers Association, June 2017), www.niada .com/uploads/dynamic_areas/5Nd7sQuZuYjQ5FCDUBXL/34/UCIR__RUNNING.pdf.

19. Kenneth Shilson, "Buy Here–Pay Here."

20. Office of Court Administration, "Annual Statistical Report for the Texas Judiciary: FY 2015," 2015, www.txcourts.gov/media/1308021/2015-ar-statistical-print.pdf.

21. Lisa Greenberg, "Special Report: Fake Insurance Cards on Rise," Fox 4, November 14, 2016, www.fox4now.com/news/special-report-fake-insurance-cards-on-the-rise.

Chapter 7

1. Huggies, "Diaper Need and Its Impact on US Families," 2017.

2. Shannon Vavra and Steve LeVine, "The Working Homeless Isn't Just a Tech Bubble Problem," Axios, December 13, 2017, www.axios.com/working-and-homeless-in-the-u -1513093474-7e6f7be3-ddb5-486b-9a1a-f8be0d4c088c.html.

3. Centers for Disease Control and Prevention, "Interim Guidance on Unsheltered Homelessness and Coronavirus Disease 2019 (COVID-19) for Homeless Service Providers and Local Officials," updated May 10, 2020, www.cdc.gov/coronavirus/2019-ncov/community /homeless-shelters/unsheltered-homelessness.html.

4. Lexis-Olivier Ray, "LA installed hundreds of hand-washing stations at homeless camps. Some are drying up," Curbed, Los Angeles, April 1, 2020, la.curbed.com/2020/4/1/21203396 /homeless-coronavirus-los-angeles-handwashing-stations.

5. Huggies, "Diaper Need and Its Impact on US Families."

6. Fred Carstensen and Peter Gunther, "Better Health for Children and Increased Opportunities for Families: The Social and Economic Impacts of the Diaper Bank of Connecticut," The Connecticut Center for Economic Analysis, 2018, nationaldiaperbanknetwork.org /wp-content/uploads/2019/02/The-Social-and-Economic-Impacts-of-the-DIaper-Bank-of -Connecticut.pdf.

7. Internal communication, June 25, 2019.

Chapter 8

1. Elizabeth H. Bradley and Lauren, A. Taylor, *The American Health Care Paradox: Why Spending More Is Getting Us Less* (New York: Public Affairs, 2013), 14.

2. Office of the New York State Comptroller, "An Economic Snapshot of East Harlem," December 2017, www.osc.state.ny.us/osdc/rpt9-2018.pdf.

3. New York City Department of Health and Mental Hygiene, "Summary of Vital Statistics 2015, The City of New York," August 2017, www1.nyc.gov/assets/doh/downloads/pdf /vs/2015sum.pdf.

4. K. Hinterland, M. Naidoo, L. King, G. Myerson, B. Noumbissi, M. Woodward, L. H. Gould, R. C. Gwynn, O. Barbot, and M. T. Bassett, "Community Health Profiles 2018, Manhattan Community District 11: East Harlem," New York City Department of Health and Mental Hygiene, 2018, www1.nyc.gov/assets/doh/downloads/pdf/data/2018chp-mn11.pdf.

5. K. Hinterland et al., "Community Health Profiles 2018, Manhattan Community District 11: East Harlem."

6. L. King, K. Hinterland, C. R. Driver, T. G. Harris, N. Linos, O. Barbot, and M. T. Bassett, "Community Health Profiles 2015, Manhattan Community District 11: East Harlem," New York City Department of Health and Mental Hygiene, 2015, www1.nyc.gov/assets/doh /downloads/pdf/vs/2015sum.pdf.

7. Christopher Wildeman, "Incarceration and Population Health in Wealthy Democracies," *Criminology* 54, no. 2 (May 2016): 360–82, doi.org/10.1111/1745-9125.12107.

8. Mariel A. Marlow, Ruth E. Luna-Gierke, Patricia M. Griffin, and Antonio R. Vieira, "Foodborne Disease Outbreaks in Correctional Institutions—United States, 1998–2014," *American Journal of Public Health* 107, no. 7 (June 7, 2017): 1150–56, doi.org/10.2105/ajph.2017.303816.

9. Margaret Noonan, Harley Rohloff, and Scott Ginder, "Mortality in Local Jails and State Prisons, 2000–2013—Statistical Tables," U.S. Department of Justice, Office of Justice Programs, Bureau of Justice Statistics, August 2015, www.bjs.gov/content/pub/pdf/mljsp0013st .pdf.

10. Centers for Disease Control and Prevention, "Infant Mortality," reviewed March 27, 2019, www.cdc.gov/reproductivehealth/maternalinfanthealth/infantmortality.htm; Centers for Disease Control and Prevention, "Pregnancy Mortality Surveillance System," reviewed February 4, 2019, www.cdc.gov/reproductivehealth/maternal-mortality/pregnancy-mortality -surveillance-system.htm.

11. Integrated Financial Engineering, Inc., "Actuarial Review of the Federal Housing Administration Mutual Mortgage Insurance Fund, HECM loans for Fiscal Year 2016," US Department of Housing and Urban Development, November 15, 2016, www.hud.gov/sites /documents/ACTUARIALMMIFHECM2016.PDF.

12. Danya E. Keene, Julia F. Lynch, and Amy Castro Baker, "Fragile Health and Fragile Wealth: Mortgage Strain on African American Homeowners," *Social Science & Medicine* 118 (October 2014): 119–26, doi.org/10.1016/j.socscimed.2014.07.063.

13. "Where Are the Best Social Benefits in Europe? New Report from Glassdoor Economic Research," Glassdoor, February 17, 2016, www.glassdoor.com/research/studies/europe -fairest-paid-leave-unemployment-benefits/.

14. Elise Gould and Jessica Schieder, "Work Sick or Lose Pay? The High Cost of Getting Sick When You Don't Get Sick Days," Economic Policy Institute, June 28, 2017, www.epi.org/publication /work-sick-or-lose-pay-the-high-cost-of-being-sick-when-you-dont-get-paid-sick-days/.

15. Lisa C. Richardson, S. Jane Henley, Jacqueline W. Miller, Greta Massetti, and Cheryll C. Thomas, "Patterns and Trends in Age-Specific Black-White Differences in Breast Cancer Incidence and Mortality—United States, 1999–2014," *Morbidity and Mortality Weekly Report* 65, no. 40 (October 14, 2016): 1093–98, doi.org/10.15585/mmwr.mm6540a1.

16. Citizens' Committee for Children New York, "Community Risk Ranking: Child Well-Being in New York City's 59 Community Districts," December 2018, www.cccnewyork.org/wp -content/uploads/2018/12/CCC-Community-Risk-Ranking-December2018.pdf.

Chapter 9

1. Jesse Bricker, Lisa J. Dettling, Alice Henriques, Joanne W. Hsu, Lindsay Jacobs, Kevin B. Moore, Sarah Pack, John Sabelhaus, Jeffrey Thompson, and Richard A. Windle, "Changes in U.S. Family Finances from 2013 to 2016: Evidence from the Survey of Consumer

Finances," *Federal Reserve Bulletin* 103, no. 3 (September 2017), www.federalreserve.gov /publications/2017-September-changes-in-us-family-finances-from-2013-to-2016.htm.

2. Angela Hanks, Danyelle Solomon, and Christian E. Weller, "Systematic Inequality: How America's Structural Racism Helped Create the Black-White Wealth Gap," Center for American Progress, February 21, 2018, www.americanprogress.org/issues/race /reports/2018/02/21/447051/systematic-inequality/.

3. Signe-Mary McKernan, Caroline Ratcliffe, Eugene Steuerle, and Sisi Zhang, "Impact of the Great Recession and Beyond: Disparities in Wealth Building by Generation and Race," The Urban Institute, April 2014, www.urban.org/sites/default/files/publication/22551/413102 -impact-of-the-great-recession-and-beyond.pdf.

4. Signe-Mary McKernan, Caroline Ratcliff, C. Eugene Steuerle, Caleb Quakenbush, Emma Kalish, and Serena Lei, "9 Charts About Wealth Inequality," The Urban Institute, updated October 5, 2017, apps.urban.org/features/wealth-inequality-charts/.

5. Jason N. Houle and Michael T. Light, "The Home Foreclosure Crisis and Rising Suicide Rates, 2005 to 2010," *American Journal of Public Health* 104, no. 6 (June 2014): 1073–79, doi. org/10.2105/AJPH.2013.301774.

6. Richard Edwards, "African Americans and the Southern Homestead Act," *Great Plains Quarterly* 39, no. 2 (Spring 2019): 103-29, muse.jhu.edu/article/723271.

7. Federal Housing Administration, *Underwriting Manual* (1936), excerpts, accessed May 6, 2020, https://ontheline.trincoll.edu/images/1936-fha-manual-226.pdf

8. Robert Kuttner, "The Wealth Problem," *American Prospect*, April 30, 2015, prospect.org /economy/wealth-problem/.

9. In the Matter of Arbitration of Bernadette Martinez v. Ditech Inc. Successor, Case number 2013-0120, June 2018, Jackson, Mississippi.

10. Michael Sherraden, "Individual Development Accounts: Summary of Research," Washington University Center for Social Development, September 2002, doi.org/10.7936 /K7M61JRR.

11. Deborah Adams, Ray Boshara, Margaret Clancy, Reid Cramer, Bob Friedman, Rochelle Howard, Karol Krotki, Ellen Marks, Lisa Mensah, Bryan Rhodes, Carl Rist, Edward Scanlon, Leigh Tivol, Trina Williams Shanks, and Robert Zager, "Lessons from SEED, a National Demonstration of Child Development Accounts," Federal Deposit Insurance Corporation, September 2010, www.fdic.gov/about/comein/seed.pdf.

12. Darrick Hamilton and William Darity Jr., "Can 'Baby Bonds' Eliminate the Racial Wealth Gap in a Putative Post-racial America?" *Review of Black Political Economy* 37 (October 19, 2010): 207–16, doi.org/10.1007/s12114-010-9063-1.

Chapter 10

1. Amanda Fins, "National Snapshot: Poverty Among Women & Families, 2019," National Women's Law Center, October 23, 2019, nwlc.org/resources/national-snapshot-poverty -among-women-families-2019/.

2. Ariane Hegewisch and Heidi Hartmann, "Occupational Segregation and the Gender Wage Gap: A Job Half Done," Institute for Women's Policy Research, January 2014, iwpr.org /publications/occupational-segregation-and-the-gender-wage-gap-a-job-half-done/.

3. John Schmitt and Janelle Jones, "Slow Progress for Fast-Food Workers," Center for Economic and Policy Research, August 2013, cepr.net/report/slow-progress-for-fast-food-workers-brief/.

4. Pamela Loprest and Nathan Sick, "Career Prospects for Certified Nursing Assistants: Insights for Training Programs and Policymakers from the Health Professions Opportunity Grants (HPOG) Program," US Department of Health and Human Services, August 2018, www.acf.hhs.gov/sites/default/files/opre/final_cna_paper_final_508_compliant_5082.pdf.

5. Department of Health and Human Services, "Characteristics and Financial Circumstances of TANF Recipients, Fiscal Year (FY) 2018," www.acf.hhs.gov/sites/default/files/ofa/fy18_characteristics_web_508_2.pdf.

6. Jacqueline Kauff, "Training TANF Recipients and Low-Income Populations for Long-Term Care Paraprofessional Jobs," Mathematica Policy Research, March 1, 2005, www.mathematica.org/our-publications-and-findings/publications/training-tanf-recipients-and-lowincome-populations-for-longterm-care-paraprofessional-jobs.

7. Kayla Fontenot, Jessica Semega, and Melissa Kollar, "Income and Poverty in the United States: 2017," United States Census Bureau, September 2018, www.census.gov/content/dam/Census/library/publications/2018/demo/p60-263.pdf.

8. Paraprofessional Healthcare Institute, "A Career Development Project That Improved Clinical Outcomes," September 10, 2017, phinational.org/impact_story/career-development-project-improved-clinical-outcomes/.

9. Kauff, "Training TANF Recipients and Low-Income Populations for Long-Term Care Paraprofessional Jobs."

10. Alexandra Kalev, "How You Downsize Is Who You Downsize: Biased Formalization, Accountability, and Managerial Diversity," *American Sociological Review* 79, no. 1 (January 29, 2014): 109–35, doi.org/10.1177/0003122413518553.

11. Hegewisch and Hartmann, "Occupational Segregation and the Gender Wage Gap: A Job Half Done."

Chapter 11

1. Jennifer Haberkorn, "Freshman House Class Brings Less Wealth and Different Economic Perspective to Congress," *Los Angeles Times*, July 2, 2019, latimes.com/politics/la-na-pol-congress-freshmen-networth-wealth-20190702-story.html.

2. Jonathan Eggleston and Robert Munk, "Net Worth of Households: 2016," United States Census, October 2019, www.census.gov/content/dam/Census/library/publications/2019/demo/p70br-166.pdf.

3. Center for Responsive Politics, "Incumbent Advantage," accessed May 13, 2020, opensecrets.org/overview/incumbs.php.

4. Center for Responsive Politics, "Cost of Election," accessed May 13, 2020, opensecrets.org/overview/cost.php.

5. Megan Leonhardt, "Alexandria Ocasio-Cortez, the Youngest Woman Ever Elected to Congress, Is Down to Less Than $7000 in Savings," CNBC, November 16, 2018, www.cnbc.com/2018/11/16/alexandria-ocasio-cortez-has-less-than-7000-dollars-saved.html.

6. Pew Research Center, "An Examination of the 2016 Electorate, Based on Validated Voters," August 9, 2018, people-press.org/2018/08/09/an-examination-of-the-2016-electorate-based-on-validated-voters/.

7. John P. Bueker, "Jury Source Lists: Does Supplementation Really Work?" *Cornell Law Review* 82, 1997; Ted Eades, "Revisiting the Jury System in Texas: A Study of the Jury Pool in Dallas County," *SMU Law Review*, 2001.

8. Ray Rivera, "Racial Comment by Republican Official in Ohio Rekindles Battle over Early Voting," *New York Times*, August 22, 2012, www.nytimes.com/2012/08/23/us/politics/ohio-early-voting-battle-flares-after-racial-comment-by-republican-official.html.

9. Terry Gross, "Republican Voter Suppression Efforts Are Targeting Minorities, Journalist Says," NPR, October 23, 2018, www.npr.org/2018/10/23/659784277/republican-voter-suppression-efforts-are-targeting-minorities-journalist-says.

10. Pew Research Center, "The Politics of Financial Insecurity: A Democratic Tilt, Undercut by Low Participation," January 8, 2015, www.people-press.org/2015/01/08/the-politics-of-financial-insecurity-a-democratic-tilt-undercut-by-low-participation/.

11. Kristen Smith, "Fewer than Half of WIC-Eligible Families Receive WIC Benefits," University of New Hampshire Carsey School of Public Policy, July 20, 2015, doi.org/10.34051/p/2020.267.

12. Kathryn Bailey, Stephanie Ettinger de Cuba, John T. Cook, Elizabeth L. March, Sharon Coleman, and Deborah A. Frank, "Too Many Hurdles: Barriers to Receiving SNAP Put Children's Health at Risk," Children's HealthWatch, March 1, 2011, childrenshealthwatch.org/too-many-hurdles-barriers-to-receiving-snap-put-childrens-health-at-risk/.

13. Arielle Levin Becker, "Still on Hold: A Solution for Long DSS Call-Wait Times," *Connecticut Mirror,* April 21, 2015.

14. Jared Bennett and Ashley Wong, "Millions of Poor Lose Access to Cellphone Service Under Trump Administration Reforms," *USA Today*, November 5, 2019, www.usatoday.com/story/news/investigations/2019/11/05/under-trump-millions-poor-lose-cellphone-service/2482112001/.

15. Free Press, "FCC Lifeline Proposal Is the Latest Battleground in Trump's War on the Poor," November 15, 2019, freepress.net/news/press-releases/fcc-lifeline-proposal-latest-battleground-trumps-war-poor.

16. Amanda Michelle Gomez and Josh Israel, "What 13 States Discovered After Spending Hundreds of Thousands Drug Testing the Poor," ThinkProgress, April 26, 2019, thinkprogress.org/states-cost-drug-screening-testing-tanf-applicants-welfare-2018-results-data-0fe9649fa0f8/.

17. "Inmate Race," Federal Bureau of Prisons, updated March 28, 2020, www.bop.gov/about/statistics/statistics_inmate_race.jsp; U.S. Census Bureau, July 1, 2015.

18. Michelle Alexander, *The New Jim Crow: Mass Incarceration in the Age of Colorblindness* (New York: New Press, 2010).

19. Robert Brame, Michael G. Turner, Raymond Paternoster, and Shawn D. Bushway, "Cumulative Prevalence of Arrest from Ages 8 to 23 in a National Sample," *Pediatrics* 129, no. 1 (January 2012): 21–27, doi.org/10.1542/peds.2010-3710.

20. Gary Sweeten, "Who Will Graduate? Disruption of High School Education by Arrest and Court Involvement," *Justice Quarterly* 23, no. 4 (2006): 462–80, doi.org/10.1080/07418820600985313.

21. Vincent Schiraldi, Bruce Western, and Kendra Bradner, "Community-Based Responses to Justice-Involved Young Adults," *New Thinking in Community Corrections Bulletin*, US Department of Justice, September 2015, www.ncjrs.gov/pdffiles1/nij/248900.pdf.

22. Daniel Romer, "Adolescent Risk Taking, Impulsivity, and Brain Development: Implications for Prevention," *Developmental Psychobiology* 52, no. 3 (April 2010): 263–76.

23. National Juvenile Defender Center, "Defend Children: A Blueprint for Effective Juvenile Defender Services," November 2016, njdc.info/wp-content/uploads/2016/11/Defend-Children-A-Blueprint-for-Effective-Juvenile-Defender-Services.pdf.

24. Press Room, "Poverty, Not the 'Teenage Brain' Account for High Rates of Teen Crime," SAGE, March 5, 2015, us.sagepub.com/en-us/nam/press/poverty-not-the-"teenage-brain"-account-for-high-rates-of-teen-crime.

25. Mishi Faruqee and Abby Anderson, "Walk in Our Shoes: Youth Share Their Ideas for Changing Connecticut's Juvenile Justice System," Youth First/Connecticut Juvenile Justice Alliance, 2016, www.ctjja.org/s/WP_YF_CTJJA_WalkInOurShoes_YouthInput_2016.pdf.

26. Payne, "People's Report," 33.

27. Payne, "People's Report," 34.

28. Lloyd Sederer, "Where Have All the Psychiatrists Gone?" *U.S. News & World Report*, September 15, 2015, www.usnews.com/opinion/blogs/policy-dose/2015/09/15/the-us-needs-more-psychiatrists-to-meet-mental-health-demands.

29. Council of State Governments Justice Center, "Confined and Costly: How Supervision Violations Are Filling Prisons and Burdening Budgets," June 19, 2019, csgjusticecenter.org/publications/confined-costly/.

30. Mack Finkel, "New Data: Low Incomes—but High Fees—for People and Probation," Prison Policy Initiative, April 6, 2019, www.prisonpolicy.org/blog/2019/04/09/probation_income/; Matthew Menendez and Lauren Brooke-Eisen, "The Steep Cost of Criminal Justice Fees and Fines," The Brennan Center, November 21, 2019, www.brennancenter.org/our-work/research-reports/steep-costs-criminal-justice-fees-and-fines.

31. "Suit Says County Violates Constitution by Jailing People Who Are Too Poor to Pay Court-Imposed Debts," American Civil Liberties Union, October 6, 2015, www.aclu.org/news/lawsuit-challenges-benton-countys-modern-day-debtors-prison.

32. Jessica Feierman, "Debtors' Prison for Kids? The High Cost of Fees in the Juvenile Justice System," Juvenile Law Center, 2016, debtorsprison.jlc.org/documents/JLC-Debtors-Prison.pdf, n93.

Chapter 12

1. Substance Abuse and Mental Health Services Administration, "Results from the 2015 National Survey on Drug Use and Health: Detailed Tables," US Department of Health & Human Services, September 8, 2016.

2. Monnica T. Williams, Isha W. Metzger, Chris Leins, and Celenia Delapp, "Assessing Racial Trauma Within a *DSM–5* Framework: The UConn Racial/Ethnic Stress & Trauma Survey," *Practice Innovations* 3, no. 4 (2018): 242–60, doi.org/10.1037/pri0000076.

3. Vincent J. Felitti, Robert F. Anda, Dale Nordenberg, David F. Williamson, Alison M. Spitz, Valerie Edwards, Mary P. Koss, and James S. Marks, "Relationship of Childhood Abuse and Household Dysfunction to Many of the Leading Causes of Death in Adults," *American Journal of Preventive Medicine* 14, no. 4 (May 1, 1998): 245–58.

4. Michelle A. Hughes and Whitney Tucker, "Poverty as an Adverse Childhood Experience," *North Carolina Medical Journal* 79, no. 2 (March 2018): 124–26, doi.org/10.18043/ncm .79.2.124.

5. Nadine Burke Harris, "The Chronic Stress of Poverty: Toxic to Children," *Shriver Report*, January 12, 2014, shriverreport.org/the-chronic-stress-of-poverty-toxic-to-children-nadine -burke-harris/.

6. Megan V. Smith, Anna Kruse, Alison Weir, and Joanne Goldblum, "Diaper Need and Its Impact on Child Health," *Pediatrics* 132, no. 2 (August 2013): 253–59, doi.org/10.1542/peds .2013-0597.

7. Center on the Developing Child, "Maternal Depression Can Undermine the Development of Young Children" (Working Paper 8, Harvard University, December 2009), developing child.harvard.edu/wp-content/uploads/2009/05/Maternal-Depression-Can-Undermine -Development.pdf.

8. Kelley E. C. Massengale, Lynn H. Comer, Anna E. Austin, and Joanne S. Goldblum, "Diaper Need Met Among Low-Income US Children Younger Than 4 Years in 2016," American Journal of Public Health 110, no. 1 (January 1, 2020): 106–8, doi.org/10.2105 /AJPH.2019.305377.

9. Joseph L. Dieleman, Ranju Baral, and Maxwell Birger, "U.S. Spending on Personal Health Care and Public Health, 1996–2013," *JAMA* 316, no. 24 (December 27, 2016): 2627–46, doi .org/10.1001/jama.2016.16885.

10. Catherine DeCarlo Santiago, Stacey Kaltman, and Jeanne Miranda, "Poverty and Mental Health: How Do Low-Income Adults and Children Fare in Psychotherapy?" *Journal of Clinical Psychology* 69, no. 2 (December 20, 2012): 115–26, doi.org/10.1002/jclp.21951.

11. Mary DeYoung, *Madness: An American History of Mental Illness and Its Treatment* (Jefferson, NC: McFarland & Company, 2010).

12. DeYoung, *Madness*, 13.

13. Anandi Mani, Sendhil Mullainathan, Eldar Shafir, and Jiaying Zhao, "Poverty Impedes Cognitive Function," *Science* 341, no. 6149 (August 30, 2013): 976–80, doi.org/10.1002 /jclp.21951.

14. Mani et al., "Poverty Impedes Cognitive Function."

15. Martha E. Wadsworth and Shauna L. Rienks, "Stress as a Mechanism of Poverty's Ill Effects on Children: Making a Case for Family Strengthening Interventions That Counteract Poverty-Related Stress," *Children Youth and Families News*, American Psychological Association, July 2012, www.apa.org/pi/families/resources/newsletter/2012/07/stress-mechanism.

16. Daniel A. Hackman, Martha J. Farah, and Michael J. Meaney, "Socioeconomic Status and the Brain: Mechanistic Insights from Human and Animal Research," *Nature Reviews Neuroscience* 11, no. 9 (2010): 651–59, doi.org/10.1038/nrn2897.

17. Felicity Thomas, Lorraine Hansford, Joseph Ford, Susanne Hughes, Katrina Wyatt, Rose McCabe, and Richard Byng, "DeSTRESS Project Final Report: Poverty, Pathology and Pills," DeSTRESS Project, April 2019, destressproject.org.uk/wp-content/uploads/2019/05 /Final-report-8-May-2019-FT.pdf.

18. Thomas et al., "DeSTRESS Project Final Report," 14.

19. Thomas et al., "DeSTRESS Project Final Report," 20.

20. Stacy Dean, Ed Bolen, and Brynne Keith-Jennings, "Making SNAP Work Requirements Harsher Will Not Improve Outcomes for Low-Income People," Center for Budget and Policy Priorities, March 1, 2018, www.cbpp.org/research/food-assistance/making-snap-work-requirements-harsher-will-not-improve-outcomes-for-low.

Chapter 13

1. Susan Aud, William Hussar, Michael Planty, Thomas Snyder, Kevin Bianco, Mary Ann Fox, Lauren Frohlich, Jana Kemp, Lauren Drake, and Katie Ferguson, "The Condition of Education 2010," National Center for Education Statistics, June 2010, nces.ed.gov/programs/coe/analysis/2010-section3b.asp.
2. US Government Accountability Office, "Public High Schools with More Students in Poverty and Smaller Schools Provide Fewer Academic Offerings to Prepare Students for College," October 2018, www.gao.gov/assets/700/694961.pdf.
3. Chris Duncombe, "Unequal Opportunities: Fewer Resources, Worse Outcomes for Students in Schools with Concentrated Poverty," The Commonwealth Institute, October 26, 2017, www.thecommonwealthinstitute.org/2017/10/26/unequal-opportunities-fewer-resources-worse-outcomes-for-students-in-schools-with-concentrated-poverty/.
4. Texas Educational Agency, "2018–19 Accountability Ratings Overall Summary: Lytle ISD (007904), accessed May 14, 2020, rptsv1.tea.texas.gov.
5. Rebecca Madill, Van-Kim Bui Lin, Sarah Friese, and Katherine Paschall, "Access to Early Care and Education for Disadvantaged Families: Do Levels of Access Reflect States' Child Care Subsidy Policies?" Child Trends, updated March 1, 2018, www.childtrends.org/publications/access-early-care-education-disadvantaged-families-levels-access-reflect-states-child-care-subsidy-policies.
6. Katherine Magnuson and Jane Waldfogel, "Trends in Income-Related Gaps in Enrollment in Early Childhood Education," *AERA Open* 2, no. 2 (May 16, 2016), doi.org/10.1177/2332858416648933.
7. Jamie L. Hanson, Nicole Hair, Dinggang G. Shen, Feng Shi, John H. Gilmore, Barbara L. Wolfe, and Seth D. Pollak, "Family Poverty Affects the Rate of Human Infant Brain Growth," *PLOS one* 8, no. 12 (December 11, 2013), doi.org/10.1371/journal.pone.0080954.
8. Jill Gilkerson, Jeffrey A. Richards, Steven F. Warren, Judith K. Montgomery, Charles R. Greenwood, D. Kimbrough Oller, John H. L. Hansen, and Terrance D. Paul, "Mapping the Early Language Environment Using All-Day Recordings and Automated Analysis," *American Journal of Speech-Language Pathology* 26, no. 2 (May 2017): 248–65, doi.org/10.1044/2016_ajslp-15-0169.
9. Douglas E. Sperry, Linda L. Sperry, and Peggy J. Miller, "Reexamining the Verbal Environments of Children from Different Socioeconomic Backgrounds," *Child Development* 90, no. 4 (July/August 2019): 1303–18, doi.org/10.1111/cdev.13072.
10. Catherine E. Llhamon and Jocelyn Samuels, "Dear Colleague Letter on the Nondiscriminatory Administration of School Discipline," US Department of Justice and US Department of Education, January 8, 2014, www2.ed.gov/about/offices/list/ocr/letters/colleague-201401-title-vi.html.
11. David Figlio, "Testing, Crime and Punishment," *Journal of Public Economics* 90, no. 4–5 (May 2006): 837–851, doi.org/10.1016/j.jpubeco.2005.01.003.

12. M. Cahalan, L. W. Perna, M. Yamashita, J. Wright, and S. Santillan, "Indicators of Higher Education Equity in the United States—2018 Historical Report," The Pell Institute for the Study of Opportunity in Higher Education, Council for Opportunity, 2018, pellinstitute.org /indicators/reports_2018.shtml.

13. United States Government Accountability Office, "Food Insecurity: Better Information Could Help Eligible College Students Access Federal Food Assistance Benefits," December 2018, www.gao.gov/assets/700/696254.pdf.

Chapter 14

1. David K. Evans and Anna Popova, "Cash Transfers and Temptation Goods: A Review of Global Evidence," *Policy Research Working Papers*, May 2014, doi.org/10.1596/1813-9450-6886.

2. Manuela Angelucci, "Love on the Rocks: Domestic Violence and Alcohol Abuse in Rural Mexico," *The B.E. Journal of Economic Analysis & Policy* 8, no. 1 (October 26, 2008), doi.org /10.2202/1935-1682.1766.

3. V. Joseph Hotz and John Karl Scholz, "The Earned Income Tax Credit," in Robert A. Moffitt, ed., *Means-Tested Transfer Programs in the United States* (Chicago: The University of Chicago Press, 2003); Bruce Meyer, "The Effects of the Earned Income Tax Credit and Recent Reforms," in Jeffrey R. Brown, ed., *NBER Book Series Tax Policy and the Economy* (National Bureau of Economic Research, 2010), www.nber.org/chapters/c11973.

4. Emmanuel Skoufias and Vincenzo Di Maro, "Conditional Cash Transfers, Adult Work Incentives, and Poverty," *Journal of Development Studies* 44, no. 7 (September 18, 2008): 935–60, doi.org/10.1080/00220380802150730.

5. Evelyn L. Forget, "The Town with No Poverty: The Health Effects of a Canadian Guaranteed Annual Income Field Experiment," *Canadian Public Policy* 37, no. 3 (September 2011): 283–305, doi.org/10.1353/cpp.2011.0036.

6. Matthew Gardner, Robert S. McIntyre, and Richard Phillips, "The 35 Percent Corporate Tax Myth: Corporate Tax Avoidance by Fortune 500 Companies, 2008 to 2015," Institute on Taxation and Economic Policy, March 9, 2017, itep.org/the-35-percent-corporate-tax-myth/.

7. Statistics Sweden, "Smaller Share of Income Goes to Housing Costs," December 15, 2014, www.scb.se/en/finding-statistics/statistics-by-subject-area/household-finances/income-and -income-distribution/households-finances/pong/statistical-news/household-finances-2013 --housing-and-housing-costs/.

8. Ruopeng An, "Effectiveness of Subsidies in Promoting Healthy Food Purchases and Consumption: A Review of Field Experiments," *Public Health Nutrition* 16, no. 7 (July 2013): 1215–28, doi.org/10.1017/ S1368980012004715.

9. "Economists' Statement on Guaranteed Annual Income," 1/15/1968–4/18/1969 folder, General Correspondence Series, Papers of John Kenneth Galbraith, John F. Kennedy Presidential Library.

10. Noam Chomsky, Peter Hutchison, and Jared P. Scott, *Requiem for the American Dream: The 10 Principles of Concentration of Wealth & Power* (New York: Seven Stories Press, 2017).

11. Glen G. Cain and Douglas A. Wissoker, "A Reanalyis of Marital Stability in the Seattle-Denver Income-Maintenance Experiment," *American Journal of Sociology* 95, no. 5 (March 1990): 1235–69, doi.org/10.1086/229428.

12. Forget, "The Town with No Poverty: The Health Effects of a Canadian Guaranteed Annual Income Field Experiment."

13. Olli Kangas, Signe Jauhiainen, Miska Simanainen, and Minna Ylikännö, "The Basic Income Experiment 2017–2018 in Finland: Preliminary results," Ministry of Social Affairs and Health, Helsinki, February 8, 2019, julkaisut.valtioneuvosto.fi/bitstream/handle/10024/161361/Report_The%20Basic%20Income%20Experiment%2020172018%20in%20Finland.pdf.

14. "Research at GiveDirectly," GiveDirectly, accessed May 20, 2020, www.givedirectly.org/research-at-give-directly/.

15. Y Combinator Research, "Basic Income Project Proposal," September 20, 2017, basicincome.ycr.org/blog/2017/8/24/basic-income-research-proposal.

16. Josh Marcus. "What Stockton's UBI Experiment Cane Teach Us About Surviving Coronavirus," *California Magazine*, April 30, 2020, alumni.berkeley.edu/california-magazine/just-in/2020-04-27/what-stocktons-ubi-experiment-can-teach-us-about-surviving-coronavirus.

17. Ekaterina Jardim, Mark C. Long, Robert Plotnik, Emma van Inwegen, Jacob Vigdor, and Hilary Wething, "Minimum Wage Increases, Wages, and Low-Wage Employment: Evidence from Seattle" (NBER Working Paper Series, National Bureau of Economic Research, revised May 2018), www.nber.org/papers/w23532.pdf.

18. Michael Reich, Sylvia Allegretto, and Anna Godoey, "Seattle's Minimum Wage Experience 2015–16," Center on Wage and Employment Dynamics, June 2017.

19. Ben Zipperer and John Schmitt, "The 'High Road' Seattle Labor Market and the Effect of the Minimum Wage Increase: Data Limitation and Methodological Problems Bias New Analysis of Seattle's Minimum Wage," Economic Policy Institute, June 26, 2017, www.epi.org/publication/the-high-road-seattle-labor-market-and-the-effects-of-the-minimum-wage-increase-data-limitations-and-methodological-problems-bias-new-analysis-of-seattles-minimum-wage-incr/.

20. David Dayen, "Whether America Can Afford a Job Guarantee Program Is Not Up for Debate," The Intercept, April 30, 2018, theintercept.com/2018/04/30/federal-job-guarantee-program-cost/.

Index

Note: Names appearing in quotation marks are pseudonyms.

spending choices, 144, 237–238
spokesperson, 258
Springfield, Mass., 167
standardized tests, 220, 226
"Stark, Alice," 70, 72–73
state legislature, 259
"Stephen" (Newark resident), 193–194
stigmatization, 7–8, 98, 181
Stockton, Calif., 246
streetcars, 96, 97
street food giveaways, 48
street life, 189
Streetsblog USA, 100
stress
    and access to hygiene, 117–118
    cognitive functioning and, 209–210
    with diaper poverty, 117–118, 232
    and food insecurity, 205
    health effects of, 124
    and housing insecurity, 68
    mental health effects of, 203, 208–209
    poverty-related, 209–210
    for pregnant women, 136
subprime lenders, 58, 104, 105
subsidized housing, 74
substance abuse, 53, 54, 196, 210, 212
Substance and Abuse and Mental Health
    Services Administration, 54
subways, 93–94
suicide, 127, 142, 151, 152
summer food programs, 50
Sununu, Chris, 120
Supplemental Nutrition Assistance Pro-
    gram (SNAP)
    barriers to participation in, 181
    cost of, 239
    and diaper poverty, 205
    funding for, 36, 37, 49, 133, 240–241
    healthy food for recipients of, 129, 242
    and LIHEAP, 89
    meal preparation expectations of, 45
    race of recipients, 3
    and SMART program, 128, 129
    and Thrifty Food Plan, 47
    utility debt for recipients of, 81
    work requirements of, 212
Supplemental Security Income, 80, 89, 132
survival sex, 67
Swan, Colleen, 20–21, 32
Sweden, 124, 241
Switzerland, 124

T

Taggart, Gina, 195
tank-based water systems, 19–22
TAP (Tiered Assistance Program), 30–31
TARP (Troubled Asset Relief Program),
    155
Tasha (Giant Laundry user), 115–116
taxes
    corporate, 239
    earned income tax credit, 238, 243
    estate, 8
    mortgage interest deduction, 53, 55–56,
        153, 239
    negative income tax, 243–244
    property, 72–73, 231
    sales, 121
    tax benefits for home ownership,
        152–153
Taylor, Lauren A., 124
team building, for advocacy efforts,
    256–257
teen workers, 231
Tempe, Ariz., 98
Temporary Aid to Needy Families (TANF),
    7n*, 252
    cash assistance from, 182
    funding for, 240, 241
    job training for recipients of, 159, 160
    and LIHEAP, 89
    race of recipients, 3
    transportation and dependence on, 102
temptation goods, 237–238
tenant unions, 74
Tenenbaum, J. Samuel, 146, 147
Tennessee, 114
Tensas Parish, La, 22, 29–30
Terra Firma, 207–208
Texas, 6, 105. *see also specific cities*
Texas A&M, 227
TFP. *see* Thrifty Food Plan
13th (film), 127
Thrifty Food Plan (TFP), 45–47, 50, 240
Tiered Assistance Program (TAP), 30–31
Time (magazine), 3
TOD (transit-oriented development), 109
toilets, access to, 113–115, 121
"Tonya" (New Britain teen), 43–44
Too Small to Fail, 232
training programs, for women, xix, 159–
    161, 171
transit-oriented development (TOD), 109

About the Authors

Joanne Goldblum is CEO and founder of the National Diaper Bank Network, encompassing more than two hundred member organizations that provide diapers and other basic needs to families across America. In 2018 she founded the Alliance for Period Supplies, which provides free hygiene products to the one in four people for whom menstruation means difficulty attending school and work. Joanne has spent her career working with and advocating for families in poverty. She has written op-eds for the *Washington Post*, *US News & World Report*, and HuffPost. She has been an ABC Person of the Week and the subject of profiles by CNN, *People*, and many other outlets. Joanne is an inspiring and in-demand speaker. In 2007 she was chosen as one of ten Robert Wood Johnson community health leaders on the basis of her work to found the New Haven Diaper Bank.

Colleen Shaddox is a print and radio journalist and activist. Her publication credits include the *New York Times*, the *Washington Post*, National Public Radio, *America*, and many more. She left daily newspapers when an editor reprimanded her for "writing too many stories about poor people" and went to work in a soup kitchen. She has had one foot in journalism and one in non-profits ever since. In states throughout the country, Colleen has worked on winning campaigns to get kids out of adult prisons, to end juvenile life without parole, and to limit shackling in juvenile courts. She is a frequently anthologized fiction writer. Her award-winning play *The Shakespeares* and other dramatic works have been performed around the country.